CHAD JOHNSON

How to Win a Heart

ONE MAN'S ADVENTURE IN FINDING AND WINNING HIS LIFELONG LOVE

ethos
collective

Identifiers:

LCCN: 2020912638

ISBN: 978-1-63680-029-5 (paperback)
ISBN: 978-1-63680-030-1 (hardback)
ISBN: 978-1-63680-031-8 (ebook)

Available in paperback, hardback, e-book, and audiobook

DEDICATION

This book is dedicated to my bride and the love of my life Jenise Cheri. Thank you for saying yes to the adventure of us and knowing the best is yet to come. To our eleven fantastic children, you are truly a blessing from the Lord, and you have made me a very happy man. To those who have married our children (or will marry our children), you are an answer to our prayers. To our five precious grandchildren (so far!), and the ninety-five to follow, seek first the Kingdom of God. Lastly, to all who aspire to be married well: prepare early and date intentionally.

CONTENTS

ACKNOWLEDGMENT

There are so many individuals who helped to bring this book to life. First, I'd like to thank Kary Oberbrunner and the entire team at Igniting Souls Publishing Agency, especially Teresa Alesch, who helped bring clarity to the book in its early stages. Along the way, there are so many other important team members crucial to marketing and producing the book, and I'd like to acknowledge a few—Gailyc Sonia (Project Manager), Faye Bryant (Marketing Coordinator), Beth Wilson (Assistant), and Raya Michelle (Website Designer).

Thank you to Allison Harp Photography for the beautiful cover and back picture and James Engerbretson for the stunning book cover. Thank you to Zach Holmes for producing the audiobook.

Thank you to my parents, Burnell and Paula Johnson, for modeling godly marriage for the past 55 years. I love you so much!

Finally, I want to thank my amazing assistant, Sheryl Sellers-Obarski. You are the glue that holds it all together. Thank you for your patience and perseverance in coordinating everyone to produce a book I'm genuinely proud of.

And most of all. Thank you to the God who made me, loves me, and gave himself for me, that I might have life and life more abundantly!

I am overflowing with gratitude.

FOREWORD

When Daddy sent me *How To Win a Heart*, I didn't get more than three pages in before tears started pouring down my face. This is the love I witnessed every day growing up. A never-ending pursuit of my mother through stressful times and rich seasons—years when we lived in a tent and trailer, and years we spent with all eleven of us kids skiing Squaw Valley for six weeks at a time.

The romance didn't end with the final pages you'll read here. The pursuit continued when I was born, when my sister followed fifteen months later, and nine more kiddos joined our family after that. Letters to Mother still showed up in the mailbox when I finished college, and Daddy still drove up in dramatic fashion to take Mama on a date in a Porsche (it didn't matter that it was borrowed) when we were as broke as church mice, and he had the weight of the world on his shoulders.

Watching Daddy and Mother build a lifelong love made marriage look rewarding and fulfilling—like something worth waiting for. Up close and personal, I could see that a great marriage took work. But the work looked so worth it, when I saw the twinkle in their eyes and the laughs they shared. Other people noticed their love too. So many times, when they were alone (without us kids) in public, someone would stop them and ask if they were newlyweds.

As a teen I craved purity and monogamy and faithfulness, because I saw in their relationship the electric passionate romance God designed marriage to be.

Money, children, and life's distractions never got in the way of Daddy's relentless pursuit of winning Mother's heart. And I'm forever grateful for his example that showed me why I shouldn't settle for anything less than the incredible man that daily pursues mine.

Kathryn Joy Voetberg
Now That We're a Family
http://nowthatwereafamily.com/

INTRODUCTION

Hi, I'm Chad, a fifty-one-year-old man who is totally in love with his woman. Yep! Even after twenty-eight years of doing life as a married couple, most days we really like each other a whole lot.

What you are about to read is our love story. A very true, straight-from-the-heart love story, written by me, from my perspective as a twenty-one year old in 1991.

Jenise has written a commentary and brief perspective for each chapter. These chapter notes are a bonus feature you can download for free at HowToWinAHeart.com.

So, yep, a romance book written by a dude!

I know. It's a bit unusual. Women write romance books and women read romance books. Aren't romantic movies even called *chick flicks*?

I am convinced that writing this book is the manliest thing I could do. As the leader of our large and growing family, I want to do everything in my power to elevate the priority and power of a godly marriage.

Jenise and I approached our twenty-fifth wedding anniversary in August of 2018 feeling extremely blessed and grateful. As we celebrated, I told and re-told the story of how we met, dated, fell in love, got engaged, and then married. In sharing this story with our eleven children and two sons-in-law, I realized that there are many lessons—some good, some bad—in our story, and I was excited to pass these lessons along to our children.

Time and love have burned the details of this story into my brain, and I have relished the telling of it many, many times through the years. I realized that someday I may not be able to recall with clarity all that happened. I wanted to put it down in writing so future generations of Johnson grandchildren and, Lord willing, great-grandchildren would know our story.

The title is a little misleading, I think. As people read our story, they suggested titles that would heighten reader interest in learning about how to start and build a great foundation for marriage. But know this: *How To Win A Heart* is not a formula. Our desire is that it will serve as a practical guide to building your own God-honoring love story. And although I wrote this book for my children and grandchildren, I hope it might be useful to you.

This book is for you if . . .

- You have a heart for Christian marriage.

- You are a young person interested in getting married someday and would like some ideas and inspiration on how to lay a solid foundation.

- You are a manly man who never thought you would read a love story, but you really do want to find and win the heart of an amazing woman someday.

- You want more romance, adventure, and creativity in your life.

- You are in a marriage that you desire to be stronger, healthier, more alive, richer, more romantic, and more Christ-honoring.

- You like love stories.

- You are a parent and would like some ideas or perspective on how to encourage your children or other young people with a vision for a great relationship.

Here are some questions you'll find addressed in *How to Win a Heart*:

- When is a good age or time to date?

- How do you go into marriage with no regrets?

- How do you deal with parents or potential in-laws when you are dating?

- What does it mean to honor your parents?

- How important are rules or guidelines?

- What are your standards in dating?

- What questions should you ask your date?

- How do you make your relationship God honoring and still have lots of fun together?

Thank you for buying this book!

All profits are going to help newlywed couples and other married couples get resources, coaching, counseling, and other help to strengthen and grow their marriages.

I hope you enjoy this book and that it will inspire you to invest in your own love story.

Chad Johnson

CHAPTER 1
THE RISK

The plane hit the tarmac at Hartsfield-Jackson Atlanta International Airport and the clock started ticking.

It was February 12, 1992, and my watch read 3:47 p.m. I was already twenty minutes late, and my mind raced through all the preplanned steps that needed to happen in a coordinated way before 5:00 p.m.

I had only seventy-two minutes until I must enter the lobby and hit the button on the elevator that would take me to the eighteenth floor of a beautiful high-rise office building on 118 Peachtree.

People bumping and shoving in the aisle jarred me from my thoughts. Here we go, Chadwick Buford (not my real name but the name I used—and still use—when talking to myself), let's do this.

I joined the line of eager-to-depart travelers and made my way into the terminal, looking right and left to see if I could catch a glimpse of Kim Gable, a dear family friend who'd agreed to help me rent a car. My age of twenty-one didn't win me admission to the most-favored-car-rental-customer category. Each rental car agency made it very clear that, no, they wouldn't rent to me unless someone over twenty-five years old signed for me.

Kim was nowhere in sight. She was probably by the luggage area. I hastily scanned the signs directing me to the lower level to retrieve my bags. When I arrived downstairs, there was nothing on the carousel; it wasn't even moving. No sign of Kim either. Yikes—4:03 p.m. My time was slipping away. I looked around for a pay phone but didn't see one. I was already amped with adrenaline working its magic, but anxiety began creeping in.

What if I messed this up? What if I missed the deadline? What if Kim forgot?

I had invested so much in this trip—over $500 just for the flight, which was a lot of money for a ski bum, I mean ski patrolman—not to mention the time off from work and new clothes I bought. They say clothes make the man, whoever they are. I didn't believe it, but I also didn't want to show up looking like a bum or someone who doesn't get it.

So some new duds were in order; everything had to be perfect! At this very moment, I was sporting a nice suit—yes, a suit. White shirt, tie, and all. I'm telling you—this was a big deal for me! A really big deal. I'd never done anything like this, and it was unlikely I'd try anything like it again.

Just then, the carousel began creeping in its clockwise circle, and what do you know? The second bag down the ramp was mine! After hoisting it to the ground, I turned and scanned the growing crowd for any sign of—

"Chad!" a voice called from behind me to the left.

Sure enough, Kim had found me. Actually, Kim and friends had found me. Trailing alongside Kim was a blonde-haired, blue-eyed boy of about twelve years wearing glasses and two young brunette girls around ten and eight years old. All seemed awfully glad to see me, and I was elated to see them.

After a brief hug and introductions, I told Kim I really needed to hustle. The clock was ticking fast, and if I didn't hit the road into Atlanta in the next twenty minutes, I'd never make it on time. We ran to the Enterprise rental counter. I don't know why it takes so long to rent a car, but it does; and that day, it took an eternity. I wasn't even needed; Kim was the renter and would sign me on as the driver.

Thinking ahead, I told her my plan called for buying flowers to present upon my grand entrance. She agreed I should run back toward the luggage carousel where I'd spied a vendor selling bouquets. As I turned to go, Kim's young son, Phillip, begged his mother to allow him to go with me. "Why not?" she said, and off we ran in pursuit of roses.

Picking out the best bunch of bright red long-stem roses took no time at all. Checking out was another story. Four, five—no—six people in front of us. The young lady running the register, or being run by the register, was clearly brand new to the job. Each product presented a new and exciting treasure hunt for her and an entirely new and different version of pain for me and for her ever-growing, waiting audience.

Oh. My. Word. I can't believe this is taking so long. Phillip kept looking up at me, wondering if my deep breathing was impatience, or if I was experiencing chest pain and having a true medical emergency.

Fifteen minutes later, with red roses clutched firmly in my grip, Phillip and I sprinted back to the Enterprise counter. Kim was gone! No! Where on earth would she have disappeared to? The agent behind the counter had no answers, but he did have the keys to the rental car.

Where is Kim? I ran back out to scan the entire surrounding area—no Kim. Not a pay phone to be found, and cell phones didn't exist in 1992. What was I going to do? I was already behind schedule. Oh well.

"Phillip, here we go!" I told him to follow me, and we ran for the car rental shuttle. On the ride over, I told Phillip he would have to make the short trip into downtown Atlanta with me, hang out while I surprised this amazing girl, and then I'd take him to his parents' home, where I had arranged to stay.

The look on Phillip's face told me it was a crazy plan and that separating him from his mother wasn't a wise idea, but I bolstered my confidence by telling myself it couldn't be avoided, and the adventure would be good for him. As soon as the shuttle stopped, we ran to the car in 27C, a nice, full-sized sedan with leather seats and some decent power under the hood. I'd need it.

A few moments later, we whizzed down Interstate 85 toward downtown Atlanta. I've been known to drive too fast at times, and this was one of those times. With my speedometer inching over 100 mph, I risked a glance at Phillip. He was slinking down in the passenger seat, pale-faced, white knuckles clutching the armrest and the door handle, and eyes glued to the dash.

I realized the trauma I was causing him and casually justified the rush. "Phillip, I know I'm going kind of fast, but it's important I get to the office building before 5:00 p.m. If I arrive after, all my weeks of planning and expenses would be a waste." I didn't feel comfortable showing up at Jenise's townhouse, so I had to make it to work before she left. "Is this scaring you?" The question elicited a quick nod from Phillip.

He managed to whisper, "My Daddy drives fifty-five," or something of that nature.

What am I going to tell his parents? The gnawing thought compounded my guilt. Phillip's father, Steve, is a CPA. Yes—that kind of guy. He's wise, lives life well planned out, schedules vacations one year in advance, never speeds or runs out of gas, pays his taxes early; you get what I'm saying. Phillip was now in full shock, realizing there are guys like me who, well, do life a little less structured. I don't know that he was relishing this revelation.

But the mission must go on! I was committed to pulling off my plan. Which off-ramp did I need? Was it Peachtree . . . Street? Avenue? Boulevard? Lane? Drive? Parkway? Circle? *Oh, no! I only wrote Peachtree.* Every off-ramp on Interstate 85 was a Peachtree something.

I started praying. *Lord, I have no idea which of these streets I'm to exit onto, but you do. Please show me because I only get one shot. If I get the wrong Peachtree, by the time I realize it, I won't have time to sort through the plethora of Peachtree options.*

I let the first Peachtree exit pass. It didn't feel right. The sign above said two other Peachtree options were upcoming. I took the second for no reason other than I just did. We turned onto Peachtree Parkway and sped through the greenish-yellowish signals heading toward the tall buildings of downtown. My watch read 4:52 p.m. Tucker Wayne/Luckie & Co., the advertising agency where Jenise worked as a receptionist, would close at 5:00 p.m. I'm not sure which raced faster, the car's engine or my heart.

"Phillip, can you help me find the address?" I looked over and saw a changed kid.

He was sitting up straight with a smirk on his face. He was enjoying the adventure! His eyes were wide as he scanned the side of the street, and then he shouted, "There it is!"

"What is?" Sure enough! Braking hard, as we were flying in way too hot, we somehow hit the driveway entrance, but not without receiving a blast from a horn and a good fist-shaking from an unsuspecting driver I'd cut off. "A full parking lot? You've got to be kidding. All this and no parking spot."

"Over there." Phillip pointed.

Man, I'm glad he came along. Wait! What on earth am I going to do with Phillip? It was 4:56 p.m. There was no time to think. "Phillip, come with me. We've got to run!"

Roses in hand, Phillip and I sprinted and weaved through the cars, hurdling a hedge bordering a perfectly manicured lawn, through the lawn, over another hedge, and across the beautiful stonework courtyard to the massive glass doors of the building. Out of breath, sweaty, and a bit rumpled from our run, I straightened my suit. Looking at my reflection in

5

the glass doors, I put my shoulders back, took a big breath, and entered the large, stunning lobby.

A security guard stood behind the big welcome counter centered in the grand space. Suddenly feeling small, I questioned myself. *What am I doing here? What was I thinking?* Why had I flown all the way from Los Angeles to surprise a girl? Did she even like me? Would she be there? Would she think I was nuts? Would she shut me down?

Ouch! Fears are such creepy things. I was half-tempted to go back to my car and quit the operation when Phillip bumped me. I looked down to see his young face flush with excitement, anticipation, adventure, and still breathing hard from our 100-yard dash to the building.

"Okay, let's do this!" I said.

The security guard realized our urgency and pointed out the right elevator. "The eighteenth floor."

I pushed the button, and we started our climb. *Phillip! What am I going to do with Phillip? There's no way I can surprise Jenise and try to explain all of this to her.* "Phillip," I said, crouching down and looking him square in the eye, "do you like riding elevators?"

Not waiting for an answer, I told him, "Here's what you'll do. When I get off the elevator, you keep pushing these buttons right here in front of you. You can go up, and you can go down, but don't get off the elevator. Got it?" Fear was in his eyes as the door opened, and I stepped into the lobby of the unknown.

The elevator door closed behind me. I was about to face . . . what? Rejection? Failure? Maybe, but for sure the most beautiful girl in the world.

* * *

6

CHAD'S REFLECTIONS

It seems kind of crazy looking back. Flying across the country to ask a girl out on a date. What was I thinking? Seems risky, doesn't it?

I firmly believe it was my responsibility to initiate, to pursue, to seek out and interrupt Jenise's life—not the other way around. It was clear early on that following my romantic interest would require me to take a risk, to step out into the unknown, and possibly suffer the pain of rejection.

We live in a day and age of passive guys and aggressive girls.

Guys, are you willing to step up and be the initiator? I know a lot of amazing young ladies who are eager to see that kind of male leadership.

CHAPTER 2
MARRIAGE

What led to my cross-country adventure? Why was I in Atlanta, on the eighteenth floor of a high-rise office building? Who was the amazing woman who'd won my heart and made any sacrifice or expense seem small and necessary? Where did my crazy, fun—so far— adventure begin?

Actually, the whole thing started when I was a kid. Yes, as a young man, I remember a married couple, Bob and Sylvia, who went to our church. They seemed not just to love but *like* each other. A good-looking couple, they were striking in appearance. Just seeing them together made me smile. I admired how he treated her, and she seemed to love the way he treated her too.

They delighted in each other. Marriage was fun for them! Best friends, lovers . . . you know, the stuff they write about in books and create in movies, except this was real. Something in the way they looked at each other and romanced each other made me want to have a great marriage someday—a marriage like Bob and Sylvia Thompson.

Call me weird, but in my late teens, I began reading books on marriage. Yep, me, a regular guy in most respects who wanted to become a marriage expert—but not so I could have a bunch of theories or ideas. I don't like theories or concepts unless they work and produce a good result. I like results, and I wanted the result of a great relationship with a girl someday. *My* girl!

So, yes, I figured I'd better start studying and soon found myself at the bookstore: *What Wives Wish Their Husbands Knew About Women; Letters to Phillip; Do Yourself a Favor: Love Your Wife; Love Life for Every Married Couple; His Needs, Her Needs; The 5 Love Languages,* and many others. I read them all and took my research seriously. I underlined, took notes, and memorized key parts.

Now, that wasn't all I did. I was a ski bum too! Not really a *ski bum* but a full-time ski patrolman at the local resort, Snow Summit, in Big Bear, California. I chased down that job as soon as I turned eighteen and received my training as an EMT. Hey, if they were willing to pay me to ski, I was willing to ski for pay! It was one of my earliest lessons in win-win situations. I spent summers working in construction or at the family business in Los Angeles while eagerly waiting for winter to roll back around.

One of those winter evenings, I sat in "Bump," the ski patrol shack at the top of the mountain near chair two. In between responding to skier accidents or emergencies, we were free to use our time as we wished. I was reading one of my books on marriage, written for single guys, and I did what the author suggested and started writing out the list of character qualities and attributes of the woman I wanted to marry.

One of my fellow ski patrollers asked me what kind of homework I was doing. I told him, and boy did that set off a firestorm of heckling, hooting, and hollering. "Chad is figuring out what kind of woman he wants to marry! Ha!"

"Well, tell us!" they said. So I did.

"I'm looking for a godly woman who truly loves the Lord and wants to live her life to glorify Him. She will love His Word and comprehend the power of God to save and give freedom. A woman who wants a man to lead spiritually and be the head of her home and understands the beauty of a man submitted to Christ and a wife submitted to her husband as unto the Lord.

"Yes, I want her to be beautiful in form and feature, inside and out. A classy woman who can dress like a lady, attend a formal event, and be the queen of my heart and lady on my arm, and yet, the next day, can put on jeans and jump in a ditch. No, she's not afraid of getting dirty or doing hard work. I want a woman who hasn't had sex prior to marriage, a virgin. Someone who will unwrap that precious and amazing gift with me, both of us for the first time together, and then every day for the next, oh, 100 years, growing in and glowing in fresh, pure intimacy.

"She must want children, a bunch of them—maybe ten or twelve. She needs to be adventurous. Yes! Having children is adventurous. And with that, a companion, someone to live, laugh, hike, and play alongside. Someone who will ski a mountain, sleep under the stars, run a trail in the moonlight, and jump off a bridge into the cool freshwater below—all with me.

"She must be a pioneer, not a settler. Someone who will move wherever in the world the Lord calls us. Must be willing to be dirt poor or filthy rich, and be the same awesome girl, unchanged by either. She cares for others as a servant and a leader. She's confident and sure of herself, and yet humble, grateful, and flexible. Comfortable in all settings whether she's attending a state dinner at the White House or loving someone who desperately needs love at a homeless shelter. A true princess, a queen. A fit woman. Interested in healthy and abundant living. Strong, athletic, capable.

"She'll be a discerning woman, wise, and able to counsel and instruct. A woman who could homeschool our children, yes, all ten of them. A woman with a positive attitude. Oh, yes, a joyful woman! I had read Proverbs enough to know that a dripping faucet isn't for me. I want a woman with a

Philippians 4 focus. Someone who'll think right about life—thoughts that are true, honest, pure, just, lovely, of good report, worthy of virtue, and praise. Yes, a girl with exactly that kind of mindset."

The list kept growing.

The entire time I was talking, the guys at Bump gave me grief. "Chad, you honestly think that kind of girl exists? Hardly. No way! If you could find even a few of those attributes, you'd be lucky, but all? Dream on, dude!"

Dream on I did. I knew a secret they didn't know.

From the moment of my birth, my mother and father had been praying for this woman who'd someday be my wife. I could confidently dream. I had an awesome, capable God who loved me and had incredible things in store for me. A God who, in Deuteronomy 28 and Psalm 1, spells out just how much He desires to bless those who seek Him and walk in His ways. And I believed Him.

That didn't keep the guys from trying to set me up with every ski bunny who hit the slopes during those years. "Here's one, Chad. She's hot. Go skiing with her. Ask her out." Within a few minutes of meeting any of the girls, including ones I met at church, camps, or anywhere else, they weren't for me.

My parents, whom I adore and respect so much, counseled me growing up, and I took it to heart. "There's no sense spending time dating around and tying heartstrings with a woman if she isn't the one you'll spend your life with." During the years between ages eighteen and twenty-one, I had a lot of friends who were girls. Some were really beautiful, nice, wonderful, and godly, but I never had a "girlfriend."

I only went on a couple of dates during that entire time. Each time, usually very early in the evening, I realized that, nope, she wasn't the one for me. Now, I realize some people may require more time to determine these things. I can't understand the couple who's been dating for two or three years and don't know if he or she is "the one" when I ask.

If a date didn't meet the criteria I had so meticulously defined beforehand, I'd thank her for going out that evening, and then a few days later, I'd tell her I only wanted friendship. The few girls I dated didn't understand, but I truly didn't want to break their hearts or have mine get tangled up with someone I didn't see myself going the distance with. This kept things simple and kept me out of a bunch of trouble, I'm sure.

Thank you, Mom and Dad. I'm grateful for the wisdom of those in my life.

* * *

CHAD'S REFLECTIONS

Many young men and young women look forward to having a special someone to share the adventure of life with. While many say that is what they want, I have found that they often have done little to prepare themselves for that kind of relationship. A great marriage is built on a solid foundation of preparation. What kind of preparation would be helpful?

CHAPTER 3
ANGEL AT FIRST SIGHT

I had seven cousins who lived next door while I was growing up. We were close, sometimes more like siblings than cousins. One afternoon while visiting my parents, my cousin Brenda met me at the gate separating our two yards. She asked me to be a part of her wedding party. It was an honor, and I gladly said yes.

As I said, I'm a fan of marriage—always have been and always will be. I like weddings too. My personality leans to the sanguine side, so any place with a bunch of people is a happy place for me, and that is only compounded when you think of the romance, dancing, drama, story, and adventure surrounding a relationship and marriage.

On April 13, 1991, I drove my 1988 Toyota 4Runner down from Big Bear to Whittier, California, for Brenda and David's wedding. As I drove into the Friends Church parking lot, I thought with a smile, *Better than the Enemies Church!* (That couldn't be good for marriage, even though that's where a lot of marriages end up going, it seems.) I had no idea that it'd be the day I'd meet the girl of my dreams!

Several hours later, after pictures and standing around visiting with the other guys in the wedding party, I walked down the aisle with Kim, a friend and bridesmaid of Brenda's. In line with the other couples that preceded us, we turned to face the audience, and my eyes fell upon a surreal and compelling image. To my left stood a large, beautiful harp of light-colored, sculpted wood. Seated and playing that harp was the most beautiful woman I'd ever seen!

"Oh, my word," I said, nudging the young lady beside me. "Check *her* out! An angel," I said in a slow, loud whisper.

The harpist was stunning. Her smile was radiant and filled the entire room with a delightfulness I hadn't felt until I saw her. Her blonde hair tumbled gently around her face, shaping her high cheekbones and revealing eyes that sparkled with joy. A long, slender neck relaxed into a perfect and graceful form of a woman, making her ideally suited gown appear as if it belonged on her. Long, willowy arms precisely evoked a mesmerizing melody from the instrument that seemed harmoniously paired with its master. It transported me. Wow! Unbelievable!

An elbow in the ribs shook me from my trance, which caused me to close my dropping jaw. I turned my view back to the center aisle and to the bride who'd completed her journey and was now standing in front of the pastor. I didn't hear much of anything the pastor said that day. My head and thoughts kept returning to that young woman.

Who was she? Was she married? I didn't see a ring. I checked, of course. *Maybe she takes it off to play. I'm sure she has a boyfriend. Probably many! Most likely.* A woman like that must have guys standing in line. I'd stand in line! *Wait a minute! What am I thinking? I know absolutely nothing about this girl. What's up with me?* Still, I couldn't quit stealing glances her way. She was truly amazing!

I couldn't wait for the ceremony to be over. Fortunately for me, Brenda asked me to video record the wedding guests, interview them, and ask them to share words of wisdom and happy wishes for the couple. Grabbing my camera, I quickly found the harpist and took my job to the heights of professionalism and attentiveness.

"What is your name?" I asked.

"Jenise Johnston," she said.

Johnston! She fit me to a T. My last name is Johnson. How perfect! Question after question, I fired them off, trying my best to be witty, funny, and interesting. I learned she was number nine in a family with twelve children. How cool was that? Her father was a real estate developer and investor; they lived not far away in Fullerton, California. She'd just finished her third year of college at Cal State Fullerton. Her family owned a Christian camp in Northern California, called JH Ranch. Brenda's older sister, Donna, had attended the JH Ranch and suggested Brenda and David hire Jenise as their harpist.

I had so many questions I wanted to ask, but I also knew Brenda would be pretty upset if she only had video footage of the harpist and none of the guests. So I tore myself away and poured myself into the task of filming the wedding reception. Halfway through the reception, my father found me and asked where my older brother Warren was. I didn't know. When I asked why, he said he wanted to introduce him to the harpist he just met. *What?* I guess he thought Warren was more ready for a relationship.

As the afternoon reception began winding down, I saw Jenise placing the cover on her harp. I made my way over and offered to help move it to her car. She accepted, and I recruited my brother David to help. While carrying the harp outside and down the steps to the parking lot, I scanned the area for a vehicle befitting such a princess but didn't see a carriage, limousine, or chauffeur.

Jenise woke me from my thoughts. "Right here."

She opened the door to the most beat-up station wagon I'd ever seen. It had to be twenty years old. Tan paint covered the areas not dented and rusted. She popped the back open and pointed for us to lay the harp in . . . there? The trunk space was filled with a skill saw, toolboxes, pipes, small pieces of lumber, straw, and a piece of old carpet laid over all that fine mess to protect the gorgeous harp I guessed cost close to $15,000.

I looked back at Jenise; she wasn't kidding. This was the vehicle she was driving, and yes, she wanted me to place the harp in there. Wow! What struck me in the moment was how comfortable she was with the situation. Here is this stunning woman, dressed like a U.S. president's wife at a state dinner, and yet she was driving this unbelievably decrepit station wagon without a hint of embarrassment or shame. I was in awe. Everything about her was awesome! What a class act. Unbelievable. I told her we should go skiing some time, to which she agreed that'd be fun. Before I knew it, she drove off, and a huge piece of me went with her. I wanted to run after the car. What was happening to me? Was I nuts? I hardly knew this woman, but something inside of me felt like I'd known her forever. We clicked. The way she looked at me just wrecked me. Something about her was different from all the other girls I'd ever met.

She was so fresh, energized, delightful, joyful, full of life. I was smitten, done, gone! I had a serious crush on this girl and was going to do something about it. Then it dawned on me—I hadn't even asked for her number! What a chump. I guess that's the penalty for being in la-la land.

I marched right back into the reception room and strode straight to my cousin Donna. "Who is this Jenise girl? I want to know everything. I mean everything!" I passionately demanded.

Donna was kind enough amid all the reception chaos to download the fact that Jenise did have a boyfriend. *How serious? They aren't engaged. She doesn't have a ring.* "The deal isn't closed until someone is married," I said. I knew I had to know much more.

Driving back up the winding road of Highway 18 that night, I couldn't stop talking about her. David was in the passenger seat and kept saying, "Quiet already. I know she's gorgeous, amazing, awesome, perfect. She is . . . blah, blah,

blah. Calm down, dude! You go to a wedding, and now you think it's your wedding. Chill out! Sure, she's pretty, but lots of girls are pretty. Sure, she's nice, but lots of girls are nice."

"Dude, you just don't get it," I told him. "She's one in a million. She's *the one!*"

He snapped back as he looked at me. "Dude, you're gone! Wacko, man. Unbelievable, Chad! Get a grip!"

We drove the rest of the way in silence as I replayed every word she'd said, recalled every glance, every smile. What a smile! *She has the best smile in the world.* I must have looked like a clown as I drove with my smile ear to ear. Mmm . . . her smile.

Dixianne Chandler and her husband, John, had one of the most amazing homes in Big Bear Lake. Set back across the street from the lake rested the coziest mountain home ever. It had a wood-burning, river rock fireplace, overstuffed leather chairs, and lots of red, green, soft, and warm blankets draped everywhere. Lamps cast a homey glow across the kitchen and living room. Like my mother, Dixianne was a great cook, and walking into that home to the aromatic smell of cornbread and chili made everything feel and smell better that night.

My brother David—fifteen months younger and my best friend—rented a room with me from John and Dixianne. It was close to Snow Summit where we both worked as ski patrolmen—heroes of the mountain, rescuing the hurt, the weary, the risk-averse, and those who'd gone way over their heads and were now experiencing the greatest of regrets. The Chandlers' home was merely a couple of miles from the mountain.

As I entered the front door that evening, Dixianne asked about the wedding. "I met the woman I'm gonna marry!"

"Really? Tell me about her," she said. David quickly made up some reason to leave the room, and I detailed every moment once again, savoring the detail.

Sleep was difficult that night. I was really messed up. What was going on with me? I had experienced my share of crushes, but this was something else. On a crush impact scale of one to ten, the others had been a five or six; this was one hundred!

Over the next few months, I plotted and planned a way to get to the JH Ranch. I visited my cousin Donna Beth several times and interrogated her further on Jenise and all things Johnston family. I learned a lot and took notes. I was on a serious mission.

I discovered that Jenise was twenty-four. Ouch! She didn't look any older than my humble twenty. I wondered if that'd be a big deal to her. I guess I always thought I'd marry a girl younger than me. I don't know why. Perhaps it was because my mother was eleven years younger than my father, but I was over it already. Four years older was fine.

Then, I found out her birthday—February 17, 1967. So, technically, she was only three years, three months, five days, sixteen hours, forty-three minutes, and ten seconds older than I was. Okay, I'm kidding about the hours, minutes, and seconds part, but it was close enough to have this work.

I also discovered that her father, Gene Johnston, was a successful real estate developer and investor. He appeared to be loaded, even though Jenise drove the most beat-up station wagon ever. I came to learn they were extremely frugal and put every extra penny to work at the JH Ranch and ministry they started. Donna informed me that Mr. Johnston had invested a large sum in purchasing 300-plus acres in Northern California, near the Oregon border.

She described the place as having an old lodge, a swimming pool, some cabins along a creek, and she told the story of Gene Johnston and his vision for turning the run-down hunting lodge into a pristine resort for Christian youth leadership. He enlisted his oldest son, Bruce, the second child of his and Joy's twelve children, to lead the development of the ranch.

Within ten years, it became a beautiful oasis amongst and surrounded by majestic mountains and pine forests. For sport, it had a large pond with zip lines, rope swings, climbing walls, ropes courses, tennis courts, mountain biking, river rafting, and various other adventures, such as hiking up Mount Shasta or cycling to the Northern California coast. The way she described it made me wish I was there. That kind of action was right up my alley. Everything about it sounded awesome.

Donna shared how Jenise was Bruce's right-hand gal in making the whole operation run. She oversaw the women's staff, keeping the kitchen spinning like a top and churning out yummy meals for 300-plus people three times a day! She told me that Jenise led concerts, sang, and shared her testimony at the "Big Top" gatherings held in a large tent. Donna spoke of her leadership, character, and strength.

After speaking with Donna Beth, intimidation seeped in. I was already in awe of this woman from afar, but the more I learned seemed to put her farther from my reach. She was the princess of rich gentlemen, living in a world far from mine, and I was sure she'd long forgotten the boy she met at that wedding back in April.

For some reason, though, I couldn't give up that easily. No! I had to know. I'd find a way to see her again and see what came of it. Maybe it was just a silly crush. Maybe this wasn't the girl I'd been praying for most of my life, but how could I be sure unless I saw her again?

The tricky part was JH Ranch didn't have any programs for single young men age twenty who wanted to meet the daughter of the owner—I checked. The soft Southern voice on the end of the line provided extraordinary customer care to those who called and gently informed me of that fact.

The only program available was for high-school-aged boys and girls and was called Second Wind. I thought I could probably pull off acting like a high schooler for a week but didn't think that'd be the way to impress Jenise. Then, Donna Beth told me about Singles Week. It was a weeklong program for "singles." Ugh. I didn't think of myself as a single person. Singles, in my mind, were the over-forty-five-year-old folks who hadn't married yet but still wanted to hang out with potential suitors just in case.

No, I didn't believe I qualified, but if that was my only way onto the ranch to see Jenise, then singles week it would be. I quickly campaigned to enlist some of my siblings, a couple of cousins, and some friends to go along. Donna Beth was a great support in this as she'd been to the ranch before and was as eager to recruit as I was to go.

* * *

CHAD'S REFLECTIONS

Can love at first sight really be a thing?

Probably not. Infatuation, a crush, intrigued, curious, interested at first sight, yes, but hardly love.

Love is a lot of things, but love that lasts is a verb with pure action and commitment. Love that lasts requires some due diligence, factfinding, soul searching, prayer, and wisdom from the Lord.

In Proverbs 18:22, it states, "Whoso findeth a wife findeth a good thing, and obtaineth favor from the Lord." What I gather from that is a wise young man is always on the lookout for a godly young woman who meets the criteria and attributes he has thoughtfully considered beforehand.

CHAPTER 4
THE RANCH

The day finally came, and after an almost thirteen-hour bus ride from Southern California—a total blast—we made the final winding turns up French Creek Road, crossed under the JH RANCH welcome sign, and entered another world as we passed over a scenic wooden bridge with a babbling brook tumbling underneath. The canopy of trees opened in front of us like a wide-angle lens, showcasing a lush green meadow with rich grasses, wildflowers, and eight horses grazing while the evening sunlight danced off their sleek shoulders.

An antique wagon, restored to its red and green with JH Ranch lettered in gold along the side, completed the postcard picture view. Wow—what a place! You could feel the stress of city living, the long drive, and a busy life flowing out of you and being replaced with a tranquil spirit of joy, rest, and refreshment. *JH Ranch, I love you already, and I just met you.*

The bus chugged up the steep lodge hill, and dozens of smiling faces greeted us. Staff members were dressed in bright red "JH Ranch Staff" T-shirts. What a welcome it was! I sat on the right side of the bus, which provided the best view of the waiting staff. My eager eyes scanned the crowd of faces for one—the one. There she was! Jenise! The blood surged through my veins, igniting whatever hormone makes you happy, joyful, excited, and about to jump out of your skin.

Her smile! Now that she was outside, it lit up the whole outdoors. Gene Johnston's daughter's smile alone illuminated all 300 acres of his ranch. She was all I could see, but she still didn't see me. I neared the front of the line to get off the bus, and there she was up close.

"Hey, Jenise," I heard myself saying. With surprise written all over her face, she seemed genuinely happy to see me. Then again, I'd never seen her without a smile. After being herded onward with the crowd, I noticed she seemed delighted to see everyone.

Every moment that week at JH Ranch delighted me. The activities seemed designed especially for the kind of guy I am. There was river rafting, hiking, camping, mountain biking, super swinging into the lake, ziplining, ropes courses, and so much more in the way of physical challenge and adventure. Almost all Jenise's family was there. I met Bruce and his wife, Heather, who was Jenise's best friend. I met Janet, Jenise's older sister, and Jilinda and Jolene, her younger sisters, and her brothers Bruce (JH director), Mark (entrepreneur investor/ youth minister), Craig (entrepreneur business owner), Doug (sales executive for Kaiser Insurance), Rick (school teacher, composer), Curt (musician), and Tim (JH staff and college student).

Intentionally, I spent much of my time visiting with Johnston family members, learning about who they were, listening to stories, and finding that we had so much in common. They were an all-around free-spirited and wild bunch. The only Johnston I didn't see much was Jenise—the one I so desperately wanted to see more of. Observing her from a distance, she worked so intentionally in serving, leading, or fulfilling responsibilities. Occasionally, I'd catch her eye. We'd exchange a glance and a smile, but that was it.

Things improved Friday evening. To my delight, on a wooden stage in the tent where all meetings were, Jenise provided a concert singing and sharing her testimony. I was transfixed! Her voice, that of an angel, resounded deep and full, lower than I'd expected, rich and clear. Her genuine passion echoed so purely throughout the tent. Jenise wasn't of this world. She picked those songs because they meant something to her, and she believed the message she shared.

This wasn't a show but a sharing of heart, and I hung on every word, lost in the moment. She was so real, open, confident, bold, and, yes, beautiful. Jenise shared how she'd come to faith in Christ during her early childhood and, in middle school, how she realized *the world* was going one way, and her faith was calling her to something different. Who was she? What choices would she make over the next five years of her life? Where would these choices lead her? She knew following and going with the flow wouldn't lead to the life of blessing she desired.

To hear from the heart of a young and strong woman like Jenise, if I wasn't gone on her before that evening began, by the time she concluded, I was done! Yes, I was head over heels in love with this woman, this angel. She was a woman of strength, courage, character, wisdom, and hard work. Not shallow and trite, but depth and substance. Wow! What a woman. As she spoke that evening, I remember thinking that her beauty was stunning, but the beauty inside surpassed her appearance.

My eyes swept the tent to witness her enchanting, melodic voice divinely touching every person with its sincerity.

Leaving the tent, I ran into Carl, a fellow I had met earlier that week at the ranch. Immediately, I sensed his awe in Jenise as well. "She is amazing!" I remember him expressing. During our walk up the lodge hill road back to the snack bar, he couldn't stop talking about her. He wished he had the courage to ask her out. Too lost in my thoughts about this incredible young woman, I said little and wondered how I could make her mine.

Back in the cabin, while my cabinmates dozed, I revisited in my mind every detail of that evening—the way she looked and stood and carried herself, her white jeans and pink and white blouse, her blonde hair, and that smile. Oh, that world-changing smile! Her angelic voice was warm, rich, and full. Her heart was so kind, so genuine, so graceful, so loving. I drifted off to sleep.

The very next day, I had my big break. For just five minutes between her busy tasks, I spoke with her. Under the big canopy where we ate our meals, she'd just finished wiping down tables. Looking so sporty and fit, she smiled as I walked up. "Thank you for sharing last night," I said. "That was wonderful."

"Thank you," she said, smiling once again. I felt myself melting into a puddle. *Oh, my word! She is too much! Why does this girl smite me so?* In the past, I'd taken great pride in being able to approach any creature of the opposite sex and confidently engage in conversation or make them laugh with a witty quip, comment, or question. Okay, seriously—most of my life had smoothly played out in that area. I really humored myself on being pretty good with the ladies.

But this was completely different. In the presence of this woman, I felt over my head, out of my league, and like a little boy in the presence of a princess. It was pathetic. Fortunately, I was way too interested in her to stand flat-footed with my mouth gaping open. We did have a brief conversation, the details of which you'd have to ask her. I was simply glad to be talking to her.

Later that day, she walked by with some young man, who—I heard through the rumor mill—was dating her, and there were even whispers of possible engagement. *No! That can't be!* Such troubling, exasperating thoughts.

During our twelve-hour drive home, the vehicle buzzed with excited chatter, storytelling, and adventure—the replaying of a group of young people who'd just experienced a remarkable week at the ranch. Each told stories of river rafting water fights, jumping off high rocks, getting roughed up in the bully ball game at the rodeo. All these adventures were very much on my mind, too, but my thoughts kept returning to one person—Jenise Cheri Johnston.

Jilinda, her younger sister by two years, had told me her middle name, Cheri. Jilinda, a firecracker and closer to my age (twenty-two), was fun, dynamic, and athletic. Some even tried to match us up that week. I spent more time with their older sister, Janet (she must have been thirty or so). Sadly, she was divorced but had a cute and outgoing personality and was talkative and more than willing to share the good, the bad, and the ugly about the Johnston family. I loved her for it! She gave me a window into Jenise, how she was raised, Gene and Joy (her parents), the ranch, and all those eleven siblings.

I hit it off with Jenise's brothers.

I can't forget Bruce giving the lake orientation to the campers. He climbed the twenty-five-foot tower and launch pad for the Super Swing, which quickly became my favorite activity at the lake. Once he was done with his talk, in a dress shirt and blue jeans, he set the microphone down and jumped out in a classic belly flop formation flying toward the water below. Every one of the 200-plus campers gasped, imagining he'd spread his guts all over the glassy water. Did he? No! Daredevil Bruce brought his hands and feet together into the jack-knife position, minimizing the pain and thrilling us all with the feat.

He was my kind of guy. Bruce was a visionary, full of crazy-fun ideas, and a great leader too. I had several brief conversations with him throughout the week and left each one knowing I could learn a lot from him and wishing for more time. One evening in the cabin, I envisioned myself a part of the leadership team at the ranch, working alongside Bruce. Leadership and impacting young men's lives in an outdoor adventure type of setting was a dream of mine, and the JH had that in spades.

We could have been twins separated at birth, though he was older than me by almost twenty years. I related to him on so many levels: He was a big-time adventurer. He'd journeyed to Hawaii on a sailboat, flown airplanes, ridden motorcycles, and ran the JH Ranch. He was handsome and his wife, Heather, was beautiful. I visualized myself dating Jenise and hanging out with Bruce and Heather and thought how cool that'd be.

I never met a man more in love with Jesus and telling others about him than Jenise's brother Mark. He was truly an evangelist and a character. He could turn any conversation into a powerful life-changing faith talk. He was a very successful entrepreneur who'd built a good business that allowed him to retire at the young age of thirty to go into full-time ministry, working with down-and-out youth in his community. He said thirty was the age when Jesus started his ministry, so it must be a good time to start his. Man, I liked Mark.

A third brother, Craig, had such a personality. Yes, all the Johnston men were made of the same cloth. Each one was full of fun stories, and each was unique with amazing qualities. Craig was no different. He was very successful in business and had started a carpet cleaning business in high school. He was a superstar football player, always late to practice because he was training an employee or dealing with a customer then evermore trying to make up time by racing over in his new Corvette. In a nutshell, Craig was very self-motivated and didn't know a stranger but could sell a drowning man a glass of water. It's not that he would, but he could.

Doug, Rick, Curt, and Tim rounded out the list of Jenise's brothers, each amazing and gifted and so much fun to get to know over the week. Along with those seven brothers were five sisters: Judy, Janet, Jilinda, Jenise, and Jolene. Judy was an incredible artist and playwright; Janet was a sales-woman through and through who could sell anyone just about anything—don't worry about the details, just give her your credit card and she'd get you going; then there was Jilinda, whom you know; and the youngest sister, Jolene, who was my age (twenty).

Twelve children, all so strong, unique, gifted, hardworking, and accomplished, yet unconventional. It reminded me of my family. I was the third of eight children—five boys and three girls. We, too, were a bit of an unconventional bunch. We did things our way and charted our various paths.

Getting into the van to head home, I felt empty. I didn't get to say goodbye to Jenise. She was nowhere around when we left. So, lost in thought on my journey home, I gratefully relived the time I spent with Jenise's family, and I pensively replayed the few interactions I had with her. The whole purpose of my trip was out of sight most of the time. Was she hiding from me? I doubt it. I sincerely doubted whether she even knew I existed. Being at that ranch, she must have a thousand young men hanging around, following her every move. Was I only another one of those? Of course not! I quickly countered that thought and tried to join the conversation in the van.

David knew me better than anyone on the planet and started razzing me. "So why are you so quiet, Chadwick Buford? You got a girl on your mind—a little crush that's crushing you? Don't worry about her, Chad. I saw her with her fiancé. She'll be fine."

It was a classic motivational speech by David Edmond Johnson. He was well-known for his quick wit and cutting humor, and this guy took great pride in saying it as it was (he still does). Well, he was right about one thing—I had it *really* bad for this girl. Maybe he was also right that she had her guy, maybe fiancé, and was fine without me. Was I wasting my time thinking about her?

After being at the ranch for the week, I decided that the whole Johnston family was a family I'd love to be a part of. I'd always said, "You don't marry a girl. You marry a family."

That was a family I'd like to marry. The JH Ranch left a big impression on me. It was all such a blessing to see a family working together to minister to others, to serve, to bless, and to grow others. I loved that!

But she doesn't even seem to know you exist, Chad. She is out of your league. What are you thinking?

* * *

CHAD'S REFLECTIONS

It has been said—and I fully agree—that you don't marry a person; you marry a family. Obviously, you don't literally marry a family, but the point is important.

The person you marry comes with parents (most likely) and siblings (most likely), and these people will play an important role in your life and marriage. Even if they are distant geographically, they are family. If the Lord blesses you with children, these people will be their grandparents, aunts, and uncles.

The blessing of family can play a hugely supportive role in a marriage, or they can be a demanding challenge.

I want to be clear here. Most people don't get to choose their family. And the "sins" of the parents must not be carried by the offspring. A believer is made new, and issues such as divorce, substance abuse, or other damaging potentials come with emotional baggage. This coupled with a family who doesn't share in faith can place a difficult strain on the marriage.

My advice is to marry a person with the most stable family background as possible. Trust that if the Lord has something else for you, He will help you thrive in that.

CHAPTER 5
GOD, I NEED A MIRACLE

By the time we arrived home after battling traffic, I was borderline depressed. Surely, much of it was due to the physical letdown from being so up all week: adventure, adrenaline, fun, late nights, busyness, social stimuli, and then *crash* . . . right back to work tomorrow.

The experience left me physically exhausted, emotionally cleared, and even spiritually drained after being on such a divine high at the ranch. I found myself more motivated than ever to grow in my relationship with the Lord, in reading His Word, and in prayer, but that all seemed so far away right now. I fell into bed that evening, praying that tomorrow would feel brighter, more possible, and promising.

The next couple of weeks were full of work, church, friends, and life as usual, but everything was far from usual in my head. I couldn't stop thinking about Jenise. David couldn't help but notice. "Hey, Chad, we ought to go over to the Poulters' house." The Poulters were friends of ours. "I heard they're inviting some people over, and I believe a couple of girls we haven't met will be there. It should be fun!"

Usually, I was the first one to jump at the chance to socialize, hang out, and meet some new people, especially new girls. As I mentioned earlier, I had many wonderful, good friends who were girls and just that—friends. My parents encouraged all eight of their children to have a lot of friends, including those of the opposite sex. But with that encouragement, they challenged us not to date or engage in a serious relationship unless two things were present:

1) We were ready and at a place in life where we could marry.

2) We would date intentionally—meaning, if the person wasn't "marriage material" for us, then we wouldn't date or have a serious relationship with that person but would remain friends.

For the most part, all of us took that to heart and modeled our dating and romantic lives that way. Though twenty-one years old with plenty of opportunity, I'd only dated two girls at that point. I appreciated the wisdom of my parents. In both cases, these girls were attractive, godly young women. They were great catches who have proven to be wonderful wives and mothers. Yet, I knew after the first date with one and after the second date with the other that they weren't for me.

In both instances, they were surprised and taken aback with the thought that we wouldn't be dating. They were certain we'd enjoyed our time together and that our friendship could progress to something deeper and long-term. Don't ask me how I knew, but I did. I'd never marry them, so we were done in that way and continued to be friends. One even attended my wedding.

Very few guys I knew were as intentional as I was, which I attribute to my parents' wisdom and counsel. They spared my siblings and me so much trauma and difficulty in relationships—in dating, engagement, and marriage. To this day, all eight of us enjoy great satisfaction in our marriages (at least to all appearances anyway; a person could fake it, but I hope not).

Besides saving myself from relationship ruin, this intentional dating worked because I strongly desired a rich, real, romantic relationship that was extraordinary. I wanted an amazing marriage. I viewed dating as the foundation building block for marriage. It wasn't only a time to have fun, feel romantic feelings, and goof around. My parents modeled the kind of marriage I wanted, a strong relationship—loving, committed, dedicated, and caring.

I'd purposed in my heart early on that I'd apply myself to building the kind of relationship that truly nourished and cherished my bride. I wanted a woman who longed to be dated, courted, and romanced for her entire life and not only during the initial months of getting to know each other. My desire was for a woman who'd become more beautiful and radiant due to the rich joy of a loving relationship and the total oneness of being fully known and loved unconditionally. Jenise sure seemed like she might be that kind of woman.

As the weeks went by after my return from the ranch, I was a conflicted mess of thoughts about what to do next. *Should I call her?* No. Her summer at the ranch held a mission she must accomplish, and I so respected her commitment to that. I witnessed firsthand how hard Jenise worked and how little time she had for anything but her work. The last thing I wanted to do was interrupt her there.

Should I write to her? No. I remembered her fiancé or boyfriend and thought if I had any chance of connecting with Jenise, it must be in person once she returned from the ranch. I knew she lived with her parents in Fullerton and had one more year to finish her studies at Cal State Fullerton. I should wait until the end of summer, only six more weeks, and then I could ask her out and make my case.

The weeks passed slowly, and it was very clear that this crush wasn't waning or going away. David continued to cheer me on in his usual way. "Hey, Chad, what's on your mind? Not the harpist, is it? She's probably married by now, dude. Time to get a new crush. Time to move on, my friend."

31

Then came grappling and tussling in the way that brothers do, and being the older brother, I had the upper hand. I'd rough him up a bit and teach him a lesson that lasted fifteen or twenty minutes before he'd begin again.

Deep down, I loved his teasing, comments, and great sense of humor. Yet at times, what he said hit too close to home. Like most fears, they're bigger in your head than in person, though you have no way of knowing that in the moment. It turns out the fiancé was never really a fiancé. Janet told me later Jenise cut that relationship off the weekend after our singles week. It had nothing to do with me, unfortunately. It'd become clear he wasn't the right one, and they went their separate ways.

As the last weeks of the summer of 1991 passed, my fears grew bigger and bigger.

In my heart, I prayed, *Lord, is there any chance Jenise Johnston is the girl for me? She matches all those things I wrote down two years ago in the ski patrol shack at the top of Snow Summit. But, Lord, she probably doesn't even remember me. How do you know, Lord, when you're to pursue or go a different direction?*

I remember reading the account in Scripture where Elisha put out a fleece before the Lord and tested him on how to proceed. The Lord answered Elisha and made his path very clear. I really wanted that too.

Well, I didn't know if this was a good idea or not, but I truly didn't want to waste my time, Jenise's time, or fall flat on my face if it truly wasn't God's will for my life. So I prayed. *Lord, if you'll cause my path to cross three of Jenise's siblings over the next week, this will truly be a sign from you.* If I ran into three of the Johnston family members over the next seven days, I'd see it as the Lord saying, "Chad, pursue Jenise Johnston until you win her heart, or she breaks yours."

Note to the reader: I'm not advocating this theological approach to romantic pursuit, but it's what I did.

The Johnston home in Fullerton, Orange County, California, was less than fourteen miles from my parents' house, where I stayed for the summer. In a city the size of Los Angeles, you never run into anyone from that far away, let alone three people. Knowing I'd asked for the impossible, I let it go and slept well that Sunday night.

* * *

CHAD'S REFLECTIONS

Looking back, I can see all kinds of reasons not to do what I did. I do believe that God is the God of miracles who speaks today and desires us to seek Him with all our hearts. As for putting a "fleece" before the Lord, there are men far more equipped to comment on that. What I do know is this—I wanted God's will in my life, and still do, more than anything. I wanted His very best in my relationships and even more so in the dating department of my life. My wisdom was not sufficient, and God's leading is what I desired.

CHAPTER 6
JUST NOT POSSIBLE

The following evening, my mother asked me to run next door where my Uncle Allan and Aunt Linda lived with their seven children, my double cousins. Yep, double cousins. My father, Burnell, and Uncle Allan are brothers; Burnell married Paula Clayton, who is Aunt Linda's sister. So cousins on both sides equals double cousins. Living right next door made them feel more like siblings, and often we went through the gate in the backyard fence that separated our two houses to borrow milk, eggs, butter, or some honey. Tonight it was butter, so I ran through the gate and knocked on the back door of their sprawling ranch-style home.

Donna Beth opened the door and let me in. "Oh, hi, Chad. Do you remember Mark Johnston?"

Johnston! Hearing the name sent a jolt through me. "Johnston! Did you say Mark Johnston?" I asked.

"Yes. He's here for dinner. Come in and say hi." Sure enough, at the table surrounded by my cousins sat Jenise's older brother Mark.

"Hi, Mark. How are you?" My mind was whirling. *Mark, here? What an amazing coincidence! Really, for real?* The very day following my prayer, here was Mark. Unbelievable! After a bit of small talk and a question about the rest of the family (although Mark didn't seem to understand what it really

34

meant), I grabbed the butter as directed and headed back to the house.

Tuesday passed with zero Johnston sightings.

Wednesday, I worked at Ceramic Decorating Company, Inc., the family business that my grandfather and his brother started in 1934. Shortly before noon, they paged me to come to the office. I made my way past the loud bottle screen printing machines and up to the front office. Standing on the porch was Jenise's older brother—*Craig Johnston*! He dropped by to see where Donna Beth worked, which happened to be the place I worked. (Always the entrepreneur, Craig later attempted to purchase the business when my father and uncle were considering selling it.)

That day, Craig offered to take me to lunch. As we talked, I picked his brain about Jenise, the whole Johnston family, business, and anything else I could think of. Craig was an enjoyable and likable guy, full of wisdom and a sharp sense of humor. Driving back to the office, I couldn't help but talk to the Lord. *Well, you've done the unimaginable already, Lord. Two Johnston family members in three days. Are you really going to do this for me? Are you going to make it clear that I'm to pursue Jenise?*

Thursday at work, the day passed without incident. After dinner that evening, I drove to the Whittwood Mall in Whittier, California. This mall had the nearest Oshman's Sporting Goods store, and I needed a new volleyball for the gym night we were planning for Saturday evening. The mall closed at 9:00 p.m., and I knew I'd cut it close. I ran through the mall's inner corridors, arriving just before they pulled down the metal-framed security gate. I quickly made my purchase and made my way back down the long interior mall between the closed shops. I saw a lone figure walking toward me from the far end. He was carrying a scooter, and as I got closer, I stopped in shock.

Walking toward me was Jenise's brother Curt, who is the brother directly older than her. He had a big grin on his face, and he said, "Hey, Chad. How are you?" His voice was quiet and soft. I don't entirely remember what I said. *Curt Johnston?* I had just run into three of Jenise's siblings in four days! I'd never experienced such a clear message from the Lord. It was obvious to me that the Lord, God of all creation, had orchestrated events in my life to tell me He loves me, listens to me, and was leading me. It was such a special moment. *Thank you, Lord!* I spent the drive home singing praises to Him, thanking Him for His goodness to me.

It was crystal clear. I was to pursue Jenise Johnston! I had no idea what that meant. Would I win and find my one true love? Would this be the heartbreak I'd so wanted to prevent? I didn't know, but I was fired up about the adventure. Let the games begin!

* * *

CHAD'S REFLECTIONS

Seeing Jenise's brothers was an amazing confirmation for me. While "proper theology" may disapprove or disagree with what transpired with me running into her brothers, for me, it was a delight to see God answer my prayer in real time, in a real way. I do believe that the God of all creation, who made me, knows what is best for me, is on my side, and wants to shed light upon my path, and did so in a powerful way that week in August of 1991.

CHAPTER 7
SHE'S DATING SUPERMAN?

Working at the Ceramic Decorating Co. the following day, I finished a big project at 8:30 p.m. I thought I ought to call Jenise before it got too late, so I went into my office and closed the door. I half-dialed Jenise's home number and hung up for the third time. *Dude, are you a chicken or what?* I could hear David chiding me in my mind, always the coach and motivator, egging me on. *Chad, you said you would never have trouble calling a girl. Just pick up the phone and call!*

I took a deep breath and dialed again. The phone rang. My breath came in short gasps. *What's up with me?*

"Hello?" a deep voice answered (definitely not Jenise).

"Hello." I tried not to sound like an adolescent boy whose voice was just beginning to change. "This is Chad Johnson. Is this Gene Johnston?"

Her father replied, "Yes, it is."

"Uh, okay. I was wondering, well, I really enjoyed meeting Jenise at the ranch this summer; I was wondering, well, uh, would it be okay if I asked her out? I'd really like to get to know her better." *There! I said it.*

The pause seemed far too long. "Well," Gene said, "you'd have to ask her."

"Okay, great! Is she there?" I could feel my confidence returning.

"No, she isn't here. She moved to Georgia," he said, like he'd just told me she was on an errand and would be right back.

What? She moved to Georgia?

He must have sensed my shock from my delayed response and repeated, "Georgia, as in the state, on the other side of the country."

"Yes, got it. I guess I'm a bit surprised. Do you have her phone number?" I asked.

"No, I don't. Joy?" His voice faded as he called out to ask his wife if she had Jenise's number.

I heard Joy, Jenise's mother, in the background, "No. Have him call Janet. She'll have it."

Gene's voice sounded much louder as he spoke directly into the phone again, "Here is Janet's number. Try her."

"Okay, thank you very much," I said after I wrote down the number.

"Good night." He hung up the phone.

What on earth? Seriously? Jenise moved to Georgia?

The phone call to Janet was easy. After I brought her up to speed on my reason for calling, my short conversation with their father, and what I honestly thought of Jenise, Janet filled me in on what was going on with her sister.

"Janet, I've never met anyone like Jenise. She's amazing. I see so many things in her that are the kinds of character, personality, and qualities I want in a wife someday. What's going on with her? When I was at the ranch, she was dating a guy named James. Are they still dating or engaged?"

Janet laughed. "Oh, no," she said. "She dumped him the weekend after singles week. That was over seven weeks ago. There's a new guy now." She giggled happily. I could tell she was enjoying torturing me, but I didn't see the humor.

"Who is this guy?" I asked. "How serious are they?"

"His name is Will Markman, and he's amazing!" She informed me that he was twenty-eight years old, six feet, four inches of tan, fit, good-looking Ironman triathlete, who loved the Lord and made over $400,000 a year as a businessman in Atlanta.

"Oh, great," I muttered under my breath. "Now she's dating *Superman!*"

I'd always been a confident guy, somehow infused with a strong dose of can-do and a positive attitude. I was up for a challenge and ready to tackle the hard things, but somehow with Jenise, I wasn't sure I'd measure up. Upon hearing all the heroics about the new guy, I ruled myself coming up way short.

Instead of four years older than Jenise, I was three years younger. Instead of having a steady career and a solid six-figure income, I was a ski patrolman making two bucks an hour above minimum wage. Instead of six feet, four inches, I came to a whopping five feet, eleven and one-half inches—if I was wearing really thick socks. I loved the Lord with all my heart but wasn't sure that'd make a difference here. The fear set in the longer Janet spoke. She seemed to be having herself some fun chatting with me and making me squirm.

When she finished giving me Jenise's number and the latest scoop, she said, "Well, I'd better hang up so you can call her right now."

"Now? Right now? It's 9:00 p.m. in California. That means after midnight in Atlanta. That's way too late!" I protested.

"Oh, no," Janet replied. "Call her now. It's Friday night. She'll be up. A bunch of young people get together there on the weekends. She'll most likely be up."

"What if she isn't?" I countered.

"Then, you'll take her by surprise!" Janet laughed. "Which is even better!"

I laughed. Janet was nuts. What a gung-ho girl! I liked her. Thanking Janet, I said I'd call and hung up the phone.

This time, I committed to dialing the phone only once. Before I called, I prayed. *Lord, you know exactly what's best for me. If it's Jenise, please let me get an open door or at least the opportunity to proceed. If not, slam the door as quickly as possible. I don't want to hurt Jenise or get hurt if this isn't your doing. You've made it clear I'm to pursue until I win her, so I will continue to do so unless you make it crystal clear we aren't for each other. Please move in such a way as to make things clear.*

"Hello, this is Jenise!"

The thrill of hearing her voice caught me by surprise. I felt an incredible surge of joy sweep over me. Yes, she still had me. She had no idea how she'd been impacting my life ever since I met her in early April. She'd somehow held my heart captive without even knowing or trying. And now I had her on the phone.

"Hello, Jenise, this is Chad Johnson. From California. I met—"

"Chad Johnson!" She laughed as she interrupted me. "I know who you are. How are you?"

"Very well, Jenise. How are you?"

"Good!" she said.

"I got your number from Janet. Actually, I called your father to ask if I could ask you out on a date."

"You did?" she said with a hint of intrigue.

"Yes, and he informed me you'd moved to Atlanta. I couldn't believe it. He gave me Janet's number and said she'd have yours. She's hysterical, by the way," I said with a laugh, and Jenise laughed too.

"Oh, yes, she's a wild one," Jenise replied.

"Well, I know it's late, and you're probably wondering what I'm doing calling you. I went to the ranch this summer for one reason." I paused. "To see you. I really enjoyed meeting you at Brenda's wedding and went to the ranch to get to know you better and meet your family. It was a blast, but you and I got very little time to talk. That whole week I watched you working, serving, and loving on people. I thought you were stunning from the moment I met you, but the night you sang and shared your testimony, I saw how beautiful you are on the inside. In fact, I saw many things in you that are qualities I would like to see in a wife someday."

Wow! Did I just say all that? Chad, you're just putting it out there. I hope you know what you're doing and don't scare this girl away in this first opportunity to speak to her.

"I left the ranch a bit disappointed that we didn't get the chance to connect. Then, I learned you were dating a guy. Janet said you aren't dating James anymore, but now there's a new guy. I believe she said his name is Superman. She also informed me that he's seven feet tall, is totally yoked, loves the Lord like no other, does Ironman triathlons every day before breakfast, and makes a million bucks a year without breaking a sweat. Is this true? Are you really serious about him?"

Laughing, she replied, "Well, the part about James is true. He is history. As for Will, well, there are always questions." I loved to hear Jenise laugh.

"Good," I replied. "Keep asking questions." A laugh came from her end of the line.

I changed the subject, and we made a little small talk about her decision to move to Atlanta. I could sense she wanted to get away from James. She enjoyed new friendships and the challenges of a new job, having harp students, and getting involved with Charles Stanley's church. It was so easy to talk with her. So fun! The minutes were brief and flew by far too fast.

I told her I should let her go and prepared to hang up the phone but wanted to be sure I had a next step lined up to continue the conversation. "Jenise, if you were closer, I'd ask you out this weekend. But since you aren't, would you care if I wrote?"

"Sure," she said.

"Great!" I was elated.

She gave me her address, and we said farewell.

My heart sang. I'd just spoken with the girl of my dreams. Every time I encountered her it was as if everything came alive inside of me. Everything! I wanted to dance, run, sing, yell, jump up and down, and shout to the world that I was in love! Crazy, I know, because the conversation that night wasn't gushy or romantic. She didn't say anything that could have been taken as anything but friendship, but she spoke with me.

She laughed, talked, seemed to have fun, and didn't hang up on me. She didn't tell me not to write to her. She said she had questions about Mr. Will, aka *Superman*. Oh, yes, to me each one of those symbolized victories. I didn't realize the anticipation I'd bottled up for the past few months and wondered what our next point of contact would be. Would there be a crack in the door for me, or would the door slam shut? Now, I knew! We'd spoken, and I was positive she enjoyed it and was glad I called. There was an opening for me to pursue, a tiny seed planted. Yes!

* * *

CHAD'S REFLECTIONS

As you can tell by now, I am old school. I believe it is a guy's responsibility to pursue the girl, that it's a young man's duty to interrupt the life of a girl he wants to get to know. Does this require courage? You bet! Is it freaky and scary at times? For sure! Is it a thrill to be in the game? Absolutely!

At times, I run into guys with interest in a young woman or with a major crush. They see potential in someone who could be a possible spouse and yet fail to act. I can think of two different guys, who, as of this writing, had a major interest in a young lady but lacked the courage to reach out and connect. Both of those young men want a lifelong, committed relationship yet are still single.

Yes, the odds against you can seem daunting. Yes, the "competition" can seem larger than life. Yes, she can say no and break your heart in two. Yes, you can keep your head down and hope someone falls in your lap.

This is not for guys only; young ladies need to take a risk to say yes to a date that seems a bit of a stretch and to share your heart in getting to know a guy while not sure if he is "the one."

To win a heart, taking a risk is necessary.

CHAPTER 8
NOT COMING HOME FOR CHRISTMAS

I jumped into my Toyota 4Runner, my heart still soaring from our phone call and began the drive home. The first song on the radio about sent me through the roof. I found myself crying as I sang along with Shenandoah's country song, "The Moon Over Georgia."

Was this too good to be true or what? What are the odds that this song would play at this time—a song about a super-rich guy from Atlanta, trying to win a girl, but she took the moon over Georgia. *All I had to offer her was the moon.*

The following day I mailed a letter to Jenise. The contents were not gushy, romantic, or overly forward. I erred on the side of newsy, providing a bit about me and what I was up to. Then I asked her some questions. I didn't want her to feel pressured. I hoped to establish a bit of a friendship and learn more about who she was, what she thought about, and what she was learning. More than anything, I wanted insight into her mindset. It's been said that mindset is everything, and more and more, I believe it's true.

Mindset is a powerful thing. It drives how we think, the way we act, and the fruit we get to reap in our lives. Wrong mindset? Wrong fruit! Right mindset? Sweet fruit! It makes all the difference in the world. It's difficult to write someone a letter and not let them get a glimpse into your mindset. As I dropped it in the mail, I counted the moments until I received a letter in return. I'm not too good at waiting. The following Friday morning, I got a wild idea to send her some flowers.

I questioned myself on the way to the flower shop. *Chad, what are you doing? You'll scare her off. You asked if you could write to her a few days ago. She's likely receiving it today or possibly yesterday. Now you're dropping flowers on her doorstep. She's dating that Superman guy. She'll shut you down. This is too much, too soon.*

Nevertheless, I drove until I arrived at Commerce Flowers on Atlantic Boulevard in East Los Angeles, a place jam-packed with flowers on the walls, on the shelves, all over the floor, and in the bathroom (I don't know; I'm just guessing). It was like navigating a maze to get to the front counter. The line was three deep, but the staff was helpful and fast.

"What can I get you?" the woman behind the counter asked, smiling at me.

"I want to send some flowers to a girl!" I blurted out.

Her smile brightened further, and she nodded knowingly, encouraging me to continue. When I didn't continue, she leaned forward, puzzled. "Yes?" she asked.

My look spoke more than words. Clearly, I hadn't done this before.

She quickly picked up on it, turned to a nice mixed arrangement, and asked, "Would you like to send something like this? A large spring mix bouquet? It's $64.99, and I'm sure she'll like it."

"Well, I was thinking more—"

Seeing my hesitation, she pointed to a much smaller version of what appeared to be the same bouquet.

"No, too small. What about some roses?" I asked.

"Oh." She raised her eyebrows and smiled. "Like that?" She pointed to a beautiful arrangement of a dozen red roses.

"No, too much, too soon! How about those?" I asked, pointing to a dozen yellow roses. I'd heard yellow roses were for friendship. Friendship seemed about right. We couldn't call ourselves more than that.

My friendly flower saleswoman took a pen and asked me, "What do you want to say?"

"Say? Uh, I don't know. What should I say?" My thoughts churned. What do you say and not seem weird, desperate, or something else undesirable? I sensed she was getting impatient. A line was forming behind me, so I blurted out, "I can't get you out of my mind . . . Chad!"

The woman smiled and wrote it down. It was true. That's exactly what had been happening since, well, wow . . . since I first met her back in April. Now it was early September, and for the past six months, she'd been finding her way into my thoughts.

What was she going to think? *Oh, well, what's done is done*, I thought to myself.

Little did I know that in Atlanta that evening, Jenise would be with a group of young people at Dr. Stanley's church for a social function. She was visiting with none other than the *Superman*, Will, when her roommate, Karen, walked in with a large bouquet of yellow roses. She handed them to her and walked away with eyebrows raised and a smile on her face as she glanced back over her shoulder. Jenise quickly read the card (with Will looking over her shoulder). She later told me she knew they weren't from him. He wasn't the kind of guy to do something like that.

"Who's Chad?" he asked.

"Oh, a guy I met at a wedding earlier this year," she replied nonchalantly.

After repeatedly checking the mailbox for the letter postmarked Atlanta what seemed a million years later, I received a letter from Jenise. Okay, it was closer to a week. "You're so sweet! Thank you for the flowers. They were beautiful!" She shared what the Lord was teaching her, what was happening with her work, how harp and voice lessons were going, and about life in Atlanta. She ended in asking a few questions.

She'd written back, and I was elated! Thus began a series of letters between us over the rest of September, October, and November. As December approached, I wondered if she would come home to see her family over the Christmas holiday. I also wondered what was going on with Superman Will. Still dating? How serious? Or was it over? Still friends? She never brought it up. She was writing to me, so I saw no reason to rock the boat, but by the time late November came around, I had to know.

Sure enough, I got a letter. It read, "I'm bummed that I can't make it home for Christmas. Funds are tight, and it appears I need to stay here." My heart sank as I read the words. I was broke, too! *Man, I wish I had the money to buy her a plane ticket.* Managing my money hadn't been a priority up to this point in my life. I worked to maintain basic necessities, such as ski gear, gas money, and lift tickets, with not much left over after I purchased sufficient amounts of the above. Plus, we were in no place in our friendship for me to offer to buy her a plane ticket.

A week later, another letter arrived. It read, "Plans have changed! I will make it home after all. I'm so excited to see my family—"

I don't remember reading the rest. She was coming back to California! Yes, yes, yes! I picked up the phone. I had to know. When? For how long? What about Will? Stuff like that.

It was so good to hear her voice. Why did my heart sing hearing her answer the phone? "Hello, this is Jenise." Aw! The conversation that followed did my heart so much good. She was warm, fun, and to my question about *Superman* Will, she said it hadn't progressed; they weren't dating, and they were only friends. *Yes!*

She met my inquiry of possibly getting together with what seemed like genuine interest. Getting off the phone, I found myself hard-pressed to find my footing. I was walking on air! It took so little from her to make my day. *What on earth is wrong with me?* Never, and I mean never, had a woman had this effect on me. And I liked it—a lot.

* * *

CHAD'S REFLECTIONS

When I heard that song, "The Moon Over Georgia," come on the radio immediately after speaking with her on the phone, it spoke to me so powerfully and somehow instilled confidence. Anytime I take a risk, I win, or I learn. As my business coach, Dan Sullivan, has taught me, taking risks is so important in life. The fruit of healthy risk-taking is full of wonderful life-giving rewards.

It is far more dangerous to live attempting to avoid risk and playing it too safe. So often, the fears we conjure up in our minds do not turn out to be real at all. FEAR is False Evidence Appearing Real.

It is often better to take many small risks than to take one massive risk. Take a risk to advance your cause. Evaluate the outcome, then take another risk based on what you find.

CHAPTER 9
A HEART NOT IN IT

The next few weeks crawled by up until I learned Jenise had landed at the Orange County Airport and was home in Fullerton. My family was planning a day trip of skiing to Big Bear, California.

I called and asked if she'd like to join us. She accepted. Her brother Mark and several other Johnston siblings also joined us at Snow Summit.

This was my world. I had worked as a ski patrolman at Snow Summit over the past five winters. I knew every inch of the small ski hill and was prepared to deliver some wow and impress this woman. In my prime as a skier, I carved tight turns, slammed the bumps, busted sweet airs, and even pulled a backflip along the way. Jenise was right there every time I turned around. She never seemed very impressed with my antics, but she impressed me with how she could hang with me no matter what the terrain or pitch.

Wow, she was a fine woman indeed! She wasn't only the most beautiful girl in the world, but she loved the Lord, and she could ski well! What more could a man ask for? Could this really be true? We piled into a fifteen-passenger van and sang songs all the way home. As I replayed the day, my heart grew fuller. With each glimpse into Jenise, my regard for her intensified.

The only disappointment was how brief her visit to California would be—only five days. The following evening, her brother Mark put on a pageant in his front yard as an outreach to the community, and, of course, Jenise sang Christmas carols. I rounded up my parents, many of my siblings, and a few cousins, and we went to enjoy the show. Hearing her sing once more delighted me beyond measure. She truly was an angel.

That weekend, I was scheduled to lead activities for young people at a camp in North County San Diego. My family and about 250 other people were going, and I agreed to help long before I knew Jenise would be home for the holidays. Driving down Friday evening seemed wrong. Jenise would be at her folks' home until Monday morning. Just two more days and I'd be out of town for the entire time? Lame.

Friday night I was scheduled to lead an activity. My heart wasn't in it. When I commit, I'm a 100 percent engaged and present kind of guy, but I felt halfway that night. My mind was in Fullerton. *What was she up to? Was she thinking of me at all?* It appeared we'd had a good time skiing and being together when we had seen each other over the past two days, but was I reading more into her friendliness than I should?

Maybe she wasn't interested. I hated the thought of it. No! She was warmer than just a friend. She wasn't flirty but friendly and open to talking and interacting and didn't give me the cold shoulder or ignore me. But there was still no real way to know what she thought unless I asked.

What am I doing here when she is there? The following morning, I woke with an immediate awareness that I needed to see her. A limited window of opportunity existed, and I couldn't miss it. I spoke with my father, who was leading the camp. I told him I wasn't present and able to put my heart into my role and asked if someone else could lead in my place. I love my father. He didn't even hesitate. "Go! We'll take care of things here. Let me know how it goes," he said with a smile and wink.

I was off in a flash. I found a phone and called the "Fullerton House," which is what the Johnston family called their Fullerton home. I believe they called it that because, for many years, the family had lived at the ranch house at JH Ranch in Etna, California. Jenise's oldest brother, Bruce, answered the phone, "Hey, Chad, what are you up to?"

"Well, I wondered if it might be okay if I came over and spent some time with your family today?"

"Sure, come on over," he replied.

"Super! I'm in San Diego, so it'll take me a while to get there."

"No problem. We'll be at the house all day. The whole family is here just spending time together," he added.

My foot felt heavier on the gas pedal than usual. The two-and-a-half-hour drive took less than two hours, and soon I was knocking on the door of an older home on a beautiful street lined with jacaranda trees. The house wasn't fancy; in fact, it was rather run down. After being at the JH Ranch and seeing the beauty of that place, this was a bit of a shock. Remembering the beat-up, old station wagon Jenise used to transport her harp, the Johnston family dynamic began to make more sense.

They definitely didn't spend a lot of money on themselves, their homes, or their cars. Bruce answered and warmly welcomed me. I immediately felt right at home. With twelve children, their spouses, and their children, the house bustled with life and energy. Great conversation animated the living room, dining room, and into the small kitchen where Jenise's mother, Joy, hustled about preparing a noonday feast.

Across the room, I caught Jenise's eye and smiled. Yes, I was there to see her, and she knew it. She seemed to like it. But what do I know? It was just a feeling I had. It was fun to go around the room and reacquaint myself with her sisters, brothers, and their spouses. Some I remembered well from the ranch six months prior, and some were new. We all gathered in the living room, and one by one they shared their talents in an informal talent show. The performer nominated the next person to sing a song, play an instrument, quote a poem, or some other talent. I could tell this wasn't their first show!

Each person seemed more talented than the one before. Curt played the piano; Bruce, Craig, and Mark played the horns; Judy did a skit, and her children acted along; Janet and her little ones sang a song; Rick performed a set of magic tricks; and then, Jenise sang. Every time she sang, I slipped a little deeper. Every set of eyes turned to me after Jenise's song, and Craig said, "Your turn."

My turn! "Okay . . ."

I got slowly to my feet and thought of what talent I could share that wouldn't completely embarrass me or make the entire Johnston family sorry they'd opened their home. I'd taken music lessons on several instruments growing up—my favorite was the five-string banjo. Piano or singing seemed to be my only options, so I made my way over to the piano and began playing the only song I knew, "Onward Christian Soldiers."

Years of piano lessons with little practice limited my repertoire. When I finished, they clapped graciously. Fortunately for me, I didn't receive a request for an encore. The whole tone of the room and the family being together refreshed me. It mirrored my home growing up—full of playful banter, storytelling of great memories, and simple delight in being together.

With my heart full, it was already time to say goodbye to the Johnstons and make my way home. Jenise and I'd had little time together, but I'd witnessed her in her natural habitat, the home she grew up in, and her interactions with her siblings. My long-held belief stands—you don't only marry a girl; you marry a family. If by some great work of God, Jenise would marry me and we were blessed with children, this amazing family would be my children's grandparents, aunts, uncles, and cousins. After a day like that, I cherished that thought every moment after.

More than almost anything, I wanted a masterpiece marriage and a masterpiece family—a family rich, full, and strong. I wanted the total of the blessing of the Lord. After that short day together with Jenise's family, I realized she came from a wonderful family. Perfect, no, but no family is. Wonderful, yes. Full of character, rich in relationship, creativity, leadership, passion, and ambition. Yes, the Johnston family would be an amazing family to be a part of.

Snap out of it, Chad. What are you thinking? You're a long way from getting anywhere with Jenise. Well, didn't Mark invite me back tomorrow for lunch after church? Yes, but that was Mark. What was Jenise thinking? I had no way of knowing. Tomorrow I must ask to find out what Jenise was thinking. Sleep came slowly that night.

With our entire church fellowship in San Diego at the camp the next morning, I didn't go to church. Why didn't I find out where the Johnstons went to church? I spent time in the Word and much of the morning in prayer instead. *Lord, show me if Jenise is the one for me. Make it clear. I don't want to waste her time or mine. I don't want to break her heart or mine. And Lord, my heart is growing fonder every moment I'm in her presence.*

* * *

CHAD'S REFLECTIONS

It is so important to listen to your heart. God gave you gut instinct, intuition. He often leads me by laying something on my heart. Finding myself in San Diego and really wanting to be in Fullerton with Jenise and her family tugged on my heart. I often think back to what might have happened if I had not listened to my heart that day. Paying attention to what you are thinking and feeling is important. Then act on it!

It felt kind of weird inviting myself over to the Johnstons' home, but I knew my time was limited. Again, another risk was in order. What if they said no? Or what if it felt awkward or strange? The opportunity to be with her and see her in her natural habitat was super important to me, so I took the risk.

In dating or intentionally pursuing someone, it is invaluable to see them in lots of different settings, with different groups of people, so that it's not only the two of you doing fun things together. I saw Jenise in a variety of settings and circumstances—work at the ranch alongside the staff, with her siblings, with my family while skiing, during her performance with others in the pageant, and then I had a full day at her home with her family. These were such valuable times, and they were so helpful in seeing what kind of woman she was (and remains). It was a delight to see how she honored her parents, how she respected her father, and how she communicated with him. It was a beautiful dynamic to see between Jenise and her siblings—how they got along, enjoyed humor, and creatively produced during their times together.

CHAPTER 10

JUST US

The next day I went to lunch at the Fullerton House. Jenise greeted me at the door—how fun! My breath came up short when I saw her. Her smile lit up the entire doorway. She looked stunning.

She welcomed me with a warm hug, and the family picked up where we'd all left off the night before, sitting around the massive table stuffed into a room far too small for it. The joyful voices and conversation of family warmed my heart as Mama Joy's cooking warmed my tummy with a chicken casserole, steamed carrots and broccoli, a hearty salad, and Bragg's Liquid Aminos for the dressing. Mama Joy was into health! I loved that. I learned later just how health-conscious she was. A healthy, hearty meal refreshed my soul.

This was the world Jenise grew up in and the example and model her mother had given her. Joy bustled about the kitchen to serve her family, taking care of every detail so everyone else could enjoy the meal. Wow! What an amazing woman. Gene, Jenise's father, was a quiet, soft-spoken man. When he spoke, everyone listened. You could sense the respect each individual had for him. He was a wise father, and his children, mostly all adults, honored him. That and so much more was apparent as we enjoyed the meal together.

As the conversation moved to the front room, I found Joy in the kitchen. "Joy, put me to work," I said, rolling up my sleeves. She was doing the dishes in the small sink in front of the window. I marveled at how small the kitchen was where this woman turned out large portions of food for her family. I joined Joy at the sink, but she turned and literally pushed me away. "Oh, stop," she said sweetly. "Go on, go on. Join the others. I've got this."

I persisted, thinking she'd allow my help. Boy, was I wrong. When Mama Joy makes up her mind, I don't know a force on Earth that can change her. So I retreated toward the front room as Jenise came through the front door. "She's not going to let me help," I said, pointing over my shoulder at her mother.

"I know she won't!" Jenise laughed. "That's the way she is." I thought Jenise was going to see her mother, but she turned with me, and we made our way to the living room.

The talk turned to what to do that afternoon, and Mark suggested we head down to Universal Studios. He said there were shops and interesting things to see. We piled into two cars, my 4Runner, and Mark's black Camaro, and headed off to the Universal Studios CityWalk. I made sure Jenise rode shotgun up front with me and her sister Jilinda sat in the back seat. The trip out was enjoyable, and we chatted about her family. We met up with the others and browsed the shops.

I don't really get excited about shopping. My approach isn't a leisurely experience but more like a hunting trip—I pick my target, zoom in, buy, and leave. I noticed what drew Jenise's attention and how she enjoyed looking, though she didn't purchase anything. I learned later how frugal, wise, and intentional Jenise was with her dollars.

Gene, who'd been an orphan and had to own his existence and sustenance at an early age, imparted his wise financial mindset to his twelve children. Each had engaged in entrepreneurial activities at very early ages, most in their early teens, to provide income for everything beyond basic food and shelter needs. Even clothing was the responsibility of the young person in the Johnston home. All the Johnston children were this way. To illustrate, when skiing the week prior, Mark showed up in a black ski bib overall set with a huge rip down one side of the leg, which he'd ingeniously remedied with duct tape. It wasn't a fashion statement, but it did the trick.

It was a thrill to be in Jenise's presence as we walked along the boardwalk. We talked, joked with her siblings, and found ourselves in front of a theater with a crowd waiting for a concert. The billboard displayed "Barry Manilow," followed by "SOLD OUT." Mark began asking guests milling about if they had tickets. Mark put his skills to work and showed up several minutes later with tickets he'd purchased for less than 50 percent of the price!

"Come on!" he said, the rush of victory still in his voice. Though I'd never heard of Barry Manilow, I recognized many of the tunes, and sitting next to Jenise made for a memory I'll always cherish.

As we exited the concert in the rain, I asked Jenise if I could drive her home—just her. "Oh, I see how it is!" Jilinda joked as she piled in with Mark's crew. I opened the door, and Jenise hopped in. I savored treating her like the lady she was. Taking care of Jenise was just fun.

* * *

CHAD'S REFLECTIONS

Money matters in relationships. It is a huge factor in how married couples interact, get along, and work together toward common objectives. What is her money style? What is his? Is one or the other a spender, saver, or in debt up to their eyeballs? Many young people pay zero attention to these things while dating or getting to know someone.

Early on, it can be useful to observe. How do they talk about money? Spend their money? Give their money? Are they generous or stingy? Risk-taker or conservative? Frugal, wise, foolish, or something else altogether?

Just being together in situations can reveal a lot. My limited time with Jenise by that point revealed some very strong tendencies—leaning toward frugality, stretching a dollar, a lack of concern with impressing others, a generosity that inspired me, a work ethic to model, healthy respect, and avoidance of frivolous debt.

All of that gave me a lot of confidence in moving forward. I knew I would need someone who was more frugal than I was; I tended to be a spender. I knew I wanted someone who would make me better than I was and not take me away from my bigger goals. Jenise, on the other hand, has said so many times that she would never spend the money I do on experiences, travel, etc. We feel that spending led to so much richness in our life, and she is glad she married me to "balance" her out. I have observed that, for many couples, finding an opposite in this area can be helpful, though not always necessary. I believe formulas on who might complement you perfectly can be risky and downright harmful. In the end, God knows who is right for you, and all the differences in the world can be overcome if He is at the center.

There is no doubt that Jenise was far more prepared for a relationship financially than I was. I had some real catching up to do to bring a healthy awareness and practice to solid financial management.

CHAPTER 11
WRONG TURN

Wonderful conversation filled the drive home. Despite the rain pounding and the thumping of the windshield wipers, I wanted the drive to last forever. It dawned on me—my exit! Scanning the nearest road sign, I gasped. Directions came easy to me, and we were nowhere near where I estimated we should be. I grew up in Los Angeles and knew the freeways like the back of my hand (and this was before smartphones and GPS), yet we drove north on the 405 freeway instead of south for close to one hour. I loved *every minute of it.*

Sheepishly, I took the next off-ramp and explained my mistake. Jenise found delight in my error. It was my joy to inform her that if she could refrain from being so engaging and distracting, I could fulfill my responsibility of getting us back to her parents' home. For the next hour and a half back to the Fullerton House, we immersed ourselves in who we were, what we liked, and what we didn't like. Jenise pointed out that the rain had stopped—as the wipers screeched away at the dry windshield. *Man, what's going on with me?*

At one point, I looked over, and Jenise had a questioning look on her face. "What are you thinking?" I inquired slowly.

"I don't know what to think anymore," she said. The look in her eyes told me that whatever this meant, it wasn't a bad thing.

Safely back at the Johnston's, we all replayed highlights from the day. Realizing it was late, I said I should get going. My parents always advised it's best to leave before being asked to leave, and I didn't want to wear out my welcome. Jenise stood up as I said my goodbyes. Walking to the door, thinking this would be my goodbye until, well, I didn't know when, I asked if I could talk to her for a minute.

Jenise had mentioned earlier in the day that she didn't know if she'd return to work on staff at JH Ranch as she had the previous nine summers. I was shocked; I thought she'd always be there. Walking from the porch to my car, I noticed the beautiful glow the streetlights cast on the jacaranda trees that covered the street with their arched branches.

"So you don't know if you'll be at the ranch this summer?" I asked as we approached my car.

Jenise replied thoughtfully, "No, I don't know yet. I can't imagine not being there, but I love my work and the students I'm teaching back in Atlanta. It feels like I'm really gaining traction there."

"Bruce asked me if I'd work at the ranch this summer," I said.

"Oh, you should!" she exclaimed. "You'd absolutely love it. It's so you!"

I loved to see the way her eyes lit up when she was excited. I could see her obvious love for the ranch. "It sounds so exciting and like something I'd love to do. I'll have to let Bruce know soon. I guess it fills up pretty quickly," I said.

"Yes, you need to confirm right away," she advised me. "They get way more candidates than they can take. Kind of a first come, first served."

"I'll go if you go," I blurted out.

She turned and looked at me. "Really?"

"Sure!" I countered. Changing the subject, I asked, "When will I see you again?"

She again looked at me. "Oh, I don't know. I guess if I come out to the ranch, maybe then."

"How are you getting to the airport tomorrow?" I asked. Without waiting for an answer, I continued. "Can I take you?"

"Really?" she questioned.

"Sure, I'd love to," I assured her.

She thought about it for a moment and looked as though she remembered something. "Oh, that probably won't work. I have to stop in Anaheim to pick up a song someone arranged for me, a soundtrack I'll be singing. It will take too much time; I don't want to trouble you."

"It's no trouble at all! What time can I pick you up?" I asked. We agreed that 9:00 a.m. would give us plenty of time to run the errand and make it to the John Wayne Airport for her scheduled departure.

* * *

CHAD'S REFLECTIONS

Making mistakes is part of any relationship. Looking back, I have a few insights. People are people, and people make mistakes. As you continue to read this story, I will share more mistakes I made, some quite embarrassing.

Here's what I have learned:

Making mistakes is easy. Owning them is hard. The quicker I own my mistakes, the better off I am. The less momentum I lose, the less progress I give up. It is rarely the mistake that sinks me, but my response to it can. Humility goes a long way to making mistakes useful and less deadly. Pride is a killer and causes mistakes to compound and multiply. Small mistakes can be laughed off and corrected immediately. Big mistakes require a sober-minded, thoughtful response and long-term action to remedy. Some mistakes have the potential to kill a relationship. Yet again, my response to the mistake is usually the deciding factor. Relationships are built on trust. Trust comes from seeing how people handle their mistakes.

CHAPTER 12
MIXED SIGNALS

I said farewell to Jenise and drove home with a bunch of mixed emotions about how the day had gone. It wasn't mixed feelings for her. No, they only continued to grow. Every conversation, look, glance, smile, and turn of her head was art, poetry in motion—absolute beauty, grace, and style. Smitten beyond measure, I was 100 percent sure of my desire to pursue this young lady, to show up on her radar, and to register as a valid contender of her heart.

But how was Jenise feeling? Yes, she'd ride in my car. Yes, she'd visit. Yes, she'd say she didn't know what to think anymore. At the same time, I didn't receive the full green light. She held back. Why? What was it? Seeing no reason whatsoever for her to do anything but fall deeply in love with me, I was definitely the wrong guy to ask.

My prayer that night was this—*Lord, please continue to make my way clear. You've promised to direct my steps if I trust in you with all my heart and lean not on my own understanding. So, Lord, I'm trusting you.*

The following day whizzed by. Our drive to Anaheim didn't take nearly long enough. We knocked on the door of a small white house on a quiet street. A gentleman, looking exactly like a composer should look, opened the door. After lengthy instructions from the man, Jenise sang along to the music, the minstrel song, "Swanee River." She was considering the song for a beauty pageant. I loved it when she sang, and I enjoyed watching her practice. The composer appeared to enjoy her performance of his music. She paid the man, and after some additional talk of future opportunities, we departed for the airport.

"That was fun!" I commented.

She glanced over at me. "Are you being sarcastic?"

"No! I enjoy doing anything with you." She turned back, seeming a bit embarrassed. It was true. The most simple, mundane, routine things—even driving in traffic—seemed like an absolute joy.

All too soon, we arrived at the John Wayne Airport parking lot. "You can just drop me up-front," Jenise suggested.

I refused. "Oh, no. I'm going to see you to your gate. You've got two heavy bags, and I won't have you lug those around."

"Well, thank you," she said.

This was long before 9/11, and security was virtually non-existent. We checked her luggage, retrieved her boarding pass, and made our way to the gate without much time to spare. The plane was almost entirely boarded, and the attendant managing the gate informed us that Jenise would need to get on.

I didn't want to say goodbye. What was it that made her irresistible to me? I hugged her, then she turned to walk toward the gate. She looked back over her shoulder with a peculiar look in her eyes. "See you this summer, maybe?"

She said it lightly, flippantly, but I thought, *There's no way on earth I'm waiting until summer to see you again.* At that exact moment, I knew! She was the one for me. I'd pull out all the stops and do whatever was in my power to win her heart.

My eyes filled with tears, and a wave of emotion washed over me, overwhelming me with gratitude, awe, and wonder as I watched her enter the jetway to board her plane. *Goodbye for now, Jenise Cheri. You've captured my heart, sweet girl. You're the one I've been praying for my entire life. Some divine day,*

I'll marry you and adore you for the rest of your life. I watched, unmoving, until the plane taxied out to its take-off point. The engines roared, and I watched as she lifted slowly and faded out of sight, tears rolling down over the smile still on my face.

I praised and thanked the Lord on the way back to the car. *Thank you, Lord, for making such an extraordinary woman. She is amazing! Awesome! Wonderful! Beautiful! Fascinating! Motivating! You're so good! She is one of your finest masterpieces.*

* * *

CHAD'S REFLECTIONS

I have found in speaking with many newlywed couples and hearing their stories that one person in the relationship often knows far earlier that the love story is going to happen, while the other may not be sure at all.

This was definitely the case for Jenise and me. I felt led to pursue her from the moment I first met her. It took me six months from meeting her to get some time with her in-person that weekend in December 1991. During that time, I continued to see my interest in her grow.

As she flew off into the skies and across the country to Atlanta, I truly felt like God had spoken to me, letting me know she was indeed the one for me. In the moment, that gave me such confidence, peace, and joy; all of it would be tested in the months ahead, but on that day it was a huge comfort.

I see a lot of young men and young ladies experience a similar knowing at some point in their relationships. They often immediately tell the person they have feelings for; in my opinion, that is nearly always a big mistake.

Looking back, I am grateful I kept that little secret deep inside and did not even think of telling Jenise of my insight. I thought it could put a lot of unneeded pressure on her. I thought it would bring a weird dynamic to our growing friendship. Just recently, I had the opportunity to observe a young man dating one of my daughters. He experienced a similar knowing and immediately shared it with her. It put unnecessary pressure on the developing friendship. Today they are not dating, and I don't foresee them dating again.

All this is to say that if you get to a place of confidence in your relationship with someone that you are sure you are going to marry them, unless you can tell they are 100 percent there as well, you might be wise to consider it your little secret. Trust that the One who revealed the information to you will also reveal it to your loved one in His perfect time.

Keep the pressure off the relationship. It seems some young men and women think sharing that insight with the other will somehow help convince that other person God is doing great work in bringing them together. Often, it can feel like spiritual manipulation being used to persuade the other to move forward. That is a major fail. A healthy relationship does not need pressure to advance. It is almost always a factor in causing the relationship to fail.

CHAPTER 13
A STRATEGIC PLAN

Shifting from praise to focus, I needed to plan a trip to see Jenise. I had no intention of waiting six months for summer. No way! I needed to jump on a plane and visit her in Atlanta to surprise her. Her birthday is February 17. Valentine's Day is the fourteenth. Ideas flowed into an adventure in the making. It would be perfect!

I called the Atlanta Chamber of Commerce and asked if they'd mail me a relocation packet. The packet included maps, points of interest, and must-do activities. Before the internet and Google, that was how we did things. After that, I dropped by AAA to get everything they had on Atlanta. The woman behind the counter asked if I was a member. She told me I had to be a member to get the information, and that it cost $59.00 per year. "Ouch!" I didn't realize I said it out loud.

The woman behind the counter laughed politely.

"I don't have that kind of money. I'm trying to surprise a girl who I like a whole lot and want to plan a trip."

"Oh, get over here," the woman said. She grabbed brochures, maps, guidebooks, and everything else within her reach that said Atlanta on it and started putting them into a bag. When finished, she looked at me with a smirk, winked, and said, "Good luck, young man. I hope you win the girl."

What a champ! She was awesome, and I let her know it. With the wind at my back, things rolled right along.

Next up, my flight—booked and done! Then, it hit me. *What am I doing?* That flight was over five hundred bucks, a big chunk of change for a ski patrolman! *Just see it as an investment*, I told myself. Yeah, an investment in my future.

Next, with the map of Atlanta, I started mapping out my plan. I'd arrive Wednesday afternoon, February 12. If everything went as planned, I'd rent a car and travel to Jenise's workplace before 5:00 p.m. to surprise her at work. The thought of surprising her anywhere else didn't sit right or make sense. If I surprised her at her church, I'd have to wait until Sunday. I didn't feel comfortable dropping by her house. Too creepy. I loved the thought of surprising her at work.

During our drive in the rain, she had mentioned that she worked for an advertising agency, Tucker Wayne/Luckie & Co., in downtown Atlanta. I researched and found it on the map. I noted the address and then noted Jenise's address about forty minutes away in Smyrna.

That evening at dinner with my parents, I told them my plan. "You should stay with Steve and Kim Gable," my mother suggested.

My memory of Kim and Steve was foggy, but I recalled a handsome couple who really seemed to like each other, and by "like," I mean in a good way. They liked to be in each other's presence—they liked each other. I always watched couples, noticed how they treated one another, spoke to one another, and loved one another. Some couples love each other, but the relationships I admired most consisted of best friends, playmates, and confidantes who truly found joy in each other's presence. Kim and Steve stood out in that way. That's all I really remembered.

I made the call, and the Gables gladly opened their home for my stay in Atlanta. It was fun to let them in on my planning and adventure, and I sensed they'd be worthy accomplices and enjoy the mission. I also asked if one of them would meet me at the airport and sign for my rental car. I was twenty-one; you had to be twenty-five to sign. Steve's work schedule wouldn't allow it, but luckily Kim could make it happen.

Bit by bit, the details slid into place. Some days, I really second-guessed myself. *Should I be doing this?* Was I nuts? What would Jenise think? Do? Not do? What if she wasn't there? What if she was too busy? Had commitments? Was with another guy? She could be dating someone; I hadn't asked her. And she—in no way—was committed to me. We hadn't even so much as hinted that something could be between us.

Yet, I felt the warmth of embers beginning to glow when we were together. Hadn't she spent time with me? Didn't she let me take her to the airport? Was she only being nice? Or using me? Some girls do that, you know. They play a guy along, get some gifts and favors, then shut him down when he gets serious.

Fear, doubt, and unknowing kept appearing. Many times in life, fear lifts its ugly head, making adventures seem unworthy, and like disasters waiting to happen. I hadn't let fear get too strong, obstacles too high, or visions of failing too real. When fear and doubt entered my mind, I remembered God's guidance in all of this. Didn't He send three—yes, three—of Jenise's family members into my life that unbelievable week? Didn't He speak to me and tell me she was the one as I sent her off on that plane a short couple of weeks prior?

I knew I must be the one to pursue. I wouldn't find a woman as interesting if she hunted me down. Yes, this was the next step. In so many ways, it reminded me of other risks I'd taken in life—simple risks. It's like a big ski jump and attempting to turn two layout backflips before landing without training and a safety net. I relished in the feeling of approaching the jump, adrenaline pumping, the blast into the air, the sensation of flying, flipping, and the powerful, sudden effect of gravity doing its thing, the earth welcoming you back with a body-slamming impact. In those moments, I feel so alive, so alert, so full of energy. It's those types of moments that make life grand and glorious. *Just go for it, Chad.*

The energy, creativity, and passion for Jenise, of life, and of this grand surprise ignited my heart. Life without courage isn't worth living. Courage is required because fear exists. *Go, Chad. Do this beautiful experiment. If you fail, you learn. If you succeed, wow! If you succeed, your life will be changed forever.* What a small thing to risk for such a great reward. I continued planning with refreshed zeal. The most romantic restaurant in Atlanta? Tux rental place? Flower shop? What had Jenise mentioned in our conversations? What did she like? Detail by detail, I planned it all.

After Jenise returned, I waited a week and a half, then I called her. We chatted about her time in California, her trip back to Atlanta, and what was new. It was fun, and both of us seemed comfortable and at ease with each other. She laughed at my attempted humor, and I hung up feeling pleased.

During the countdown, I worked full-time as a ski patrol-man at Snow Summit. Filling my days seemed to make the clock tick a little more quickly. I skied, rescued damsels in distress, ate all-you-can-eat pizza at the local pizza place, and spent time with David and our friends Roger Williams and Jeremy Wright. All the guys on patrol and Bonnie, Debbie, and Dee, the gals we worked with, knew of my head-over-heels fall for the blonde girl in Atlanta.

Conversation, razzing, and harassment electrified our atmosphere in the Patrol Shack Bump at the top of chair two. "So Chad, what's next?"

"I'm flying to Atlanta to ask her out on a date. It'll be a surprise!"

"What? You're nuts, dude. She has no idea you're coming? Are you crazy? She'll run the other way, man." Every one of them agreed.

Many discussions about the type of girl I wanted to marry had taken place. "Girls like this don't exist. She is off-the-charts unbelievable, and if I'm going to show up on her radar, I better act, and act now." I knew she wouldn't be available long. Girls like Jenise? No way.

About ten days after the last call, I called Jenise again. She was warm and almost flirty! "Hello, Chadwick Buford." My real name is Chad Allan (Allan, after my father's only brother). My siblings nicknamed me when they learned my parents chose my name after reading a book, *The Little Shepherd of Kingdom Come*, about a character called "Chadwick Buford." David took great delight in using it in front of Jenise. I hadn't realized she noticed. It thrilled me to hear her say it.

Our conversation that evening was a bit warmer, more enjoyable, and even had romantic undertones—nothing overt, but a new level of feeling. As I began our goodbyes, Jenise playfully challenged, "Why don't you sing me a goodnight song?"

"What?! Me, sing? A goodnight song?" Then, an idea hit me. "Jenise, you're the singer. Why don't you sing me a song tonight, and I'll call you tomorrow night and sing you a song."

She laughed and challenged me. "Are you stalling?"

"Yep! Sure am," I admitted.

The sweetness of her warm, rich voice filled the line as she sang, "May tomorrow be a perfect day; may you find love (*Did I just hear her say that?*) and laughter along the way; may God keep you in his tender care—till he brings us together again." She cleverly finished with, "Good night, everybody." *Man, I love this angel! She is awesome!* She was a fun girl, a fun song, a fun, fun, fun way to finish our conversation. "Don't forget," she added, "tomorrow night, you're up!"

As soon as I hung up, I started my research. *What will I sing to her?* She'd said a "goodnight song." *How about a lullaby?* My mind went to the only lullaby I knew, which started, "Lullaby and goodnight," but I didn't remember any words beyond

71

that. I usually just hummed along the rest of the way. Then another idea hit me: *I'll write my own words using that tune.*

The words flowed freely. I'm not a poetic genius, but I was pleased with the result.

* * *

CHAD'S REFLECTIONS

Writing this chapter got me so pumped again! It has been over twenty-eight years since these events took place, but the excitement of the adventure came rushing right back at me.

Every relationship is different, and every love story is special! What makes love stories special, in my opinion, is when someone takes a risk and steps out, goes out on a limb, and shares a piece of their heart. Both Jenise and I did that in this chapter. I started planning this amazing surprise. I couldn't wait to interrupt her life and make my interest truly known in a bold way that couldn't be misunderstood. A DTR kind of action ("define the relationship"). My children are keeping me current with the DTR acronym.

Jenise gave me a hint that she was open to more than just friendship when she requested I sing her a goodnight song. It was a simple risk.

Such risks can only be wisely made when the groundwork has been laid and due diligence has been done on some level. It might be foolish to meet a girl in passing and then book a trip across the country to surprise her if you had no idea of who she really was. It might be foolish if Jenise asked me to sing her a goodnight song the very first time I called her.

Wisdom is a such an important part of life. James 1:5 tells us that God promises to give us wisdom when we ask Him for it. I want to take wise risks, not foolish risks.

Risking well is a rewarding part of a relationship-rich life.

CHAPTER 14
JENISE'S LULLABY

I called Jenise the following night. She was her usual self, light-hearted, fun, and a bit playful. Near the end, I acted as if I'd sign off without singing. "Well, I'll talk to you later, Jenise."

"Hey, now," she interrupted, "I believe you owe me a song!"

"You were serious about that?" I said, laughing. "Okay, but don't say I didn't warn you. You're a great singer. I'm a listener of great singers. That's why we go so well together." I was pushing my luck, but she didn't stop me, even lightly laughing. "But since you asked," I continued, "you shall receive. I even wrote the words . . . just for you."

"Really? How fun!"

"Here goes. Lullaby and goodnight, may God keep you, my darling. (I was waiting for her to slap me across the phone line, but I kept going.) Lullaby and good night, may you rest in sweet, sweet peace. May the Lord, up above, fill your heart with His love, and your sleep shall be still, as you rest in His will. Lullaby and good night, may His angels watch o'er you. Lullaby and goodnight, may you dream of only me!"

I paused, not knowing what she would say. "Aw . . ." she almost sighed. "That's so sweet."

No, I thought to myself. *You're so sweet.*

Another week passed, and, with it, my excitement grew about my forthcoming trans-American adventure. Eight days before liftoff and with all the details in place, I called Jenise to visit once more. Her tone seemed different; she seemed reserved. It was nothing dramatic, so I wrote it off that she may be tired or had a rough day at work.

Near the end of our conversation, she mentioned casually, "I'm so excited. I'm going to Tennessee for a retreat with all the young professionals at our church."

"Oh, how fun! When is this?"

"Not this weekend but the following," she said.

"Ohhh." It came out as a whisper. I quickly recovered, ignoring the hollow feeling in my gut, like someone had just punched me. "Very cool." I remember nothing else we said, just that I got off the phone quickly. Here I was planning my surprise date with Jenise in Atlanta, and she wasn't even going to be in the state of Georgia. Unbelievable!

Okay, what to do? My mind rolled through my options. Do I tell her I'm coming and blow the surprise? Do I change my flight and pick another weekend? Do I find out where the retreat will be and then show up? I went to bed that night with my plan. In the morning, I'd call Charles Stanley's church in Atlanta, find out where this retreat would be, and register for the event. Then, I'd let Jenise know when I got there that I was going to the retreat too. Simple. Problem solved. Or so I thought . . .

The phone number to the church rang, and a sweet southern drawl answered, "Hello, how can I help you, honey?"

"Hi, my name is Chad Johnson, and I'd like to talk with someone in charge of the young professional group there at the church."

"Okay, sir, that'd be Susan. Please hold, and I'll connect you."

Susan was warm and welcoming but quickly informed me that the young professionals retreat taking place in Gatlinburg,

Tennessee, was booked full, with a waiting list six people deep. "Would you like me to put you on the waiting list, honey?" she drawled.

"Ma'am, you don't understand." I told her about my dilemma. Although very willing to listen, she didn't succumb to my sob story. I was number seven on the list of "young professionals" waiting to get into the retreat. She added that if she were me, she wouldn't get her hopes up, but if a space became available, she'd call me. Before I hung up the phone, I asked her what the hotel's name was where the event was to take place.

A call to the hotel confirmed the worst—it was completely sold out, along with all other hotels in town. I considered camping in a rental car in the parking lot. Thinking it through, however, explaining how I got into the retreat and where I was staying would sound awfully creepy.

I sat down and placed my head in my hands and began to pray. *Lord, you know every detail of my life, and every detail of this journey to win Jenise's heart. You can make a way for me to attend this event. That'd be nothing for you. Please make a way, Lord.* I believe in miracles.

When the phone rang the very next day, Susan was on the other end, saying, "We have an opening, sir."

I didn't even question how. "Yes, ma'am. My Visa number is . . ." I was in! Retreat, here I come.

The few days remaining flew by. Thinking ahead, I visualized how I wanted the weekend to go. Wearing a sharp suit and tie, I'd surprise Jenise at work right at quitting time. I realized I didn't have a suit, so I ran to my 4Runner and drove to Nordstrom. I purchased a shirt that nearly broke me financially, yet I loved that shirt. I appreciated high-quality and luxury goods, but sadly only had a ski patroller's income to bargain with.

The gentlemen who offered to help me had a full lineup of fine suits laid out in all their glory for me to choose. The choice was easy. A really sharp black getup that just looked like a million bucks. Putting on that jacket felt oh, so right! The problem was it was a million bucks—or might as well have been. *$1,300.00 for a suit*! "Uh, I'm going to need to think about it," I stammered. That was almost as much as I made in a month, and I had little in savings, and most of that had gone toward the airfare. Before I left the store, I bought a nice Façonnable green and white striped shirt. It was ninety dollars, and I absolutely loved the way it looked and felt.

My father told me about a men's suit store in Los Angeles in the garment district where I could get a really decent suit for a fraction of the price. Several hours later, my wardrobe was set for adventure. This was getting real. The clock was ticking. I could feel my anticipation rising. I could hardly sleep that night. My thoughts ping-ponged between excitement, anticipation, fear, and doubt.

Would Jenise and I have a breakthrough? Would my dream come true? Would Jenise respond in kind to my obvious advance and undeniable overture (as in my direct way of letting her know she's the one)? Would she appreciate that I was head over heels, that my heart was in the open, and that I was vulnerable to her every look and thought? Would I win the day? Would she turn my way and say yes to me, to us? Could this dream really come true?

Or would this be the worst experience of my life? Would my heart be broken for the very first time? It was one or the other. There was no third option. Win or lose; yes or no; ecstasy or agony. And the only way to find out was to get on the plane in the morning and take the leap.

The weather was typical of Los Angeles—sunny and seventy-two degrees—when I arrived at LAX Terminal Two. I waved farewell to my father, who'd given me the biggest hug ever. Then he looked me in the eye and said, "May the Lord give you wisdom, Chad." Smiling, he said, "Go get her!" I think he was feeling it more than I was. Forty minutes later, I sat in the middle seat between two people, one of whom was far too large for the space allotted. I didn't care. We were in the air. There was no turning back.

I opened my journal and wrote, *Dear Lord, I'm on my way. I believe you're leading me. You've opened so many doors. You've made my path clear. There's so much I don't know. Jenise seems like she's the one for me. I've never met anyone like her—nobody even close. I feel as though I'm going off the biggest jump on skis that I ever have. Now I'm in the air. I don't know how I'll land. But I'm trusting you to make it clear. Show me your perfect will, Lord, and I pray it's for Jenise and me to make a match that'll last forever. In Jesus' name, Amen.*

A quiet calm came over me. *This will be fun. I'm sure of it. I'll enjoy the ride, give it my all, and trust the outcome to the One who has everything in His hand. If it wasn't in His will, then as much as I think I want this to work out, I don't. I truly want God's best, and only His best.*

My regard for marriage was so great. This wasn't a whim or careless adventure for me. Never had I pursued a girl in this way. A marriage should stand the test of time, and the person who made up the other half of that relationship was absolutely vital. Do I believe there's just one right person for everyone? I don't know, nor do I waste much time thinking about such things.

Up to that point in my short life, I'd never felt that way about a woman, not even close. And somehow, during the excitement, a joyful peace and confidence in the Lord's leading overcame me. Before I knew it, the flight attendant began her spiel.

Well, here goes. Time will tell. Let's do this, Chad!

* * *

77

CHAD'S REFLECTIONS

The birth of a vision, the death of the vision. In any endeavor, there is the initial blast of inspiration. The idea is formed, and endorphins flow through your body. You feel the rush of excitement when visualizing the outcome of your adventure in full and living color as you work through the details of actually planning, buying the tickets, and hitting the roadblocks (The retreat is full!). It is easy to see the vision wilt and sometimes even die; that is such a natural reaction.

Looking back over the past fifty years of my life, I have seen this happen so often. I have learned it is often better to expect it. Take some time to visualize all the things that could potentially go wrong and obstacles that can block the way or pop up and surprise you.

I am a very optimistic person, and I always see the bright side—the cup is half full—but I have found that preparing for hardship in advance can make it far easier when it shows up.

It is easy to dream, but a real man shows up when dreams get off track and there doesn't seem to be a way forward. I have found that turning to the Lord and praying about my situation opens me up to seeing Him work in new and different ways.

Proverbs 3:5–6 says it so well: "Trust in the Lord with all thine heart; and lean not to thine own understanding. In all thy ways acknowledge him and he shall direct thy paths."

After all, as a child of God, I only want what is His best for my life. It was important for me to get to a place where my heart could truly say, *If Jenise is for me, then nothing is going to stand in the way. If she is not, then, Lord, I want what you have for me instead.*

CHAPTER 15
SURPRISE!

The elevator door opened, and I took a deep breath. I gave one last glance to young Phillip before I stepped into the grand lobby with a large mahogany reception desk to my left. "Oh, my gosh!" shrieked the most beautiful blonde girl in the world. Jenise, who was sitting at the desk, leapt to her feet and ran squealing out the door and into the lady's room.

Oh, no! What on earth just happened? This isn't good. Definitely not the reaction I was hoping for . . .

My eyes quickly surveyed the opulent reception area with marble floors and walls and huge glass windows overlooking the city of Atlanta—a very prestigious, luxurious, and professional setting. Hardly the place for a woman to be running and shrieking. Before I had time to collect my thoughts, a professionally dressed woman opened her office door. She studied me standing in front of the elevator, a questioning look on her face. A handsome (in my opinion), tan-faced, young man of twenty-one years, cleverly dressed in a dark suit, holding a dozen red roses, and smiling ear to ear.

"Can I help you?" she asked.

"Well, maybe. I just dropped by to surprise Jenise, and I guess it truly was a surprise because she just ran out of the room. Yes, that was her, shrieking." I nodded toward the hall she'd bolted down.

"You must be the ski guy from California."

Was it the sunburned face with goggle eyes that gave me away? *Wait! Did I just hear that? Jenise talked of the ski guy from California with her co-workers?! That's definitely me.* "Yes, that's me!" My spirits soared with this new revelation. *She's talking about me!*

Jenise reentered the room and seemed much more composed but still a little shocked. Turning, she introduced me to her co-worker, who quickly excused herself with a wink, saying, "I'll leave you two to yourselves."

Jenise blurted out, "What are you doing here?" She gave me a brief hug. Her look was one of curiosity, subdued excitement, and concern. *Uh, oh! What have I done? Was this a good call?*

"I was just in the area and wanted to drop by and give you some roses," I said nonchalantly as I presented the flowers.

She took them in hand and gave me a wry smile, "In the area, huh? How convenient."

I quickly expressed how much of a surprise I knew this was, and seeing she was still at work, I'd wait in the lobby so she could wrap up her day.

Back in the elevator, my mind reeled with questions. Was she glad I was here? Did she like me at all? I thought she did, but her responses seemed mixed—half excited and positive, but somehow reserved and unsure. I can't blame her. I popped in out of nowhere. We really had only enjoyed phone conversations and some letter writing. During her visit back home just six weeks ago, we definitely didn't have the DTR talk. *She must be wondering what I'm thinking.*

The elevator chime interrupted my thoughts—ground floor. As the door slid open, I realized I'd forgotten all about Phillip! The security guard had figured out he was joyriding the elevator (my instructions) and asked him to wait in the lobby instead. Phillip seemed genuinely glad to see me and eagerly shared his elevator adventure, wide-eyed and breathless.

I leaned down and whispered, "Phillip, I saw the girl I came to see. Now I'm waiting for her to come down and visit for just a few minutes. Can you hang out on the other side of the security desk until I finish speaking with her? I'll come to get you as soon as we're finished."

His head was nodding the entire time I spoke. We quickly walked to the other side of the counter. The guard seemed well-versed in what we were up to and gave me a wink, smile, nod, and thumbs-up. The elevator door opened behind him, allowing several employees to pile out into the lobby. "Goodnight, Jenise," the woman I'd met upstairs sang out a little louder than necessary. "Have a great evening!"

I sure hope we do, I thought as I approached Jenise.

"Shall we visit outside?" I asked. She nodded, and we exited through the big glass entrance doors and walked toward the parking lot. Neither of us said much of anything at all. I turned and faced Jenise. I could sense she was feeling awkward, nervous, and very much ill at ease. *Oh no*, I thought, *this isn't good! She isn't happy I'm here. What have I done?*

"Chad, I had no idea you were coming to Atlanta! I teach a harp lesson at 6:00 p.m. (it was 5:15 p.m.). Tomorrow I work all day, and Friday I'm taking off for the weekend. I'm going to a young professionals retreat in Gatlinburg, Tennessee. I don't return until Sunday evening!" This all flowed out rapidly as one long sentence.

"Jenise," I said, "I know I've come out of nowhere, taking you by surprise. It makes total sense that you have plans and commitments, and in no way am I expecting you to break those commitments or drop what you're doing and spend time with me. I took a big risk coming out unannounced. I am truly excited about seeing Atlanta, the underground, the Coke factory, and all the other amazing things in the area.

I'm also excited about spending some time with our family friends, the Gables."

Now, I'm afraid I didn't tell the whole truth here. *Really, Chad, you want to see Atlanta? The Coke Factory? I don't even drink Coke!* I realized I put her under tremendous pressure and wanted to put her at ease. It was important to me that she continued to fulfill her commitments, or at least most of them.

"By the way," I continued, smiling wide, "as for the retreat, Jenise, I'm also scheduled to attend."

"What?" she gasped. "It's full! You can't go. They've sold all the tickets. In fact, there's a waiting list."

I grinned and said, "I know, I was on that waiting list for a short while, but a space opened up, and I'm registered and going to be there." Her face was hard to read, and I consider myself a quick study on mannerisms and expressions. What was she feeling or thinking? Was that expression on her face concern, fear, curiosity, joy, or a mix? I couldn't tell, and she didn't seem eager to tell me, so I continued.

"Jenise, you have your harp student commitment. Please have a wonderful evening. I'd like to speak with you later tonight if you're okay with that?" I asked.

She said, "I'll call you when I'm done teaching, and we can get together and catch up."

Well, that was good news, but I lacked comfort as I walked toward my rental car. My thoughts were spinning at a billion waves a minute. *What have I gotten myself into? She isn't sure whether she's glad I'm here. In part, she appears delighted, curious, and flattered I took such a bold step and traveled here to surprise her with flowers in hand and her as my only agenda, but something else is going on.* I found uncertainty written all over her face. Perhaps it was fear or concern, and she has questions whirling through her beautiful mind.

Beautiful! Yes, she's beautiful. Man, I'd forgotten how beautiful she is. I couldn't control my heartbeat; it pounded with anticipation, beating in full, measured depth. How this girl moved me! *She's amazing, just amazing*, I thought. All at once, I realized the complete delight that only a few moments with her, speaking with her, and being near her brought me.

Get a grip, Chad. She's a long way from being anything more than a friend to you. She seems to be pulling away, not drawing near. What if this is an epic fail and this whole trip is for nothing and a waste of time, money . . . everything? If tonight she tells you she thinks you're great and only wants to be friends? No! That could happen, you know, Chad. She might totally blow you off, and then what?

How quickly a man can plunge from the lofty heights of romantic optimism and the next instant find a vast void in the pit of his being. Since my youth, my mind has been a volatile organ, whimsically vacillating from the very peaks of glory to extreme overwhelm and sorrow. I quickly readjusted my inner dialogue. *No, Chad, you're on an amazing adventure, regardless. Life is short. Take risks. Jump. Don't go through life with regrets of having not tried and always wondering, "What if?"*

"Hello, Chad," said the high-pitched voice of my young friend, Phillip, jarring me from eating my mental soup. I'd forgotten about Phillip!

"Let's go, Phillip. Everything go okay in there? Was the security guy nice?" I had to get this boy back into his parents' care, who must be sick with worry over their disappearing child.

The ride through Atlanta to Marietta, just north of the city, was a much different ride. We enjoyed an animated conversation about school, his family, and running. Phillip, an academic, noted that science, math, and learning were his thing. Yet, during our mad dash through the parking lot, over the hedges, across the lawns, and into the Tucker Wayne/ Luckie & Co. building, Phillip had awakened a newfound love—running. He loved it! For him, this became an adventure.

* * *

CHAD'S REFLECTIONS

Surprises sure do spice up life! I remember so well the feeling of anticipation, curiosity, and frankly more than a little bit of fear as I showed up in Atlanta unannounced. I was committed to showing up in Jenise's world and making my great admiration known.

There are good surprises and bad surprises in life, it seems. There are those random phone calls sharing bad news, like a friend who lets you know that he just lost his brother to an accident or someone you love has cancer and is now fighting for their life. Many of those surprises choose you. You wouldn't choose them if you had a choice.

But what about the surprises you choose? The creative way you decide to take action, take a risk, jump in with both feet? Surprises like that are at the core of learning and growing and at the epicenter of a joy-filled life. These are things like an unexpected card in the mail, traveling a long distance to delight a friend unannounced, taking off the second half of a day, and picking up a friend or family member for a picnic.

Some things make for a great surprise. They're unexpected, unrealistic, unreasonable, over the top. They can be extremely frugal, expensive, creative, thoughtful, considerate, invested, or well-planned out.

Surprises are romantic.

CHAPTER 16
WHAT ABOUT THE AGE DIFFERENCE?

Once at Steve and Kim's, Kim showed trust and great confidence that I'd return her beloved son. Her faith relieved my worry. That evening, I enjoyed the comforts of a home-cooked meal and southern hospitality at its finest. These friends of my parents easily became personal friends to me too. I found Steve and Kim to be fascinating conversationalists.

After dinner, we retreated to the living room. I learned all about them. Steve's work as a CPA and CFO allowed him the freedom to use his strengths. He ran the day-to-day business of the restaurants and resorts his boss owned. Thoroughly engaged, I noticed myself being drawn to the world of business. For a moment, I considered becoming an accountant, a CPA. That'd be a great skill to have, and Steve made it sound like so much fun! I considered him a man of confidence and character and admired his relationship with his wife, who adored him. They had a nice home in a nice neighborhood, played tennis together, were active in their church, and had three awesome children.

Lying in bed that evening, I reflected on the topic of accounting and thought, *You nut job. You, a CPA? You hate math and school. You haven't even graduated high school!*

At age sixteen, I snuck out the back door of high school by taking my proficiency examination, setting me free to pursue learning elsewhere. I'd long vowed not to let school get in the way of my learning. I don't know what I was thinking, but what was clear was that no matter what I decided to do, I'd be able to do it. Nothing seemed too hard, out of reach, or big to conquer. I'm not sure where this feeling came from, and I had virtually no experience to validate that. It was just a gut feeling that said someday I'd make it. I'd accomplish something great and impact others in powerful ways. I thank my parents for giving me that kind of foundation and confidence.

Now back to the living room. The phone rang, interrupting our visit. It was Jenise! The sound of her voice quickened my breathing as she invited me to come over to her apartment. What was it with her? She started to give me directions, but I interrupted and rattled off her address. I noticed her surprise. "Oh, okay, I'll see you shortly." I couldn't sense anything beyond that. *Oh, well, she invited me over.* I gladly accepted the opportunity.

After only a ten-minute drive, I pulled up to a townhome she co-rented with her friend, Karen Hatfield. Jenise met me at the front door, and once more her warm smile took me aback. Her blonde hair with loose curls softly framed her face. She was vibrant, joyful, energetic, and full of life. Oh, how I liked this girl!

Karen met us in the kitchen, and Jenise introduced us. Karen was about thirty years old and a flight attendant for Delta Airlines. She looked every bit the part—attractive, friendly, upbeat, and outgoing. She was so welcoming. It made me happy to see that Jenise had such a good friend. We chatted for a bit before Jenise and I moved to the living room.

In the small, well-appointed living room, Jenise sat on a couch, and I sat in an armchair facing her. Immediately, I sensed her discomfort. I jumped right in, "Jenise, I want you to know I can only imagine how you feel. Out of nowhere, some guy you barely know shows up from 3,000 miles away. You must have serious questions."

"Chad, I have no idea what's going on with us or where we are. I enjoyed spending time with you back in California, but . . ." She faded off.

"But what?"

"But, you know, the age difference and everything," she said.

The age difference weighed heavily on my mind. It was my greatest fear as I planned this grand adventure. She was three years, three months, and five days older than I was. Not that it mattered to me at all, because it didn't. I'd have pursued Jenise at ten, twenty, thirty, fifty years—well, I guess at some point it'd get weird, but a measly three years? That's nothing. But maybe it wasn't nothing because Jenise brought it up like it was something—as in, it was the first thing she said.

I attempted humor as I often do. "Jenise, I'm truly grateful for the time you spent with me in California. The best babysitter I've ever had!" She took it just the way I intended, throwing back her head and laughing.

I added, "You know I like you. I like you a lot. All of our time together confirms what I told you back in August—that I saw so many amazing qualities in you that I'm looking for in the woman I will marry someday. It's been wonderful getting to know you through our letters, your visit back home, and our phone calls. I know we haven't defined us beyond friends, and I hope I haven't made you too uncomfortable showing up like this, interrupting your rich and busy life! You're probably wondering how I could fit into your jam-packed schedule and what, if any, obligation you have to entertain or host me. Please be perfectly at ease, Jenise. I'm totally self-contained and excited to be in Atlanta. I've always wanted to explore the south, and here I am. It's so important to me that you feel no pressure at all."

Still not herself but more at ease, Jenise said, "Chad, I've enjoyed our time together and getting to know you better. I guess I didn't know your expectations for me. My weekend schedule is completely full. Tomorrow (Thursday) I work from 9:00 a.m. to 5:00 p.m., followed by another harp lesson in the evening. Then Friday . . ." She paused.

I jumped in once more, "I know you have the retreat in Gatlinburg, but I'm going, too!"

"Yes, but—" she halted.

"But what?"

"Well, a friend, Jim Price, asked me to ride with him, and I agreed. I had no idea you were showing up."

"Of course not, Jenise," I said, trying to seem calm. "There is no way you could have. I knew I was taking a risk showing up unannounced. I guess you've gotta do what you've got to do," I said casually. "You said this guy's name is Jim, right? Not Will or James?"

I guess it sounded sarcastic, which she picked up on because she shot me a look and quipped, "Very funny, Chad. Yes, Jim, *not* Will," which let me know she heard me—loud and clear.

"Just trying to keep them all straight," I said, smirking casually. Inside, I was anything but calm or casual. Some other guy! My mind raced. *What guy? Who was he? Why haven't I heard about this guy? How serious? This is seriously messed up!* Thoughts flashed like lightning through my head while I made gracious small talk that ended our little visit. With my head pounding and my heart heavy, I left Jenise's townhome.

* * *

CHAD'S REFLECTIONS

We all have ideals about the person we are going to marry—their character, what they believe, their height, hair color, personality, etc. I took the time to write down the list of things that were important to me in my future wife. The list was long and varied, but nowhere on the list was age.

I think it is so helpful to write down a list of desired qualities and traits you are looking for in a spouse. I suggested this in the notes after Chapter 3.

Most critical is the list of non-negotiable items. Here are some of mine:

- A born-again believer in the Lord Jesus Christ

- Someone who loves and believes God's Word, the Bible

- A woman who wanted to be a wife and mother and saw that as a noble calling

- Not a career woman

- A woman who was a learner and grower

- A woman open to the possibility of having ten kids and who saw children as a blessing

- Open to the idea of home birth and home schooling our children

- A woman willing to go against the culture and swim against the current

- A woman of action who appreciates adventure

- An attractive woman

- A joyful, cheerful, smiling woman

- Someone with a positive mindset and an upbeat, can-do attitude.

- A hard worker and go-getter

- A woman with a heart for others

- A woman who did not drink alcohol or do drugs

- A woman who prioritized her health

CHAPTER 17
SO I CALLED STEPHANIE

What on earth had I done? Was I just making a fool out of myself? Had I read Jenise completely wrong? Was she being nice, taking a few calls and leading me on? Was I reading more into her friendliness than she intended? Who was this chump taking my girl to Gatlinburg?

Listen to me. The realization that she was nowhere near *my girl* was hitting with full, life-sucking force. I had no reason to expect that she wouldn't see other guys or even date and build relationships. She wasn't mine. We'd never had the conversation to solidify such a thing. She had no way to read the persistent thoughts revolving in my mind ever since I had met her almost a year before at Brenda's wedding.

A startling awareness of the image I'd created hit me. That image was falling like the raindrops that drenched me as I ran to my car—the vision of the wonderful, ideal future with Jenise, the girl of my dreams, the image of her liking me back and eagerly rejoicing in my arrival, ready to drop what she was doing and leap into the delightful, romantic relationship that I imagined. Inside my car, I wanted to sit and cry. No, I wanted to yell. *Lord, why did you have me come out here? Didn't I hear your voice? Weren't you leading me to take this jump, to risk it all, to invest big and interrupt her life? Where did I go wrong?*

Driving away, I fought the urge to take the exit to the airport, get on a plane, go home, run from it all, and quit. Ugh! I hate the word quit. I couldn't quit. I rehashed the conversation over and over on the drive back to the Gables' house, looking for a glimmer of hope. She laughed at my jokes, seemed to enjoy visiting, and didn't seem offended I'd come. She didn't shoot down ever being an item and didn't say she only wanted to be friends, nor did she say she was in a relationship. Yet, on the other hand, she seemed uncomfortable, unsure, and not at all at ease.

Couldn't she cancel the ride to Gatlinburg with this guy friend and tell him a friend from California had shown up and was hoping to drive her to the retreat? I had no right to expect that. She probably didn't want to. I knew Jenise was quite the catch. She always had guys sharking around her, trying to win her. She'd been proposed to three times and by guys who seemed to have it all together. What was I thinking? Maybe I was way out of my league, over my head. I was shooting for the moon—a dreamer. I always have been, but maybe this was too much.

Some girls do like me, I told myself. Didn't Stephanie think I was something? She was beautiful, nice, sweet, a wonderful Christian girl, and everyone thought she was a catch and perfect for me—everyone but me. Nobody shimmered like Jenise. Nobody!

Ever since that first day at Brenda and David's wedding when I first laid eyes on her, heard her voice, and saw her smile, I was hooked. She was unbelievable, like a dream, only better. She was so real, so genuine, so fresh, and pure. So what are you doing, Chad? Get a grip. She isn't interested. The rain and my toxic thoughts wouldn't stop until I parked and ran to the red front door of the charming Southern white house the Gables called home.

It was late—11:30 p.m. I went directly upstairs to the guest room prepared for me, and my mind went back to Stephanie.

She thinks I'm okay. She believes there's something in me to like. I know it was weakness, insecurity, and wanting to be liked. Okay, I wanted to be admired and appreciated. Apparently, my frail ego had taken such a hit that I decided to call Stephanie. It was only 8:30 p.m. in California. It was pathetic, but I called her anyway. We didn't talk long or of anything important, but only had a brief chat catching up as it'd been some time since we'd spoken. I enjoyed her friendship, and while she may have wanted more, the conversation was warm, fun, and affirming. It somehow boosted my confidence a bit.

Wonder filled my prayers that evening. *Lord, did you really lead me to take this adventure? Am I hearing you correctly? Am I just chasing my desires? Is this a rabbit trail purposed to grow me and teach me something? Did you lead me here for a dead end? A zero?*

Romans 8:28 had always been a favorite verse of mine. "And we know that all things work together for good to them that love God, to them who are the called according to His purpose." It was one that I leaned on. I also loved what Proverbs 3:5–6 tells us: "Trust in the Lord with all thine heart; and lean not to thine own understanding. In all thy ways acknowledge him and he shall direct thy paths."

Lord, I do believe you've shown me many things regarding Jenise—this whole trip, our relationship (or what I think our relationship could be). Please show me the way. I do trust you. I'm yours and truly want your best. If Jenise isn't the one for me, please make it completely clear and obvious, so I don't waste her time and mine and both of us can honor the other and have zero regrets.

Sleep came quickly after that. Sleep has always come quickly for me. Waking in the morning to the smell of breakfast wafting through the house reminded me of home. I savored the moment lying in bed and thinking of the adventure that lay ahead today.

* * *

CHAD'S REFLECTIONS

I am not proud of the fact that I was so rocked by Jenise's hesitancy, nor my response to it. But that is the way it went.

If life went perfectly as we envisioned it, wouldn't that be great? I don't think so. I think God knows far better than I know. My perspective is so often limited and small. There is so much sweetness that comes from just taking one step after the other and leaving the results to the Lord.

Proverbs 16:9 says, "A man's heart deviseth his way; but the Lord directeth his steps." When I run into a roadblock, I can forget that. I can turn to my ways (calling Stephanie) to try and bolster my confidence instead of turning to the Lord in faith.

The Scripture verses I have memorized over the years have come to bless me and serve me so well in life. When life throws a curveball, the very best place my mind can go is to the promises of God. I love having promises from Scripture available to me wherever I go. If I take the time to hide God's Word in my heart, they are so easily brought to mind in the moment of my need. To meditate on truth from God's perspective always brings peace and restores my soul.

Philippians 4:8 tells us how to think as believers. Psalm 100:3–4 tells me how to enter His presence with thanksgiving and praise. Romans 12:2 reminds us how to be transformed by the renewing of our minds.

CHAPTER 18
A PHONE CALL

After a delightful breakfast with the entire Gable family, I pulled out my relocation packet and set out for downtown Atlanta. I made my way through the Atlanta underground, enjoying the mass throngs of people flowing through darkened corridors, shops, and eating places. From there, once in the bright light of day once more, I visited the Coca Cola factory and world headquarters.

A free tour with over 100 different soda tasting opportunities tickled my taste buds. Growing up in a home with no soda pop or other sugary drinks, well, I guess I was really living it up! Ha! All sugared up, I journeyed through the company and enjoyed learning the story of Coke's founding and growth.

Business always interested me—most likely from exposure to my father and uncle's bottle decorating plant in Los Angeles. Ironically, the soda pop business had put them on the map sixty-five years prior. Their plant provided labeling for Pepsi Cola, Aspen, Dad's Root Beer, 7UP, and many more during the heyday of returnable glass soda pop bottles. It was quite a green process and ahead of its time, now that I think about it. I always imagined I'd start my own business. I'd attempted custom mug and T-shirt businesses, but neither performed as I thought they could. Thoughts and dreams of bigger things filled my mind as I left the factory—yes, dreams of a bigger future and business success.

Next on my agenda was a drive through the fine neighborhood of Buckhead, an upscale community adjacent to Atlanta. Seeing the big, beautiful homes stirred visions of the day I'd live with my family in a grand, welcoming home full of children, life, joy, and fellowship. Yes, I was a dreamer. My $1,900 per month ski patrol income wouldn't keep the lights on and the lawns mowed in this neighborhood, nor would it make the mortgage payment, but dreaming is free, and I was good at it!

Dreaming fueled me and put me on the airplane to Atlanta. Successful people I'd come across, a network marketing company called Melaleuca, and leadership and personal development books challenged my thinking and taught me to dream and consider all that was possible. As an intentional reader, I chose books like *The Magic of Thinking Big, How to Win Friends and Influence People, The Power of Positive Thinking,* and *See You at the Top,* among so many others.

I believe God gives us gifts and abilities that allow us to realize our destiny. I believe anything is possible if you put your heart and mind to it and give it your consistent, persistent, and never-give-up all. I didn't have much to show for all this dreaming except for a few scattered and minimal successes. Somewhere deep inside, I was confident I'd find a way to fly—I just knew it. My dreams equaled big dreams. My future would be big, grand, and glorious. Even though I was young, broke, and hadn't graduated from college, I'd win big in life and fulfill the dreams the Lord put on my heart.

My dream of finding a woman who resembled my mother—a woman of grace and beauty, strength and dignity, honor and of great faith, a woman pure and noble—brought me here. I saw all those qualities in Jenise. The total package. *How did my thoughts end up here? I was thinking about business, homes, dreams . . . ah, yes, that's why. Dreams.*

What was Jenise up to? How was her day going? Now that I'd seen her office, I could easily imagine her—professional, sharp, joyful, and a blessing to everyone around her—going about her daily duties. I knew she worked hard. This stood out at the JH Ranch last summer. During our visit last evening, she said she taught harp lessons again tonight and would be unavailable. Just then, a wild hair idea. I know—another one! I don't know where it came from. What if I called her roommate, Karen, and asked her out? Oh, I liked this.

Jenise was the one who said some guy was taking her to the singles retreat. She didn't have time for me. For all I could see, she had no interest in me beyond friendship. I took a big risk and invested in what was a lot of money for me. I looked at my watch. She'd be getting off work and heading to teach. I wondered about her student. Was it another guy who liked her? Was it someone else trying to make his presence known in a sneaky way? Why was I so jealous and petty? *She is in no way yours, Chadwick Buford*, I said to myself.

I made the call. "Hello, this is Jenise," she cheerfully proclaimed. My heart soared.

"Jenise," I said, catching my breath and trying to be nonchalant. "What a surprise! I thought you were teaching a lesson."

She laughed. "I am—just had to drop by to get my music and change."

"Well, I don't want to hold you up. Actually, I was calling to speak with Karen. Is she there?"

A long silent pause . . . "Karen? Uh, yes, I think so," she said hesitantly.

"Oh, that's super. Can I speak with her, please?"

Another pause . . . "Okay," she said softly. "Karen," I heard her say as she held the phone away from her mouth, "phone is for you." I was getting a bit of a kick out of this whole thing. I could tell it took Jenise by surprise, and she couldn't tell what I was up to, which was all very good and well.

Karen picked up the phone, and I asked if she was available that evening, if I could buy her dinner, and she could show me Atlanta. Lighthearted and fun, she chatted away, "Oh, I wish I could!" She had an evening mandatory flight attendant training, a safety course. "Otherwise, I'd so be up for that."

"No worries," I replied. "Jenise is busy, so you came to mind."

"Wait!" Karen interjected. "I know a group of girls who are getting together to eat dinner and watch a movie. They'd love to have you along!"

She gave me the number—mission accomplished. That worked out perfectly. If Jenise had any interest, this should flush it out. If not—oh, well. Better to know than be clueless with hope and delay reality. I made my intentions clear with the trip, flowers, and implicit heart on my sleeve. Having declared myself in such an obvious way, she knew where I stood. I wouldn't grovel or act like a desperate puppy, even though I was in so many ways. That wasn't my style. I'd act as if it were no big deal and let her know I could get other girls to pay attention, and just maybe she would reevaluate her priorities. The relationship ball was in her court.

Back at the Gables' once again, great conversation sweetened the dinner table and made the meal that much more delightful. Their young children turned out to be bright and superb conversationalists, interesting and replete with humor. Exceptional as students, they overflowed with stories of their studies and projects. That dinner reminded me of growing up around a similar family meal table, one that held eight siblings, my parents, and room for a couple of family friends or relatives to be stuffed among us. I always looked forward to family mealtime. Back at home, there was always room for one more at the Johnson dinner table.

Laughing, talking, sharing, and storytelling of the day's adventures, failures, and lessons filled that table with life, love, and a multitude of memories. Oh, how I treasured those times. Oh, how I longed for my own future family table with a passel of little ones circling around it, filling the room and my life with energy, enthusiasm, and adventure.

The phone rang late in the evening, and Kim answered. "It's for you," she said brightly with a fun and curious expression on her face.

"Hello, this is Chad."

"Hi Chad, this is Jenise." There was no need for her to tell me. Her voice was my favorite sound in the universe. "Are you in a place where we can talk?" she inquired.

"No, but wait a second, and I will be." I pointed at the phone and gave Steve and Kim a smile and a thumbs-up as I headed to the guest room. I could tell Steve and Kim, both romantics at heart, loved every twist and turn of this little drama unfolding in their home. In not too many years, they'd be going through all of this with young Phillip and his sisters.

I closed the door behind me and braced for the worst. What was on her mind? Had my call to Karen offended her? Made her angry? Maybe she had some time to process and was calling to let me know she wasn't interested and was serious about this guy she was going to the retreat with. I held my breath and said, "Hey, Jenise. What's up?"

"Well, I've been doing some thinking, and . . ." She paused. Ugh! I felt my heart in my throat like it was beating its way right out of my mouth. My breathing was coming in shallow gasps. This was it. She'd be dropping the bomb and saying the words every guy on the planet dreads hearing—something to the effect of "I like you a lot but just want to be friends."

Lame, lame, lame! I don't want to be friends. I want to be far more than friends. Boyfriend-girlfriend, fiancés, husband and wife, passionate lovers, and together forever, 'til death do us part. The whole bit. All of it. No! No! No! Not friends. I have plenty of friends and want so dearly to have her as my own. Not a shared relationship, not one of many, not anything but her and me. All these thoughts raced spastically across my mind in that slow pause.

Jenise continued, "Well, I know you came all the way out from California, and I think it wouldn't be right if I were busy the entire time. So," she continued while my mind raced ahead. *This is better than I hoped. Maybe this would be . . . good?* "I've told Jim Price, who offered to drive me to Gatlinburg, that a friend surprised me, and I thought I should go with him."

Joy flooded my soul, and I cried out, most likely far too exuberantly, "That's fantastic!" I truly felt like Jenise plucked me from the pit of despair and thrust me to ecstatic heights of blissful sublimity! She said no to him and yes to me! If that wasn't cause for utter delight, I didn't know what was.

"So what's the plan?" I asked. "When can I pick you up? Where can I pick you up?" Jenise laughed, and the sound played on my ears like a babbling brook gaily running over a rocky stream—cleansing, refreshing, and sparkling with life.

"Well, I have a few errands in the morning, so I guess 11:00 a.m. would be good."

"Perfect!" I replied. "I'll see you then. Have a great evening."

"You too."

"I already have!" I said, smiling. I know she smiled too. I could feel it over the phone.

"Good night," she said.

The second I hung up the phone, I dropped to my knees beside the bed. Lord, you're so good! You did a work in her heart. She said no to him and yes to me.

Then I thought to myself, *Just because she told him she was going with me to the retreat doesn't mean that she's mine. In fact, she could feel obligated because I showed up on her front steps. Maybe this isn't what she wants but what she feels like she ought to do, only to be nice, kind, or civilized.*

Well, Lord, I continued, *you know all that, and I'm grateful nonetheless. The future will take care of itself, but this is a positive from my perspective, and I'm so happy.*

I jumped to my feet and ran downstairs to share the good news. "She's going to the retreat with me!" I blurted out as I stepped into the family room. The whole Gable family cheered.

* * *

CHAD'S REFLECTIONS

As a young man, I was full of dreams. There were big things I wanted to do, achieve, and see happen in my life. I think God plants little seeds in our hearts as young people, visions of what our life can be, the people we will become, the places we might go, and the things we might do, much like He did with Joseph in the Bible so long ago.

Sometimes things happen that cause those dreams to die, disappear, or fade. Life has a way of bringing failure, disappointment, doubt, and fear.

I think it is important to take all of this to the Lord. I only want dreams that are from Him. I want dreams that are right, good, best, and at the center of His will. My heart can be led astray. I can be tempted with things that are not best for me. There is a lot of comfort in knowing that I can cast all my cares upon Him for He cares for me. He says in Scripture that He will give me the desires of my heart.

My desire is to be a husband and to love my wife forever. I want to have children together and enjoy times around the family dinner table with the ones I love—these were good dreams and a good vision.

CHAPTER 19
VALENTINE'S DAY

After sweet, dreamy sleep, I woke, realizing I'd really be getting to spend the better part of the day with Jenise. I wished I could jump out of bed every day with this enthusiastic, robust confidence and expectation for the day ahead. Admittedly, I'm not much of a morning person. I come alive and get cranking in the evening. This morning was different—I was high on life. With a quick breakfast at the Gables' and the children off to school, I was off as well.

It was, Friday, February 14, Valentine's Day. How cool was that? My route took me by a Hallmark shop where I picked out a humorous and fitting card for Jenise that I'd present at the proper time if it presented itself. Just in case, I picked up a couple of romantic CDs. You never know, but the last thing I wanted to do was be presumptuous in this drive to the retreat. After all, fewer than twenty-four hours earlier, she was commuting with another guy. Still up in the air, our relationship was undeclared and wide open. *Lord, give me wisdom on how to act or advance my cause today.*

Jenise's radiant smile filled the doorway as she answered my knock. What. A. Beauty! Every time I saw her, I was blown away, almost overwhelmed by her presence. *Her smile . . . does she always wear it?* Karen greeted us, and after some small chit chat, I loaded Jenise's bags into the trunk of the Lincoln

102

Continental I rented. I asked for the most luxurious vehicle they had. This was before the days of exotic car rentals; otherwise, it would've been something far sportier and more fun. This baby sported full leather, a big engine, and lots of room. Less than thirty minutes later, we were flying up Interstate 85 to Hwy 23 on our way to Tennessee.

From the second she was in the car, our conversation was rich, varied, and didn't slow until we arrived at our destination, almost four hours later. I had prepared a list of questions during my flight and asked them one by one as we rolled along. Virtually everything was on the table: faith, doctrine, theology, family, marriage, standards and values, habits, goals, parenting, birth control, child training, education, home education, home birth, business, investments, finance, childhood highlights and low points, and on and on.

The landscape passed by outside our little bubble of discovery. Every answer, comment, response, and question was right. Not perfect, but right. I loved Jenise's confidence, strength, and willingness to speak her mind. She was direct and forthright, succinct, and clear in her expression, and a straight shooter who didn't pull any punches. She showed a humbleness, openness, and eagerness to learn. She was a great listener, asked good questions, and was genuinely interested. An extra plus was that she thought I was funny! Who doesn't appreciate that in a woman?

The charming scenes of Gatlinburg were soon welcoming us. Time flew by far too quickly. Perched on a hill, the ten-story hotel overlooked the downtown area of Gatlinburg. Five beautiful young ladies, excited and laughing, greeted Jenise with warm hugs and welcomed us as we unloaded our belongings. They surrounded me as Jenise made introductions. Once again, I was pleased to hear whispers, "Oh, this is the ski guy from California." To know Jenise spoke of me with yet another crowd made my heart dance on this Valentine's Day. Each lady was a delight to meet, fun and playful in spirit.

We all rolled our luggage into the hotel lobby and registered for the event. After agreeing we'd meet back in the lobby, the girls escorted Jenise into the elevator and off to their rooms to stow luggage and freshen up. The elevator slowly—and I mean slowly—lifted me to the ninth floor. A stocky young man named Guy answered door #915.

We quickly hit it off. He was about four years older than me, loved the Lord, and enjoyed all things outdoors and sports. He was eager to talk, and I enjoyed meeting him, but I hadn't come to the other side of the country to make a new friend. Well, I guess I did, but I intended on a *girl* friend—that is, a *girlfriend*. Politely excusing myself, I hopped back in the slow-moving elevator. It stopped on the floor directly below to pick up a short man in his late twenties. I noticed he was wearing a nametag indicating he was part of the same event but didn't notice the name.

I stuck out my hand. "Hello, I'm Chad Johnson; I'm out from California."

"Oh," he said dully, looking down and avoiding my out-stretched hand.

"I'm Jim."

He made it very clear he had no intention of speaking further. My head snapped back to look at his name tag. Jim Price! No! What were the odds? An awkward silence sucked the air from the elevator as it painstakingly lowered us to the lobby, one . . . floor . . . at . . . a . . . time. Floor seven . . . six . . . five . . . four . . . three . . .

Two sets of eyes were fixated on the numbers lighting up one by one. The pace was torture. When the "L" lit up, like racehorses at their gates, both of us readied for the gun to start the race. As the door cracked open, Jim—even more motivated than me—bolted through the gap. He nearly knocked down a woman, and not just any woman—Jenise! The only woman in the whole hotel lobby. Her hand flew up as she stood there with her eyebrows raised, eyes and mouth wide open, and the funniest expression I'd seen yet on her face.

"That was Jimmy," I said flatly, pointing after his quickly reducing frame scrambling through the lobby and out the front door. I don't know why, but both Jenise and I burst out laughing. You couldn't have set this up! It was like a scene straight out of a movie. Jill and Anne joined us, and they, too, found the whole thing hysterical.

We shared dinner in the banquet room, and I enjoyed meeting Jenise's friends. During the uplifting session that evening, my awareness centered on who I sat next to, Miss Jenise Johnston. I was in her presence. That was enough.

Back in my room, I was cautiously elated. Jenise gave no sign in word or deed that we were anything but friends. Full of questions, the guys back in our hotel room quizzed me, "So how do you know Jenise? Are you guys a thing?" They heckled me and gave me grief, letting me know through it all that they thought she was an amazing catch, with a *good luck to you, buddy, if you can pull it off.* My prayers that night mirrored the night before, only this time, they were full of praise and thanksgiving for allowing me to take this princess to the ball.

Saturday morning broke cold and clear, with low temperatures and snow glistening on Gatlinburg's ski hill. I had a perfect view from my hotel window. I fought the desire to go buy a ticket and take some runs. I love skiing! I mean love, love, love skiing! There's something about the freedom of speeding down the mountain through the trees with all of God's great creation proclaiming his awesome wonder. Yes, it feels like worship.

At breakfast, since there was no room at the girls' table, I joined the guys. A twinge of angst surfaced. *Why did Jenise not save me a seat?* Oh, well, no big deal. *Guess I should've arrived early and saved one for her. Come on, Chad! You can do better than this!* The guys' table showcased typical rollicking guy talk. I really found it easy to connect with this crew. Then again, I rarely find a person I don't like. I love people and find them fascinating. I love learning about them, discovering who they are, what they think, what they do, and what they want to become. Eager to learn and grow, I found myself challenged, encouraged, and inspired by these conversations.

A session followed breakfast, and aside from a casual greeting from Jenise, we stayed in separate crowds. Girls and guys. I started to worry that this wasn't going in the right direction. Jenise wasn't cold or hostile—aloof and distant perhaps? After an awesome day yesterday, I wondered if I did something or said something wrong? Maybe she had time to think last night and had thought better of all this, of us. Lunch was on our own, and I decided it was time to assert myself once again. I didn't intend to hang with the guys or to see Gatlinburg. I was here to see Jenise.

I purposely walked alongside Jenise as we all left the meeting hall and asked, "What are you doing for lunch?"

Jill overheard me and answered in her sweet Southern drawl, "Us girls are going downtown to Gatlinburg. Want to come along?"

I turned to Jenise. "Jenise, are you going too?" I asked, wanting to be clear that I was only interested in going if she was.

"Sure," she said cheerfully.

"Then I'm in too," I quipped.

It was a short walk to a variety of cafés, restaurants, and shops. We ended up at the base of the ski hill I could see from the hotel. It thrilled my heart to see skiers shooting down into the base area with smiles wide. Noisy and joyful banter energized our lunch table of about six girls and three guys (my two roommates joined us).

Walking down, Jenise seemed distant—not avoiding me completely, but walking on ahead and conversing with the gals and other guys. My intentions had been clear. I only wanted to attend if that's what Jenise wanted. She knew I traveled to the East Coast to get to know her. The exact feeling I'd had two days earlier when she had informed me she was going with Jim (or "Jimmy," my nickname for him) crept back in.

Knowing what worked last time, I decided it was time to see what Jenise wanted. So I sat between Jill and Anne, paying no mind to where Jenise sat or what she ate. I aimed to appear as though she didn't exist, period. Engaging in playful conversation and banter came easily; they were great girls! Lunchtime flew by. I worked hard not to notice Jenise, look her way, or pay any attention to her. It was not easy and not fun, but I tried to make it look both easy and fun.

Our little entourage meandered past the cutesy shops afterward, and I stayed away from the cutest girl on the planet. *Maybe it will backfire this time*, I thought to myself. Does she really not care? The ride up seemed so fun and warm, but now she seemed so far away. *Wait, here she is, walking right beside me.* In fact, she bumped Jill out of the way. "Move over, sister," she said playfully. I continued talking with both Jenise and her friends, giving her friends equal, if not more, time and attention. I sensed Jenise making efforts to connect, converse, and get my attention. Maybe she did care. Maybe she was interested in more than just being friends.

"Do you want to go ice skating?" I was looking directly at her when I asked.

"Sure," she replied. "Sounds fun!"

The ice rink was only fifty yards away, and soon we were lacing up. As Jenise put on her skates, I decided not to wait for her and headed out on the ice. She had taken one step toward me. I was not about to smother her with attention. I made plenty of moves to let her know just how interested I was. It was time for her to take a few more steps my way. After all, love is a game, a dance of sorts, or so I had been told. Nobody wants something too easy to acquire. It must be rare or a risk to be precious.

Racing around the rink, my few prior times on ice paid off. I felt right at home. The guys busted out fast laps around the lightly trafficked ice. The girls joined the counterclockwise pattern, huddled together and laughing gaily. We blew by them again and again. Several of them, including Jenise, took off after us. We easily outpaced them back around to the girls who stayed at a slower pace. I pulled up short and skated with them, all of us having a grand time.

The brisk air, exercise, and fun music created a festive atmosphere. I'm a physical guy, an active, adventurous risk-taker. I love being physical, doing physical things. Any sport, anytime, anywhere, and I'm in. Being outdoors in God's awesome creation fires up something in me that is so zestful, so real, like a natural high—and I felt it right then.

Jenise skated up beside me. I looked over, and our eyes met. "Want to skate with me?" she asked.

"Let's go," I said, and we took off, leaving the other skaters behind. With wide smiles, the wind flew past our faces. The ice passed beneath our skates, and our breath came fast as we skated around and around. The music, her smile . . . what a magical moment. *I love this girl.* She was savoring this and wanting to be with me too. I glanced her way and witnessed her angelic, glowing smile and blonde hair flowing in the wind. *She's the one. I know she's the one!* I'd never felt that way, ever. Never even close. Everything about her moved me—every look, glance, expression, and mannerism. Everything! I loved the way she skated boldly, with a sense of adventure, and a willingness to risk. Eager to go beyond her comfort zone, she had spirit; she had fire. She was a woman to take on life with, a woman to climb mountains with, to ski the steeps, swim, hike, mountain bike, run, and skate with—and skate we did.

"Do you want to try and skate like figure skaters in the Olympics?" she asked.

"You mean like this?" I suggested, taking her hands in mine, and attempting to skate backward with her pushing me. Oh, the simple thrill of holding her hand. My heart rate soared to a whole new level, and my heart sang as I held her hands in mine. What strong hands she had and such long graceful fingers. Her eyes met mine, and we laughed at my awkward backward skating ability, but neither of us cared one bit. We were close, we were holding hands, we were looking at each other, and we liked it. All of it!

I could tell we had just made a big step toward us, toward her and me being far more than friends, so much more than friends. It seemed as if the group we came with faded away into the background as we played together on the ice. The romance of it all—Jenise, the music, the ice—swept over me. *Thank you, Lord,* I breathed as we weaved among the other skaters who became invisible. Just Jenise and me. Our eyes didn't want to look away. We were laughing, playing, chasing, catching, wanting to be caught, and not wanting to be released.

We didn't notice the others leave the ice for a sweet treat at the snack bar. No, we went around and around and around, as if in a trance, a mesmerizing dance, never wanting it to end, wanting forever to be just like this—us, enraptured, together.

The referee woke us from our dream with a sharp whistle and instruction to exit the rink for Mr. Zamboni to do his magic. I let go of her hand as we exited the ice and made our way back to the bench. Once out of the skates and into our shoes, we joined the others. "Hey y'all," I said in my best Southern accent. "Didn't see y'all leave. Weren't you having any fun?" I asked.

"Not nearly as much as you two were," Jill shot back with a grin and knowing eyes. She laughed. "Nope, not nearly *that* much fun!"

A sled for tourists to sit on and pose for pictures sat nearby in front of a snowy mountain scene. "Hey, Jenise, come on over," I said. "Let's take a picture." I sat down. Then she stepped into the sled and sat just in front of me. My legs went around her, and she leaned back on my chest. She wore a white jacket with a white fur collar that framed her face so perfectly. The sweet scent of her perfume wafted over me—oh, my word. *She is unbelievable*, I thought to myself. Our heads close, smiles genuine, and click—we took the picture. I didn't want to move. I could have sat there all afternoon, but we made our way out of the sled, and others piled in to take their pictures.

The crowd broke into smaller groups depending on interests or plans like shopping or heading to the hotel. I turned to Jenise and asked, "Will you go for a walk with me?"

"Yes," she said. The way she looked into my eyes and the simple way she answered wasn't flirty but very open and eager, which thrilled my soul. *What a doll*, I thought, as we said our farewells to the others.

"You two be good," Jill cried cheerfully over her shoulder.

"Of course," I replied with a lovesick grin on my face.

* * *

CHAD'S REFLECTIONS

Okay, that day was magical! I hope you can feel the electricity that was in the air. This was the biggest move forward in our relationship.

Every relationship is different. No two love stories are the same, ever.

It is so important to live your story and to be led by the Lord in how you choose to win the heart of the one you love. The pace, the starts, the stops, and the pauses are all a part of the wonderful dance of dating and courtship.

When you look back on your love story, it is so easy to see the dips, the turns, the highs, and the lows as important parts of getting you to where you are today. In the moment, however, each one of those is such a big deal filled with uncertainty, unknowing, questions, zero answers, guessing, hoping, and wondering.

Something that kept coming back to me throughout the journey was this—I truly only wanted God's best for Jenise and me. Nothing less. If she was not the one for me, I wanted to know—and the sooner, the better. If we were not right for each other, then God had something better in store for each of us. As hard as that was to say and believe in the moment, in my heart I knew it was true.

It was so critical to remind myself of that often during the time. I was pursuing all-out but trusting the Lord would make things clear in His time.

CHAPTER 20
THE NEW COWBOY IN TOWN

Jenise and I strolled up the hill along the winding sidewalk toward the hotel. The sun shone brightly; the weather was cool but comfortable. We came upon a picnic bench on a grassy knoll overlooking the town below, and we talked. Oh, boy, did we talk—of personalities and what animals we'd be. I said an eagle or lion, and Jenise said a dolphin. I loved that. Dolphins are joyful, playful, and beautiful. We shared our dreams, visions, and ideals. Jenise knew her mind and communicated well. She got my humor, and we laughed often. About two hours had passed when Jenise looked at her watch and said, "Oh, we better get going. I'm singing with Wayne Watson tonight and need to get changed before dinner."

Heading up the path toward the hotel, oh, how I wanted to hold her hand. We'd left the euphoric highs of the skating rink far below, and now in the quiet, I felt much more at risk. Despite fearing her response, I reached over and took her hand.

She playfully responded, "Aren't you bold?" with a twinkle in her eye, but she didn't let go of my hand.

"Um, if I recall correctly, it wasn't me who asked if we could skate like in the Olympics. Who's bold here?" I laughed. Why did everything seem so right with her hand in mine? Hers was the hand I wanted to hold for the rest of my life, before an altar and witnesses, while she labored to birth our children, throughout our great ups and downs, while we played life like a movie—a movie we'd one day replay with our children, grandchildren, great-grandchildren. Yes, this was the hand I wanted to hold as the sun set sweetly on our lives, someday far in the future. I was a dreamer, and as we sauntered along that path, my dreams were coming true.

We met for dinner. She looked for me when she stepped off the elevator, and I was waiting right there to pick her up—no *Jimmy* coming out of the elevator this time. Though it seemed impossible, Jenise, glowing, looked even more beautiful than earlier. I wore my green and white striped Façonnable shirt that I'd dropped what felt like three days' pay for at Nordstrom. For some, that might not be a big deal, but for a twelve-dollar-an-hour ski patrolman and JCPenney kind of guy, it was a big deal. I'd always liked nice things—real nice things.

I liked to say I had caviar taste on a beans-and-rice budget, and I splurged on this trip in every way—from the flight and the car to the singles retreat. Not for a minute did I question an expense; it was one of the best investments I had ever made. Had I skated alone that afternoon, I may have thought differently. That's the nature of risk, though. You never know until you try, until you write the check, step off the edge, or fall backward. I felt on top of the world, like a million bucks.

With Jenise sitting by my side, we enjoyed a delightful meal and joyful conversation with friends. We moved into the Mountain Room for the concert, a grand room with a big stage where Jenise would sing with the praise and worship team upfront. "Save me a seat," she whispered.

"But, of course, my dear," I answered.

Soon we stood and sang praises to the God of all creation. I'm a passionate guy and not afraid to shed a few tears . . . okay, a lot of tears. I feel deeply, and I like that about myself. It makes life a more enriching experience. I want to live fully and experience all the wonders of life richly. Once more in the moment's magic, Jenise's angelic voice carried me away with her sincere heart and resonant voice. Overwhelmed, I asked, *Lord, can life be this good? Can too many things go right? Can this all be real?* I had somehow imagined this moment, and it was now happening in slow motion.

I was falling madly in love with a godly, pure-hearted, and stunningly beautiful woman. Wayne Watson, who, according to Jenise, was quite a big deal in the Christian music world, joined her on stage. Growing up on hymns and hymns alone, I'd never heard of him. His voice was unbelievable! Their God-gifted voices together—singing life-giving words of God's love, grace, mercy, and salvation—I could listen forever, as could the audience of 350. Again, I saw Jenise's unique, God-given abilities of blessing, serving, and leading others. She had so much to offer.

The concert ended, and Jenise—the star of the evening—made her way to her seat, right next to me! The whole thing seemed surreal. The speaker gave a short message, and then we rose to pray. I took Jenise's hand in mine until "Amen." Next on the agenda was a country dance—of course! Nashville wasn't too far away, and country was my thang! Reflecting now, I marvel at the grace and goodness of the Lord. I grew up listening to many of those songs. Country music often tells stories of loss, pain, depression, drinking, prison, and infidelity—messages of death—but it also tells uplifting stories of faith, hope, and love—all messages of life. What I love the most is that it's catchy and fun to dance to.

I bled cowboy joy for my brother Warren Johnson, a cowboy through and through. From the top of his flat-brimmed, 4X beaver-felt Stetson to his tight Wrangler jeans and real-deal cowboy boots, Warren was country to the core. Even though he grew up in the concrete jungle of LA, our grandfather, Warren Clayton, gifted him the cowboy gene. Warren, one of my heroes as well as my older brother, had me fully convinced country music was the only music. As a kid, I even read his old

Western Horseman magazines and sent away for information on becoming a bull rider or a rodeo clown. Fortunately for me, neither panned out.

One year earlier, I traveled to Jordan Valley in central Oregon. If you're a cowboy and anywhere near Oregon, you know it's home to one of the finest rodeos and country dances in the state. One evening, I showed up in what I called full cowboy costume with my Wrangler jeans, boots, hat, and all. It must have looked legit because, twice, real-deal cowboys asked if I was riding. "No, not tonight," I replied honestly— not tonight or any other night, most likely. Warren and the sweet young ladies of Oregon taught me to swing dance. I left that weekend with many moves and later practiced with my sisters and friends at our home in Hacienda Heights and at other functions in the area. I'm not saying I was all that, but I felt pretty confident I could hold my own if these Southern boys could cut a rug. The last thing a cowboy trying to win a woman wants to do is sit on the sidelines while somebody else twirls his girl around the room.

The music started, and Jenise was by my side. She had never danced that way before, but from a biblical perspective, swing dancing works much like marriage. The man leads the way with his lady following his lead and simple cues. As we danced up a storm, Jenise's eyes widened with wonder, and she just beamed.

"How on earth did you learn to dance like that?" she exclaimed.

"I'm a cowboy, Jenise. Didn't you know that?!"

We both laughed, then sat one out and talked. I explained the whole Jordan Valley dance lesson as we watched others dance along to the music. Most of the guests had never tried swing dancing. Jenise's friends expressed interest, so we taught them the moves throughout the night. It was so much fun! Others caught on, and we danced the night away.

Although Jenise and I practiced several advanced moves off to the side, I only had time to teach her the basics. She caught on quickly, and we soon conquered them with speed and comfort. During breaks, we joined the others to visit. Everyone was having such a great time. The music came on, and it was a fast tune, a good one.

"Time to dance, girl," I said, as I reached for Jenise's hand. We flew out onto the floor and danced away. As the song picked up pace, so did we, our bodies moving perfectly in time, synchronized in close rhythm.

We added more advanced moves and a circle formed around us, which gave us more room to swing to the music. I soon sensed that most of the dancers had stopped to watch. With bright smiles, they clapped to the beat and cheered us on as we danced. We weaved in and out, move by move—the pretzel, the ticktock, and other moves with fun names. Halfway through the song, I told my radiant Jenise I was going to flip her. Wide-eyed but ready, she nodded and smiled. We had practiced in the corner earlier.

As the song reached its finale, I swung Jenise around, placed my hands around her waist, and she jumped, throwing her head back. Her whole body formed a graceful arc as she backflipped over my arm, landing right perfectly on her dancing feet, keeping tempo the entire time. Our little crowd went wild, clapping loudly and smiling with delight! Still holding her hand, I walked Jenise back across the dance floor to the perimeter. We were both flush with the excitement, the exercise of dancing, and the thrill of being in the moment.

What a moment! We could've been stars on a movie set with all the world orbiting around us. The dancing continued, along with more teaching in the spirit of everyone having the best time. Growing up, I always made sure everyone had a good time, and that continued to be a concern and focus of mine. I'd approach the quiet, young lady sitting alone and ask her to dance. Almost always, I'd be the first on the dance floor. I'm hardwired to be the icebreaker and make it easier for everyone else to have a good time. Not to mention, it was fun for me too!

The entire night, everyone festively and fully experienced the fun, and Jenise and I were in the thick of it all. Even though we weren't with each other for every dance or every moment, we were constantly aware of where the other was. I was fully aware that I had Jenise's full attention, and I loved it! She definitely tuned in to *Chad Radio 100.1.* It was about time. Every risk from jumping on that plane to planning this wild escapade was beginning to bear fruit. It was beginning to seem like a good idea, after all.

* * *

CHAD'S REFLECTIONS

I have heard it said that "success is when preparedness meets opportunity." Another quote I love is, "There is always a prepared place for the prepared person."

That evening, swing dancing was on the agenda. I had no idea that would be happening, but because I had practiced before, I was prepared when the opportunity arrived.

Please don't misunderstand me. I don't think it would have mattered a bit if I did not know how to dance—it just made it more fun and memorable because I did.

Life has a way of presenting opportunities to us. Growing up, I always tried to participate in activities that came my way. I didn't sit on the sidelines. I didn't hold back because I didn't know how or was afraid to look like a beginner or amateur.

I am convinced that a beginners' attitude is healthy for humans. A willingness to try new things, develop new skills, and take new risks is good for us. When you do, it can make you appreciate new opportunities or shine in moments that just show up.

CHAPTER 21
ENCHANTED EVENING

Toward the end of the night, I asked Jenise if she wanted to go for a walk. She didn't need to nod—her eyes said it all. We slipped out the side door and headed down the long hall back to the lobby. "Will you be cold if we go outside?" I asked.

"Yes," she replied.

"Let's go get our jackets then. Meet you here in five. Last one back has to do push-ups!"

"Hey, no fair!" she cried, pushing me away from the elevator door. She pushed the up button, and the door opened.

We both jumped in, and I said, "You're right. This is no fair. My room is two floors above yours. I don't stand a chance!"

"Are you surrendering?" she taunted.

"To you? Never!" I responded confidently.

"Bring it on!"

The door opened at the sixth floor, and off she went.

"Take your time," I yelled after her.

My sprint to the room and the mad dash back to the elevator did me no good. Jenise stood there, leaning against the lobby wall. She yawned and covered her mouth, "Oh, you're here," she said in her sleepiest voice. "How long have I been waiting? I fell asleep."

"You punk!" I replied.

She burst out laughing. "Okay, on the floor. Give me ten." She added, "Good ones."

I hit the lobby floor and began to bang out ten perfect military push-ups. "One, two, three . . ." she counted along with me. I hit number six when from around the corner came Jenise's contingent of friends from the dance.

"What on earth is going on here?" they joked.

"Oh, I see how this is going to go!" Jill exclaimed loudly. "Jenise, it didn't take you long to get things under control."

By then, I'd finished my push-ups and jumped to my feet. "Come on, Jenise," I said, grabbing her by the hand and leading her through the crowd of her laughing friends. "Places to go, people to see. Bye, y'all!" My best Southern drawl dragged the words out long and laboriously, bringing a laugh from the group.

The cool air refreshed our faces as we exited the front doors and walked along the paving stones and down the steps. Both of us were quiet and breathing in the fresh mountain air. We followed the sidewalk around to the right. The heat of Jenise's hand warmed me to the core. *This is how life is supposed to be. A woman by my side—not just any woman, but this one. Jenise Cheri.* It was so incredibly right. I knew love wasn't a feeling but a commitment to put someone else before yourself. What a joy to experience a love that seemed to incorporate both!

Gatlinburg's twinkling lights came into view as we rounded the corner of the hotel perched high above the city. We stepped onto the vacant deck that cantilevered out over the hill. It was now covered with round tables and umbrellas, but earlier it had been full of people dining and enjoying the sun. We stopped at the railing, where the lights of the city matched the twinkling of our hearts. We turned and faced each other, and I took both of her hands in mine.

She looked up, her eyes saying, *Well, aren't you bold?* but she didn't take them back or speak.

"How are you doing?" I asked.

"Really good!" she replied. "How about you?" she countered with a mischievous look.

"Never been better," I said, smirking.

"Never?"

"Never, ever, ever," I repeated. "I don't do this every day, you know."

"What, sweep a lady off her feet?" she inquired softly with warm humor in her voice.

"Is that what I'm doing?" I questioned mockingly.

"You know what you're doing, Chadwick Buford!" I loved hearing her call me that. She used it now with full effect.

"Today has been one of the best days of my life. Every bit of it," I said. "Wasn't ice skating fun?"

"The whole day has been fun," she agreed. "I had no idea you could dance like that."

"We could dance like that," I corrected her with a twinkle in my eye.

"Yes, I suppose you're right," she said. "I didn't know I could dance like that."

"Are you cold?" I asked. She nodded, so I brought her close, wrapping my arms around her. The smell of her hair washed over me once more. *Oh, boy,* I said to myself. *Chad, you better be careful. She is too much.* The top of her head came right to my lips, and I kissed her hair lightly. We stood, not saying anything, just feeling our hearts pounding close as the lights twinkled their happy silent song below us, serenading us and dancing for us.

This is really happening, I thought to myself. *I'm holding the woman of my dreams.* For the past nine months, ever since Brenda's wedding, she'd been ever in my thoughts, my prayers, and my plans—and here she was in my arms. Could this be real? *Lord, do dreams really come true? Dreams like this?*

"Jenise," I said softly.

"Yes," she replied, looking up. Our lips met with a warm welcome and eagerness that both thrilled and surprised me.

My entire world became silent and still, and nothing mattered except for this glorious moment. My soul sang, my heart beat out of my chest, and my whole being was enraptured with this woman of strength, beauty, and character.

"Wow!" Jenise said breathlessly as we parted. She pushed me back slightly.

I let go of her and jumped up and down. "Oh! My! Gosh! What on earth? You! Are! Completely! Unbelievable!"

"You're hysterical!" Jenise was now laughing.

"Come here," I said, holding out my arms. As she came into my arms, I held her close again and said, "One more." Slowly our faces came together. Once again, the fire of our passion met, and I was lost in the blanket of her sweet love. The all-encompassing nature of our embrace silenced my other senses. Every wild and natural part of me as a man came alive with a ferocious intensity that thrilled me and scared me at the same time. I pushed her slowly and gently back, not wanting to let go. At last, we parted, and Jenise leaned forward. I pulled her close, hugging her head to mine.

"Jenise," I said, almost breathless. "Come on, let's go." I turned back toward the way we had come, taking her hand in mine. As she came alongside, I put my arm around her shoulders and held her close. "You're amazing! I can't even believe any of this," I said. "You're too good to be true! Slap me if I'm dreaming." She laughed, and the sound of it delighted my soul and flooded me with warmth.

"Where are we going?" she asked.

"I'm taking you right into this hotel, and you'll go to your room, and I'll march myself up to my room. Then, I'll try to go to sleep but will be utterly unable to, maybe forever now. I think you have completely ruined me."

"Ruined you?" she questioned.

"Yes, what is everyday life supposed to be like now that I've experienced heaven?"

"What's wrong with heaven?" she asked warmly.

"Absolutely nothing," I whispered. "That's the problem."

The elevator ride up was far too short, and as the door began to part at her floor, I stole another peck. "More heaven?" she asked, her eyes twinkling.

As she left the elevator, she said, "Sweet dreams, Chadwick Buford."

The door shut, and I looked up toward the heavens and cried out to myself, *Thank you, Lord. You have done a miracle tonight, and I praise and thank you for that. Please direct my steps. Lead us in the way we should go. Oh, how I want her with every part of my heart, soul, mind, and body. She is a treasure, rare. A beauty so precious. A heart full of gold. Oh, Lord, she's worth protecting, worth waiting for, worth anything. Please make me worthy of loving her and leading her. Give me wisdom in the way I conduct myself. Let me hold high standards and keep our relationship pure.*

* * *

CHAD'S REFLECTIONS

In this day and age, physical affection in relationships is considered to be no big deal. Kissing is no big deal. Premarital sex is no big deal. But that is not what the Bible says.

I do want to share a word of caution. Scripture is very clear on the importance of saving yourself for sexual relationships in marriage and that sex is a beautiful gift to be unwrapped in the context of a committed, lifelong, marital relationship.

So, in that light, kissing is a big deal. It can be a very intimate part of a romantic relationship. It can lead to hard-to-manage physical affection and can prematurely ignite a fire in two young lovers. It may also bring unneeded distraction from getting to know each other.

My desire was to honor Jenise in every way. Something I heard well into our marriage was that the goal in dating was to treat a woman the way you would want someone to treat your wife prior to marriage. I know for a fact that I would not be excited about someone kissing my wife—when we were dating, before we were married, or even before I knew her.

In looking back, I don't regret kissing Jenise that night in Gatlinburg, largely because I did end up marrying her. What I do regret is the couple of young ladies that I kissed prior to her whom I did not marry.

Jenise and I have been able to coach and counsel hundreds of newlywed couples over the past fourteen years. Not one of them has ever said they wish they had been more physical with their spouse prior to marriage. Not one of them has stated that they wish their spouse had been more sexually active in prior relationships. The opposite is categorically true. Many married couples have to overcome, pray through, and fight spiritually to move to a healthy place because of baggage they brought into the relationship from past premature physical or sexual activity.

The Johnston Family

Rededicating ourselves
once again after 20 years

1979   1999

The Gene Johnston Family

The Johnston Family at JH Ranch

With Mama Joy, hug master extraor-
dinaire, at her 90th birthday.

Somewhere in Colorado while bik-
ing 3,200 miles across the USA

Ski patrolling with my brother David at Snow Summit

Biking 3,200 miles across America. Left
to right: David, Dwight, Chad

First date on Jenise's birthday—February 17, 1992

After ice skating in Gatlinburg, TN

Ecstatic to be with her!

Never wanted to let go, Gatlinburg, TN.
The day everything changed.

Dancing up a storm on that magical night!

Showed up at Jenise's work to pick her up for our birthday date.

Taking time out of my bike trip across the USA to spell out my love in the salt flats of Utah

Celebrating our engagement with a BBQ!

Chad and
Jerise
Johnson

This is the Lord's doing;
it is marvellous in
our eyes.

This is the day which
the Lord hath made;
we will rejoice
and be glad in it.
Psalm 118:23-24

August 15, 1993

Our wedding invitation

Kissing on our wedding day

*Left to right: Joy & Gene Johnston, Jenise
& Chad, Paula & Burnell Johnson*

Singing my heart out with Jenise. My apologies to those who had to listen.

Chad & Jenise with Chad's family at the wedding

Jenise & Chad with their family

CHAPTER 22
SMOKY MOUNTAIN PRAYER

The room wasn't as dark and quiet as I imagined it might be. When I walked in, my roommates and another young man were playing cards.

"What's up, Chad?" Guy sang out. "How's the romance going?"

Before I could say one word, he kept it up, "Whoa, dude! You're completely smitten! Something went right tonight, didn't it?! Talk to me, Chad. Open up, buddy. We need to know the details. We're your support team here, ya know? We have your back!"

I was floating on air, and apparently it was obvious.

"What's up?" I repeated. "Oh, nothing much. I just had the best day of my entire life, that's all! I'm so in love, my heart hurts! Jenise Cheri Johnston is an angel, and if I'm not mistaken, she has a thang for yours truly! I think I'm gonna die!" I flung myself down on my bed, landing on my back. "I'm gonna die!"

They burst out laughing. "Seriously, man. What's going on?"

"I'm not kidding. Today it all came together." I detailed the ice skating, the walk, the talk, the concert, the dance, the deck, the kiss. When I got to the kiss, they started whooping and hollering like it was New Year's Eve. The people in the next room pounded on the wall for silence.

"Shhhhh!" I said, but the guys were all fired up and thoroughly enjoying making a big hoopla drama until the pounding sounded again.

"Quiet, guys. We don't want to be a bad testimony." They reluctantly muffled their laughing and funny quips while slowly winding down.

"I'm going to bed," I said. "I need to get my beauty sleep. If tomorrow is anything like today, I'm going to need it." This set off another volley of muffled comments.

Sleep wouldn't come. I could have had three cups of coffee, and, as a non-coffee drinker, it only takes one to ignite me. I wanted to run, to fight, to bust out of my skin. *I kissed Jenise Cheri Johnston, and she kissed me back!* Could this really be? Would I awaken to find it all a dream? No! This was happening. I was in love with the most beautiful and precious girl in the world, and she'd kissed me! My heart wouldn't slow down; instead, it was trying to jump out of my heaving chest.

"You going to be okay over there?" A voice in the darkness interrupted my thoughts.

"Uh, yeah. Sorry. Am I being too loud?" I asked.

"Just sounds like you're running laps," came the voice.

"Guess I'm a little wound up."

I tried to force relaxation, rest, and sleep, but it was no use. I was amped. I decided to go for a run. I put on my shorts and running shoes and quietly left the room. The cool wind outside did nothing to slow my breath. The temperature had dropped ten degrees. Though much darker, the twinkling lights beckoned me, so I ran the trail toward town. Though it was a short run, by the time I reached the ice-skating rink, now dark, I was ready to return. Back into the hotel room and careful not to wake the guys, I grabbed a quick shower and slipped into bed.

My unfinished prayer slipped away as I faded into a deep, full sleep. A pillow hit me in the face with a rude awakening and the resounding voice of Guy the next morning. "Wake up, love bird! Time to rise and shine. We have romance in the air and breakfast in fifteen."

Up and dressed in a flash, I entered the lobby with my roommates. When I scanned the café where breakfast was served, Jenise's blonde hair easily stood out amongst the crowd. I made my way over and tapped on her shoulder. She turned, our eyes met, and one look told me last night wasn't a dream but a living and gorgeous truth. Jenise Cheri was my girl.

"Good morning, sweet girl," I said quietly.

"Good morning, handsome boy," she replied. Why such a simple exchange would make my heart sing like a bluebird on a golden spring morning, I don't know, but it did.

"Are you hungry?" I asked.

"Starving!"

"Let's fix that," I said, grabbing her hand and leading her through the tables and chairs.

"Where are you going?" Jill asked as we weaved our way toward the buffet line.

"With him," I heard Jenise say, once more finding the smallest little words or phrases to mean the world to me.

Playful conversation energized breakfast time between Jenise and me, as well as our friends, who were a bit electrified by the apparent connection Jenise and I were experiencing. I noticed Jenise's friends getting a kick out of the two of us; she'd brought them up to speed too. Everyone enjoyed giving us a bit of grief!

I'm sure the session was great, but I missed most of the content due to Jenise sitting by my side. I lost myself in her presence and savored every moment. Before I knew it, our lunchtime passed. We shared warm goodbyes with our new-found friends and loaded our luggage into the trunk of my rental car.

Our drive through Gatlinburg brought to mind the treasure of memories made just the day before, and soon the fir-tree-laden forests of the Blue Ridge Mountains were beautifully painting both sides of the road as we traveled. Conversation and discovery of each other continued so freely. We traveled the reverse path we'd taken to the retreat, but the return held a new and grander perspective. All of God's glory was on display as the early morning rain subsided and the sun broke through the clouds with rays of brilliant wonder, shining forth on the rolling green forested hills that seem to go on forever. The road was like a black ribbon weaving across the hills and out of sight, carrying us on.

The road led to a curve topping a hill, revealing the majestic view in awesome wonder. My heart overflowed with gratitude. The God of all creation—He who had created the heavens and the earth, the breathtaking scenery that surrounded me both in and outside that vehicle—loved me, cared for me, brought me to this place, and gave me favor with this extraordinary woman beside me, a woman I had longed for, prayed for, and yet still wondered if she was only a figment of my imagination. No, this was real. She was real. And I was beyond grateful!

"Jenise," I began, "I just want to pray and thank the Lord." I paused. "Thank the Lord for everything . . . you, me, this trip. What He's doing in bringing us together." She looked as if she didn't know what to say. She didn't stop me or disagree, so I continued, "Are you okay with that?"

"Of course," she replied.

There in the car, driving through the Smoky Mountains of Tennessee, we prayed, and I cried out to the Lord in praise and thanksgiving: "Lord, you're so good! You hear the prayers and requests we put before you. I'm here with Jenise, in this beautiful place, which is evidence that you answer prayers. I thank you for the way you've brought Jenise and me together and that you know every detail of our lives. Lord, I ask that you go before us in every step we take. Direct our hearts to you first, and then to each other. Keep us pure in thought and deed, that we honor you and each other in all that we do. Use our budding relationship to glorify you and bless each other and many others. Lord, we entrust the future to you and rest in your plans for us, whatever they may be. In Jesus' name, Amen."

When Jenise looked into my eyes, tears were rolling down my cheeks. She looked surprised and a bit taken aback. "Sorry, Jenise, I don't mean to scare you. You don't understand. This is a really big deal to me." It was clear that Jenise had no idea just how serious I was about her. This wasn't routine. As I've said before, I had many a "girl friend," but never a girlfriend. I had always been intentional with my interactions and involvement, or lack thereof, with the opposite sex. This whole experience with all the sweep-her-off-her-feet romantics was a first in my lifetime. Not my modus operandi, not normal.

When I was praying, I knew with all my heart that she'd be the one. My one and only! She'd be the woman I'd spend the rest of my days with. The thought was sweetly overwhelming. The answer to my dreams and prayers was holding my hands. Somehow, I knew the rest of the story, not in fine detail but with enough clarity to elicit a deep sensation of blessing, gratitude, and delight.

I wanted to pull the car over and give her a big ol' hug— and a kiss—but I kept driving.

I'd long resolved to keep honor in dating, meaning:

1. Don't give in to the erotic or sensual.

2. Keep physical and emotional energies in check.

3. Respect her as if she were to be someone else's wife.

Guess I'd already failed in that—a huge part of me felt as though holding her hand and kissing her, for sure, had crossed a threshold of not measuring up to that standard. I wanted to honor and protect Jenise. I was laying a foundation for a lifetime relationship of trust and commitment. I wanted her to see that I'd be a trustworthy companion and keeper of her heart someday.

The miles flew by as we continued to unwrap the glory of the weekend. It was late when I pulled up to her condo, and I knew better than to go inside. I helped carry her bags to the front. Before I turned, our lips met once more. The stars twinkled brighter and the night quieted, making our breathing the only sound.

"Good night, Jenise Cheri," I said.

"Good night, Chadwick Buford," she whispered.

"Go in the house, girl, before I go crazy," I instructed her while nudging her slowly away. She closed the door slowly while peeking through the shrinking space.

"Hey."

She stopped. "Yes?"

"What are you doing tomorrow?"

"Work," she said.

"I know, but after work."

"Oh, I almost forgot!" she gasped. "I have a voice lesson tomorrow evening!"

"Any chance you could cancel it?" I inquired. "It just happens that somebody important to me has a birthday tomorrow."

Jenise lit up. "Oh, you're right! I totally forgot."

I had no idea what a big deal it was that I remembered her birthday. As number nine in a frugal family of twelve children, birthdays were often forgotten, overlooked, or downplayed as unimportant. While Jenise was confident of her parents' love, she carried some hurt from the oversight and the appearance of the lack of care in that area of her life.

"I'd love to have the pleasure of your company and have a little celebration together if you can make it work."

She smiled with her bright and thrill-me-to-my-soul smile and responded, "Yes, I'll make a call first thing tomorrow and cancel my voice lesson."

"Would you be so kind as to wear the outfit you wore last week to work, that black and white dress?"

"Wow, you notice everything," she laughed.

"Not everything," I continued. "Just everything about you. Good night, Jenise Cheri."

"Good night," I heard her reply before I walked, skipped, and leaped down the walkway to my car.

* * *

CHAD'S REFLECTIONS

During our dating relationship, there were several standout points of confirmation for me, and that travel day in the Great Smoky Mountains was one of them. I remember so vividly sensing the Lord laying on my heart once again that Jenise was the one for me. He said this was no fling or short-term interest. This was the woman I would be spending the rest of my life with. It was almost overwhelming emotionally. I was so happy!

I wanted to be the spiritual leader in our relationship. This was a role that intimidated me to be honest with you, but it was important to me to have the Lord in the center of our relationship. So I did what He laid on my heart to do. I asked Jenise to pray. This became a part of our relationship going forward. Not just at mealtimes, but when we were together, when we were apart, when things went well, and when things got hard.

Scripture has so many promises about what God is willing and able to do on our behalf—if we only seek Him and ask Him.

Sometimes, I make spiritual leadership harder than it needs to be. Can it really be so simple as to initiate a time of praying together? Reading Scripture together? Asking questions about how the other person is doing in their relationship with the Lord?

CHAPTER 23
HAPPY BIRTHDAY SCAVENGER HUNT

The morning broke clear and beautiful with my mind on my mission. I ate a quick breakfast with the Gable family. They were all over-the-top elated with reports of my successful weekend. Reviewing the whole thing again was a rich experience for me. Then I was off to Atlanta for a day of "Happy Birthday to Jenise" prep!

My first stop was the one-hour photoshop, where I dropped off the roll of film from our weekend retreat. The nice man behind the counter said he was a bit behind, and it'd be more like three hours.

I told him, "No problem, I'll only pay you one-third the price." He laughed with me as I quickly added, "No worries." Nothing in the world could get me down. I was walking on air. How couldn't I be? The whole weekend seemed like a dream, yet it was all so real.

After a short drive, I pulled onto Peachtree Parkway and into the parking lot of Tucker Wayne/Luckie & Co. Yes, I was lucky! No, I was blessed. I walked into the same fine foyer as I had several days prior and greeted the security guard at the front desk.

"Mr. California is back!" he chuckled. "Must have gone well over the weekend?"

"Yep! Amazing!" I gave him a thumbs-up as I waited for the elevator door to open. After a quick trip to the eighteenth floor, the elevator opened, and a surprised Jenise greeted me. I whispered so as not to disturb those working in their offices with doors opened. "Can I borrow your car?"

"Sure. Is something wrong with the rental car?" She looked concerned.

"Kind of," I grinned as she handed me the keys. "I'll get it back here by 5:00 p.m. See you then." I squeezed her hand, gave her a quick peck, and left.

I found her Honda Civic hatchback, which I had already fondly dubbed "The Wondersled," by its gold and tan color making it easy to spot amongst the black and silver imports surrounding it. Apparently, these advertising execs brought home some serious dough. The Wondersled was old but reliable. Before we left for the retreat, I noticed the winter rain and snow had done a number on it and decided to get it detailed for Jenise. Pulling up to the car wash, I saw the little sticker in the windshield. The oil change was past due by fifty miles. How fun! I'd also get the oil changed.

The attendant moved quickly upon my request. It'd be about two hours, and fortunately, I always have a book with me. This book? *How to Win Friends and Influence People*, the old classic from Dale Carnegie. Time flew by, and the detailed car I stepped into was a far cry better than the one I drove up in.

I dropped the vehicle back at the agency and drove to the flower shop, Peachtree Petals. I briefly shared my whirlwind romance story with the owner and informed her I wanted two beautiful bouquets, one I could hand Jenise when I picked her up, and another one for a special surprise. She became creative when she learned there was no budget and suggested two truly wow bouquets for the evening.

Earlier, I told Steve and Kim money wasn't an issue and asked them for a dinner recommendation. It was funny I said this—I was virtually broke, yet I truly meant it. I justified any amount as an investment and shared that with anyone who mentioned the cost. For fine romantic dining, they suggested Aria in Buckhead. I remembered Buckhead from my drive around the previous Thursday afternoon and liked the idea of dining in style in that fine town. I asked the florist the same question to compare.

"Hmmm . . ." She pondered for a moment. "If you really want to spoil her rotten, go to Aria." That sealed it for me. "You should be able to get a reservation seeing that it's Monday evening." She picked up the phone and dialed before I could say anything. "Hello, can I get a table for two this evening?" she asked gaily. Covering the mouthpiece, she whispered, "What time?"

"I pick her up at 5:00 p.m., so let's say 6:00 p.m."

"6:00 p.m. Thank you," she said as she turned to me, hanging up the phone. "You're good to go!"

"Thank you so much. Can you give me the address?" She wrote it down on a little card and pushed it across the counter. "One last question for you—is there a tuxedo rental shop nearby?"

"Wow!" she drawled dramatically. "You really are going all out!"

"Well, this young woman is the real deal, so it better be good," I laughed.

"Your flowers will be ready after two," she said as I walked out the door.

Twenty minutes later, an earnest man poked and prodded me. "You look real nice. Real nice. You have a lady to show?"

"Yes, a good lady," I smiled.

"Good, good! You look real nice! She'll like this! She'll like the clothes, real nice. She'll know you're a big man in these clothes." I couldn't help but smile further. He was quite the dramatic salesman, although he was only affirming my already-made decision.

I nodded. The image reflected in the mirror agreed. I never felt sharper, more dapper, and more respectable looking than in a tuxedo. My logic was that I'd already shown up wearing the only suit I owned, and I wanted to show up and create a little shock and awe. I wanted Jenise to know that she was special—real special—that her birthday was a big deal in my book, and that she was a big deal. My tuxedo shop host was kindly pulling on my sleeve, trying to get my attention, "Sir, you need to take that off."

"Oh, yes, will do."

A few moments later, Mr. Tux had walked to the back room, saying, "It'll be ready in an hour."

Now, for a gift. What could I get the most amazing girl in the world? I didn't want to go over the top. My financial resources were indeed limited. I knew money spent isn't the measure of a gift well-given. It's all about heart, soul, intention, meaning, nuance, and romance. Then it hit me. I knew Jenise loved music. I'd played some romantic classics on a tape cassette I'd purchased specifically for the drive up to Gatlinburg. "Edelweiss" was a favorite of both of ours.

I found a shop with collectibles, gifts, and handcrafted items. On a shelf, I spotted the most beautiful wooden music box with intricate wood inlay of a tulip on the top. When I opened the music box, the music chimed as a music box does. My heart stopped. "Edelweiss." Could it be? I stood dumbfounded as the music swept me away. Coincidence? I don't think so. The song played on until the tiny motor ran out of energy and was ready for a wind up once more.

"Do you like it?" The voice at my elbow startled me. I turned to see a smiling woman.

"Yes, I do. I like it a lot. I'll take it." The woman rang me up while asking who it was for. I detailed our short story once more with pure pleasure.

Leaving the gift store, I had one more thing on my mind. Over the weekend, I noticed Jenise's black leather pumps (her favorite pair) had a hole in the bottom of the shoe. At one point, she slipped them off, and I took another note—size nine and a half. I said nothing and filed it away for future action. *Well, now's the perfect time to remedy that*, I mused.

At Nordstrom once again, I lost myself in the vast sea of women's shoes of all shapes, sizes, styles, and colors. A kind, young woman, seeing my bewildered expression, rescued me, "Can I help you find something in particular?"

"Why, yes, you can. I'd like a pair of black leather pumps, size nine and a half," I proclaimed with my shoulders back, chest puffed, and as manly as can be.

"What size heel?" she asked.

"Oh, uh . . ." My confidence withered as I realized I had no idea pumps came in different heel heights. It made sense. I wish I'd paid better attention. "I don't really know. Can you show me a couple of options, and I'll pick one? They're not for me," I stammered with a twinkle in my eye.

She laughed. "I was guessing they weren't."

I knew the right ones immediately once I saw them and was speedily on my way. The sun was beginning its descent, and I needed to get cracking, or I wouldn't be able to pick up Jenise on time. I made my rounds to the photo shop, florist, tux rental store, and one final, very critical, stop. Aria! Driving up, I knew I'd picked the right place. The valet greeted me, and I explained my mission.

"Leave the car here. We aren't open yet, so it'll be right here when you get back." The valet led me to the front door and let me inside. He walked me to the receptionist's desk and introduced me to the young woman and the gentleman standing next to her. "Mr. Johnson, this is Miss Anderson and Mr. Foster. I'll have your vehicle for you when ready."

I turned and requested to speak with the manager. "Absolutely, Mr. Johnson. Just a moment," Miss Anderson said, and then turned and left the room. Mr. Foster offered me a drink of water. I gladly accepted it.

Everything about the place spoke of class, elegance, formality, and luxury. How fun! This was a whole new experience for me. As one of eight children, we didn't eat out often, and when we did, it was never like this place. I couldn't recall being in such a nice dining establishment ever! I soaked in every inch of the space, the decor, music, smell . . . everything. I could get used to this.

Someday, maybe this would be the norm rather than the rare exception. Not that it mattered too much. I did appreciate luxury, though, and the ambiance and aesthetics of a place always mattered more to me than most. Some of my siblings scoffed at places like Aria. The manager interrupted my reflection with a warm, "Mr. Johnson. How can I assist you?"

"I have a dinner reservation this evening at 6:00 p.m. If you'd be so kind, I'd like your assistance to make the woman joining me feel like she's the most special person in the entire world."

He smiled and nodded as if to say, *Go on.* His smile widened as I laid out my plans. "Perfectly wonderful!" he exclaimed. "It'll be just as you wish."

He called Miss Anderson and Mr. Foster over and brought them up to speed. Turning back to me, he said, "I'll also inform your waiter this evening. In fact, wait right here, and I'll introduce you now." A tall gentleman in his mid-fifties, fit, tan, and distinguished looking, was passing. He stopped and greeted us warmly. The manager introduced us.

I asked to pay in advance to keep things simple. I gave them sufficient cash to cover all courses and a generous tip in advance for Mr. Blatchford. He grinned and assured me, "It'll be a delight to make sure your evening is magical, Mr. Johnson. All details will be in order."

Driving away, I couldn't help but smile with anticipation of all the evening would hold. Arriving at the Gables' home,

I grabbed a shower and dressed in my crisp black and whites. I was so pumped! When I came downstairs, Kim whistled. "Wow," she said. "Pulling out all the stops, huh, Chad?"

"It's the last evening. He's got to close the deal," Steve chimed in with a wry grin. "Now, Chad, don't blow this. You know, it all comes down to right now." I loved his joking. "What did you decide on for dinner?" he asked.

"Aria!"

"Good man," he replied. "You're good to go!"

"I don't always act on wisdom, but sometimes I get it right."

"Aria won't disappoint," he reassured me. I nodded and told them all I had done that afternoon. "Perfect!" Steve exclaimed.

"Aren't you romantic?" Kim commented with a bit of a pout. "Poor girl, she doesn't stand a chance. Blessings on your evening, Chad, and remember whose you are," she said. Familiar words. My mother said them many a morning as I walked out the front door on my way to Los Robles Elementary School and Orange Grove Junior High. How I appreciated her subtle reminder to behave myself in a way that was honorable and right.

"Thank you, Kim," I said. "I will."

By then, I knew my way around Atlanta like a regular taxicab driver, and soon the immense outline of Tucker Wayne/ Luckie & Co. loomed ahead as I pulled once more into the parking lot. My watch read 4:45 p.m. *What a joy! I was on time.* Time has been a nagging dilemma for me since birth. When I was growing up, everyone who knew us teased us as operating on "Johnson Time," which unfortunately was not a compliment. It typically meant arriving fifteen to thirty minutes late with screeching tires and our large family piling out of a van driven to its mechanical limits.

I had the luxury of walking the same route I had so valiantly and desperately run with Phillip four days earlier. It seemed like ages ago, as so much had transpired since then. I was entering the place that a few days prior held questions and the possibility of great rejection. Now I strode in, confident I'd be met with joy and anticipation.

The security guard greeted me. "Looking sharp, young man, real sharp! Good to see you again. Is there a particular blonde you're here to see?" His smile glowed brightly, and a wink revealed his authentic joy. You could tell he loved people and his work. He continued, "You're missing your young sidekick; Phillip was his name? Are you not?"

I laughed, "He was unable to make it, had other plans."

"I see," the kind man said. "Tell Phillip hi for me and treat that blonde woman well. She's a fine one."

"Yes, sir, I will." The doors of the elevator closed, and it was just me and my reflection—a sharp-dressed, young man, looking dapper in his tux, with a flower bouquet of large white lilies in his hand. Dramatic and romantic, he was ready to spoil his angel rotten.

The doors opened, and I stepped into the foyer of Tucker Wayne/Luckie & Co. Advertising Agency. Instead of the lone Jenise sitting at her receptionist desk, it surprised me to see a small gathering of eight to ten colleagues surrounding her. She'd just finished unwrapping a small box that held a gift card from the group.

They all turned when I walked out of the elevator, and one of the women whistled and said, "Oh Jenise, never mind that," pointing to the small box Jenise held in her hand. "Your real gift just arrived!" She then pointed at me. Everyone laughed, including me.

Jenise stood up as I walked over. I hugged her and handed her the flowers, then stepped back with my arms held wide and began singing, "Happy Birthday." The entire group joined me as Jenise held her flowers close and flashed her bright and beautiful smile, her eyes looking straight into mine, saying more than words could ever say.

The crowd of well-wishers said their goodbyes, and Jenise made her way into the bathroom with a duffle bag she pulled from under her desk. "I'll be just a minute," she said, wrinkling her nose and giving me the cutest look. "Miss me," she added as she disappeared around the corner.

Little turkey. She is so stinking cute! Man, what a doll!

Just a minute was right. She returned almost as quickly as she left, and if I thought she looked amazing when she'd left a moment earlier, she looked even better when she returned. She wore the black and white dress as I'd requested, and her hair was pulled up and away from her face, revealing all her radiant beauty. She looked as fresh as a tulip in spring, bursting with vibrant color and vitality. Wow!

"Ready," she said. "Did you miss me?"

"Tons and tons!"

I put my arm around her and took her duffle bag in my other hand. She picked up the flowers from her desk and smelled them.

"How did you know I liked lilies?"

"I didn't. Just got lucky, I guess. It seems like that's happening a lot right now, and I like it."

"Blessed," she corrected me.

"Yes, blessed is right," I agreed.

"Can you take a picture of us?" I asked the security guard as we passed through the lobby.

"Sure, my man. You two look like a million bucks!" As he tilted his head to one side, he asked, "You two going to get married?"

"Working on it, my man!" I replied cheerfully.

Jenise laughed, "Hey now."

CHAD'S REFLECTIONS

I had been admiring Jenise, getting to know her by witnessing her at the JH Ranch, writing her letters for several months, seeing her in person with her family and my family, calling on the phone, and speaking very intentionally for hours about make-or-break matters. Now, almost ten months into my interest in her, I finally was at a place where I could express myself romantically in a very direct way.

And I was so excited that this time had finally come. Up until this time, I never had the freedom to express myself intentionally in a romantic way. It was game time!

Every story is different. I encourage you to take the time to get to know someone before you pour on the romance in abundance. Many relationships start with sparks and romance and don't build roots, don't tackle hard subjects, and don't get real about important things.

Romance is right in the correct place, but beware of building a foundation on romantic feelings and actions. Love is really getting to know someone deeply. Romance is icing on the cake; and don't get me wrong—I love icing!

Life is full of responsibility and duty—work, projects, deadlines, events, and must-dos; romance is the joy that fills those spaces between and makes sunshine brighter and skies bluer.

In thinking about relationships at a young age, I realized that relationships are not efficient. They require time that isn't focused on production, growth, or income. Love requires an investment in the things that life holds most valuable, such as time, energy, creativity, relationship, and money.

CHAPTER 24
THE PRINCESS AND HER SHOE SALESMAN

"Miss Johnston, your carriage awaits," I said when I opened the door to our rental car. After giving her a quick peck on the cheek, I gently shut the door, walked around to the trunk, and fished out her new pumps. Then, I knocked quietly.

Surprised, she opened the door. "Yes?"

"I've been informed that the princess has no glass slippers to wear to the ball this evening," I said in my best sophisticated English Duke voice. "Is this true?" I said with a smirk and a raised eyebrow. I knelt at the side of the car, careful not to mess up my tux, and asked her to present her feet to me.

She laughed gaily, asking again, "What on earth are you doing, Chad?" I gently removed her right black pump. "Good thing I didn't wear hose with holes in the toes," she exclaimed with a smile.

"Good thing, indeed," I agreed, still carrying on with my sophisticated impersonation. "Good thing, indeed, for holey hose and holey shoes would be quite an unsuitable combo." I held up one of her shoes, revealing the free passing of air from the inside to the outside.

She gasped, "How did you know that? You little turkey! Put that shoe back on!" She didn't seem embarrassed at all, just surprised I possibly could know. I reached behind me and placed the shoebox down on the parking lot asphalt in front of me. Taking off the lid, I pulled out a brand new, shiny black leather pump. Jenise gasped again. "Where did you get those? What size are they?" Meanwhile, I slipped it on her foot. It fit like a glove. "How did you know?" she said in breathless awe.

"I pay attention," I said, grinning, "to everything about you." I looked up. She was crying. "Oh, I'm so sorry," I blurted out. "Please forgive me. What did I do?"

She was wiping her eyes with her hand. "Forgive you? Why, for messing up my makeup?" She laughed softly. "You're too sweet to me, Chad. Seriously, you've got to stop. That is so kind of you. I still don't know how you knew. You even got the right size. You are so sweet!" While she was regaining her composure, I slipped the other old shoe off and fitted the second new pump.

As I was putting the old shoes into the empty box, a woman with greying hair walked briskly by in a dark business skirt and a white blouse, wearing high heels herself. Looking our way, she gave pause seeing me on one knee, in a tuxedo, but looking like a shoe salesman at Neiman Marcus. I smiled at her. "Ma'am, do you see any shoes you like? I'll be right with you." All three of us laughed hysterically.

"I won't even ask," replied the woman as she continued her quick pace, laughing to herself.

"Let's get out of here before she calls security," I said as we both laughed again.

Pulling into the valet lane at Aria, Jenise commented, "Wow, this looks fancy . . . I mean, expensive."

"It's free for you—and a good investment for me," I noted, then laughed.

Her look said it all. The door opened, and the valet I had met earlier greeted me. "Why, good evening, Mr. Johnson.

So glad to have you join us. Good evening, Miss Johnston," he said, looking over at Jenise.

The look on Jenise's face was priceless. She didn't say a thing except, "Good evening," while eyeing me out of the corner of her eye.

The valet opened her door, and we made our way into the reception area. Miss Anderson and Mr. Foster smiled and greeted us as we approached the dark mahogany receptionist pedestal. "Good evening, Mr. Johnson." He turned to Jenise. "You must be Miss Johnston. So glad to have you with us this evening. Please, right this way. Your table is ready."

Jenise held my hand and whispered in my ear as we proceeded down the dimly lit hallway toward our specially reserved table, "What's going on? They all act like they know us. What are you up to? You turkey!" She squeezed my hand and pulled down on it for emphasis.

As we came to our table, Miss Anderson stepped aside, making a sweeping gesture with her arm, "Please." Our booth, positioned twelve inches higher than any other table in the room, commanded a view of the entire restaurant, including the outdoor gardens lit with white, twinkling lights. A single candle burned brightly, and next to it sat a beautiful perfectly arranged table bouquet that matched the one I gave Jenise earlier. On the other side of the candle sat a framed picture of Jenise and me from our ice dancing adventure in Gatlinburg.

Looking around, Jenise covered her mouth in shock and whispered, "How?" She turned to me and asked, "Chadwick Buford, what on earth are you doing?"

She needed no reply. I said nothing and watched as she soaked it all in.

"This is so sweet," she said as she scooted into the booth. She pulled the picture close to examine it better and said, "You're so stinkin' handsome."

I leaned in close to inspect the photo. "I see what you're saying." She elbowed me.

"These flowers—they're amazing! They go with the other ones. How beautiful! When did you have time to do all this?" she asked.

"While you were working for a living today. I had all sorts of time."

Our attentive wait staff came to the table and again addressed us as Mr. Johnson and Miss Johnston. "Are you ready to order?" I asked for a couple more minutes as Jenise's eyes poured over the menu. She wasn't looking at the entrées. Instead, her eyes went straight to the à la carte (sides) section.

"Do you know what you want?" I asked.

"Yes, I think so," she replied. "I'd like a baked potato and a cup of soup."

I looked at her in surprise. "Jenise, this is a steak and seafood restaurant. You can have anything you want. Don't you want a filet? Salmon? Lobster?" I asked, using my eyes to convince her.

She pointed to the respective prices to what I'd suggested, $42, $38, and $57. "These mean dollars, right? This is outrageous!" she whispered under her breath.

"That is why you want a baked potato and a cup of soup?"

She nodded. "That's what I usually get. I love baked potatoes and soup!"

"Jenise, it's your birthday, and I want to spoil you rotten. Please order something fun, something fine that's a splurge for you. It'll thrill me if you do this."

"But it's so expensive—"

I interrupted. "Not for you. It's free. A gift, from someone who's very excited about doing this for you."

"Okay," she replied. "Thank you."

She gazed deeply into my eyes. I could sense her vast and sincere gratitude in hers. This was a big deal for her. She didn't take this for granted. She was so humble and unassuming. No pretense. No entitlement. Frugal, humble, and grateful. *Wow! Is she real? God, you really made a woman like this?*

The meal arrived in perfect order: appetizers, first-course salads, entrées prepared to perfection, and stately desserts. The food, the lighting, the music, the service, and the company was exquisite!

I was still so full of questions and wanted to know everything there was to know about Jenise. She was surprised I had so many questions left after our conversations during our travels. Each answer delighted me and affirmed her character, revealing the richness and depth of her soul even more. She was clear, direct, strong, capable, confident, content, grateful, and positive. *Seriously, is she real?* I was falling head over heels for this woman. Nope. Rephrase. I was a goner before the evening started. Each moment in her presence drew me in deeper and far beyond the point of no return.

As she finished her roasted chicken—I found out later she chose the cheapest entrée on the menu—the waiter walked casually by to fill our water and suggested that Jenise check the bottom of her plate. Caught off guard, she cautiously lifted the edge of her plate.

As she did, I leaned in and said, "Boo!" She jumped back, dropping the plate with a clatter on the table.

The waiter laughed, and Jenise playfully slapped my arm. "You!" This time, she picked it up quickly and turned it over, revealing an envelope taped to the bottom of the dish. It had a hand-drawn picture of a tulip laying on its side. She carefully released the card from the bottom of the plate and opened it. I loved watching her face as she read it. She looked as if she'd cry. Her eyes moistened, and she dabbed at them with her napkin.

Turning to me, she whispered so softly I could barely hear, "You. What are you doing to me?"

"Just letting you know that I like you . . . quite a bit," I whispered back.

Splitting dessert is so romantic, and indeed we did. I knew she'd order the chocolate brownie with vanilla ice cream and chocolate shavings sprinkled on top. Sure enough, that's what she chose. Our spoons clinked together, our eyes locked, our lips touched, our lives met, and our entire world intertwined for just a moment—a moment I wanted to last forever. Was this what love felt like? Oh, how I wanted more of this precious creature!

"Let's go!" I said.

"Where?"

"Wherever we want!" I said cheerfully. "Actually, I have a plan."

"Of course, you do. All right, let's go!"

The hospitable staff gave us a remarkably warm farewell, and the valet did what valets do in grand style. The tip mirrored the outstanding service and received a raised eyebrow from Jenise. Then, we were off to downtown Atlanta.

The Sun Dial restaurant in Atlanta has a top-floor revolving restaurant. After a brief walk past a lot of luxury automobiles parked outside, we made our way through the nicely appointed Westin Peachtree lobby. We waited with a small group outside of the elevator for the doors to open, then began our ascent to the seventy-second and top floor, which was 723 feet above the city.

Jenise and I must have been beaming because a middle-aged woman next to us in the elevator asked, "Are you two newlyweds?"

The couple standing right next to her looked up and laughed, "We were just saying the same thing!"

"Yes, how did you know?" I said in mock surprise.

"Chad Johnson!" Jenise gave me an elbow to the ribs. "Very funny," she quipped as she turned to the small audience now laughing along. "More like our first date," she added, feeling obligated to clarify while joining in on the laughter.

I added, "She's right. The first date of 10,000 more to come." They all laughed, and I kept on. "You think I'm joking."

We all laughed, but I sure did like the feeling of others seeing that we went together as newlyweds.

What a compliment! I envisioned always having a love that others recognize as new, sweet, fresh, adoring, and romantic like a newlywed couple—never stale, tired, boring, old, lethargic, or dying. So many couples stop holding hands, stop playing together, stop making their relationship fun and exciting. Yes, there was so much to learn from newlyweds. I determined early in life and confirmed again, right then, that once married I wanted to be newlyweds for life.

Married! A simple word with such profound meaning and importance. Yes, I really wanted to be married—not to just anyone but to Jenise Cheri Johnston, the girl on my arm, the woman by my side. The elevator doors opened, carrying me back into reality and us into a most breathtaking view. "Wowzah!" I exclaimed under my breath. "What a view!" Jenise turned to look at me, and I quickly added, "And the skyline outside isn't bad either."

"Very funny boy," she responded. "Aren't you a smooth one?"

"Not joking," I replied. "I'm living in an ever-present place of beauty."

A young hostess interrupted our playful bantering and asked, "Can I get you a table?"

"Oh, no—" Jenise began to say.

I interrupted her. "Oh, yes! Thank you."

"Right this way," she turned, grabbing two menus as she walked past the host station.

Jenise looked up at me, bewildered. "What are you doing?"

"Enjoying the view," I quipped.

She pushed my arm. "Very funny! We've already eaten," she said seriously.

"I know, but go with me on this," I countered.

Our hostess led us to a table next to the window with a stunning view of city lights all aglow. A sea of towering buildings with a multitude of shining, twinkling colors called out their nightly song. The city traffic buzzed far from our ears as the live music played from the simple guitar and solitary voice singing of love, warmth, and happy times. *What a moment.* A life well-lived is but simple moments savored in a carefree, timeless way. We shared a piña colada with one straw, holding hands, voices low, and our hearts and minds opened to each other in even deeper conversation.

The clock struck midnight, and my princess was getting sleepy. Though she had no glass slipper to lose, her prince knew it was time to be getting her home. Thirty minutes later, our rental car pulled up in front of her apartment. I ran around and opened her door, and hand in hand, I escorted her to the door, carrying her flowers, picture, and card from the restaurant.

"Goodnight, my love," I whispered, holding her head close to mine. The sweet scent of her hair brought a gentle swell of longing. To be a man, holding a woman is a powerful thing. A beautiful thing. A dangerous thing.

"Good night," she answered back. Our lips met, both hungry for more. She pushed me slowly away. "You better go," she said softly.

"Yes, I'd better go," I agreed, pressing in for one more kiss.

"Oh, no, you don't," she exclaimed playfully and turned away. "Off you go."

"You make me crazy, Jenise." I cried.

"Good! Go home crazy," she laughed.

"Happy Birthday, beautiful woman," I said as I turned toward the car.

"Thank you, Chad. It was by far my favorite. Ever," I heard her say.

* * *

CHAD'S REFLECTIONS

Having chemistry is important. People in love should really desire each other. Romance is awesome and such a sparkling, fun, playful, and important part of relationships!

Romance is often the first thing to show up in a new relationship—dressing up, flowers, dinners, love letters, creative actions, and investments that have no expected return.

I believe it is the awareness that someone has been thinking of you, planning in advance, creatively investing their time, energy, and sometimes money into making you feel special that makes romance so powerful.

Romance is often the first thing to go in many marriages. How sad is that? Why is that so?

I wanted so much to set an expectation early on that I would be romancing Jenise from day one until the day we died. Romance would be a part of our dating life now, for sure, but I wanted it to be even more so a part of our married relationship, forever.

CHAPTER 25
TERRIBLE!

The next morning, I delightfully shared the entire story with my hosts, the Gables. Steve and Kim were so fun to share with, interested in every detail, and excited about the whole love story.

Feeling so alive, I went for a long run after breakfast. Love has a way of making the simple profound and the grey colorful. Living things seem so much more alive, and the skies are even bluer. I praised the Lord with my voice, speaking out loud my gratitude for His many blessings, for His favor in my life, and for His working out the details of this crazy adventure in such a powerful and positive way. I love giving thanks and going through people who have blessed me so much, one by one, name by name. Running is the perfect time to give thanks, and on this day, it was oh so easy.

So many times, when things aren't going well, when I'm in despair, frustration, doubt, or overwhelm, the power of thanksgiving is even more important but so much more difficult to come by. Cultivating the ability to think thoughts of praise continually is one of the chief instructions of Scripture.

1 Thessalonians 5:18 says, "In everything give thanks."

In everything? How is that possible? My mother once pointed out that it doesn't say, "For everything give thanks," just, "in everything." It's a big difference. I'm not saying I need to be grateful I missed the mark on something. In failure, I need to say, "I'm thankful that . . ." and fill in the blank with what I'm thankful for in that situation. I can be thankful I'm still alive, able to grow, the situation isn't worse, and that God's grace is sufficient for me even in my weakness. There is always, always, always something to be thankful for.

Back at the Gables' house, I packed my bags and took some time to journal, enjoying the downtime. My life was so fast-paced. Having a few hours of rest, reading, and recording the weekend's experiences settled my soul. After I said my farewells to my gracious host family, I drove to the airport, returned the car, and took a shuttle back to the terminal. My eyes combed every inch of the massive space—searching, searching, searching—and there she was!

That blonde-haired, bright smiling Jenise Cheri was walking—no, running—toward me! I dropped my bags and ran toward her. She jumped into my wide-open arms, and I swept her up, spinning one full circle before gracefully placing her on her feet once more. Our lips met, and with our full embrace, the world disappeared. Breathless, we pulled apart.

"Well, good to see you too!" Jenise exclaimed with her smile shining bright.

"Oh, how I missed you, girl," I admitted. "Missed you badly. How am I supposed to go away and leave you here all alone?"

"I don't know about all that, but I do know that if you don't get to the gate, they'll leave without you, and you won't have to worry about that," she said, laughing. We held hands as we ran down a long corridor, and, as we rounded the corner, we found ourselves in a crowd of people waiting for the direct flight from Atlanta to LAX. We made our way to the far side of the crowd to an area separated with a glass display case. I set my bags down and took both of her hands in mine.

"Jenise Cheri, I got you a little gift for your birthday but forgot to give it to you." I lifted the brown paper sack that held the finely gift-wrapped music box out of my bag.

"Chad, you need to stop! You already gave me so many birthday gifts. Look at these! My new shoes." She looked down and pointed at her foot that she'd lifted. "You cleaned my car and changed the oil." She started to tear up. I didn't know it yet, but acts of service is her number one love language from the book *The Five Love Languages* by Gary Smalley. "The fancy dinner, flowers, pictures of our weekend, dessert at the top of the world, hugs and kisses, kind words. It's all too much, Chad. What are you trying to do to me? Spoil me rotten?"

"Yes, that's what I'd love to do!" Feeling bold, I added, "For the rest of your life."

"Stop that!" she countered quickly but with a smile that told me what I suggested wasn't unpleasant to her.

The loudspeaker interrupted us, "Now boarding for flight 2549 to Los Angeles . . . Gold Elite, Super Mega Flyers, Champions of Flight, First Class, and all other people who fly way too much may now board at their convenience." The young man making the announcement seemed proud of his sense of humor.

"They're calling me, Jenise," I joked. "Okay, in all seriousness. Here's the gift I got for you," I said, handing her the small gift-wrapped package. She opened it quickly and smiled with delight as the paper came free, revealing the superbly crafted wood inlaid music box.

"How beautiful," she whispered.

"It reminded me of you," I whispered back.

She opened it, and the simple melody of "Edelweiss" began playing so tenderly, plunking out its well-known tune.

"It's perfect," she whispered again.

"Like you," I whispered back.

She turned her eyes away from the music box to meet mine. Tears glistened in her eyes. "Thank you, Chad Johnson. Thank you, thank you, thank you." I held her close. The music box serenaded us, two young lovers lost in the moment's melody.

She looked up once more. "I have something for you too!" Reaching down, she picked up an eighteen-by-twenty-four-inch cardboard card that I could see she made herself. "This is my thank you card to you. These words and pictures remind me of you." She began to read them off, one by one. "Handsome, strong, faithful, visionary, smart, sharp, fun, witty, humorous, loving, kind, athletic." The words and pictures went on. Three full pages. Pictures of snow skiers, lovers, a heart, dancing, a Bible, ice skaters . . . there were so many pictures and words that generously laid out the parts of me she knew so far and all we experienced together that magical weekend.

"This is amazing! When did you have the time to put this together?" I asked incredulously.

"Today at work. I told you I'm only supposed to answer phones, do filing, and greet guests. Today was slow, so I was able to fit it in here and there."

"You're unbelievable! You have no idea how much this means to me. I will treasure this forever."

It was my turn. My eyes welled with moisture. My heart full, I took Jenise again in my arms, holding the card behind her back as I held her close.

The speaker barked once again, announcing the final call for Flight #2549 to LAX.

"You've really got to go," she said.

Not wanting to let her go, I looked down into her beautiful green eyes and gave her one last kiss.

"Goodbye, Jenise Cheri."

"Goodbye, Chad Johnson."

Both of us sounded like two lovesick birds.

I let her go, picked up my bags, and ran the short distance to the gate. The heavyset black woman behind the counter said as I approached, "Thought I was going to have to come over there with a pry bar to get you two apart and put you on this plane myself!" With a bossy smirk, she added, "Better run along, young man, before they fly off without you."

I turned just before the door leading into the jetway and looked back over my shoulder. There she was, Jenise, the woman of my dreams, the one who surpassed all the criteria I could ever dream up, the woman of whom there was no equal, none even close.

"Go on, git!" the woman behind the counter barked at me, no longer smiling.

I grinned when my eyes met Jenise's. She waved and nodded. Then I ran down the long, empty jetway—my heart soaring, my feet barely touching the ground.

I recounted the whole weekend in my head the second I hit the seat. Wow! So much had transpired. It went so much better than I could've ever asked for. Jenise was my girl. No doubt about it. No, we hadn't discussed it or had the DTR talk, but I just knew. Surely, she knew too. I guess I should've communicated more clearly about that, but it seemed unnecessary. I knew I shouldn't assume things. Well, guess I'd have to call her to make sure. We must be on the same page.

I opened my journal to where I compared flying to Atlanta and surprising Jenise to flying off a massive ski jump I'd never attempted before. The speed, the thrill of take-off, the airtime, the adrenaline rush, and then, the ever-most-critical part, the landing. It's upon landing that everything becomes obvious. Was it a good jump? If you overshot the landing and hit hard in the flats, your knees hit you in the face, giving you two black eyes and jarring every bone in your body to the core. Then, no, it wasn't a great jump. Or, if you come up short, it'll be the same outcome.

I'll never forget the day I missed a landing. My job was to flag the largest jump I'd ever seen at Snow Summit Ski Resort. It had an exceptionally steep take-off, a twenty-five to thirty-foot gap where the snow was at a normal run level, and an extremely steep landing. The following day, Suzuki Samurai was sponsoring a big air contest. Professional snowboarders would be busting off this jump in full view of the base lodge.

David and some of our buddies—Roger Williams and Jeremy Wright (some of the young patrolmen who had been dubbed The Young Guns)—were also working that day. They placed bamboo poles and red banner tape to keep skiing guests from accidentally launching off to their near-certain injury or possible death. Upon seeing a perfect take-off, I told The Young Guns, "This is the perfect double backflip jump." I'd become very comfortable pulling off single backflips from the halfpipe or other well-built jumps. It'd been in my mind for quite some time to try a double, and this looked like my moment.

I had them stand to the side as I dropped into a tuck from the top of Miracle Mile. The closer I got to the jump, the more I questioned my speed. Too much? Not enough? Neither option was good. One thing that's been true about me for as long as I can remember is once I commit, I commit. And for better or worse, I followed through.

As I flew off that jump, I arched my back and went into a full, laid-out backflip, what a rush! One rotation, amazing! Second rotation, and—oh no! I saw the steep landing ramp go by underneath me, my body spinning too fast and going too far. The drop from so high to the very flat landing was terrible! I had over-rotated and landed nearly flat on my back, knocking myself unconscious. According to David and Roger, I had just rag-dolled until coming to a complete stop some distance beyond. I didn't move. Long story short, I dislocated my shoulder and wound up with a serious concussion.

Though I didn't complete the routine successfully, I went for it; I jumped. I completed the two-plus rotations. And I lived. For that, I was grateful. I never wanted to be the guy going through life watching jumps from the lodge, never taking risks, never shying from success because of the potential for pain. I valued the willingness to risk, to dare, to try. I knew

I'd most likely get hurt, lose, fail, or even look bad. But in doing so, I'd fully live.

Now, when I compare this jump to my trip to Atlanta, I had a rough take-off, but the path smoothed out once in the air, and the landing was definitely a ten! That's the goal—all the elements coming together and executing correct speed, a balanced take-off, sweet moves in the air, and pegging the landing. Yes! That's a sweet jump!

The journal slipped from my fingers and fell unnoticed to the floor as I slipped into a dreamy rest. Jenise. Jenise and I skiing. Going off jumps. Living life as a grand adventure.

The loudspeaker disturbed me from my sleep. "Please put your seat belts on, tray tables up, and seats in their upright position. We're preparing for landing."

Getting off the plane, I resolved to appear as dejected and depressed as possible. I'd spoken to my parents early on when things weren't going well. I thought it'd be funny to act as though the whole trip was a failure. Walking through the door of the terminal, I spotted my parents standing off to the side with several of my younger siblings. I held my head low, not meeting their eyes and shuffled at a slower pace, trying my best to look despondent. It worked initially, as my parents approached with concern written all over them.

"How did it go?" my father asked.

But when I looked up, I couldn't even pretend. The sparkle in my eye could've caught them on fire.

"Terrible!" I blurted out, smiling so big my face hurt. "Just terrible! I'm lovesick!"

Seeing the joy on their faces was a delight to me. Both my mother and my father knew me so well and had known almost every detail along the way, so this victory was a shared one. It was a fresh and real story filled with low points that made the highlights that much sweeter, and it tumbled out fast and free as we made our way to baggage claim.

* * *

CHAD'S REFLECTIONS

When we said our goodbyes, Jenise and I exchanged gifts. I gave her the music box, and she gave me a hand-crafted, heartfelt care she created specifically for the moment. In his book *The 5 Love Languages*, Gary Chapman lays out the five major ways we can show affection to one another. It is so interesting how we attract and are attracted to people who have different love languages. According to Chapman, everyone has a primary love language that is the number one way that person feels loved. We can all appreciate all five love languages, but there is usually a descending order of importance for each individual. The five love languages he identifies in his book are:

Acts of service, gifts, words of affirmation, physical touch, and quality time.

Which one is your primary love language? If you are dating or married, what is your beloved's primary love language?

Jenise's primary love language is acts of service, and mine is words of affirmation.

Finding out the love language of the one you love is a great aid in being able to meet their needs and fill their "love tank." If we want to be relationship rich, we must always be investing. Knowing what makes the greatest deposits is a great advantage.

CHAPTER 26
AN UNRETURNED HUG

I rode up the chairlift. The morning air found any exposed
skin begging for cover and cut through me like a blade.
The snowmakers made the most of the low temperatures.
They never missed a chance to add to the snow base on the
mountain. With so much sunshine in Southern California,
man-made snow was a persistent need.

Making up for minimal snowfall that year, every snow gun
on the mountain blasted its frozen fury into the air. The roar
was deafening. Somehow, every gun aimed directly at the chair
I was sitting on, which was moving altogether too slowly for
words. I loved it! My love for snow, mountains, skiing, and
for all of God's creation has been a part of my life since I was
a child. Whenever possible, I went outdoors and searched for
some activity or adventure.

Conversation with David and Jeff Shelton was impossible
with the way we were all bundled up. All three of us hunkered
down and waited to unload. Finally, inside Bump at the top
of chair two, we soaked up the heat as the smell of wet clothes
and coffee washed over us.

"How's lover boy?" Tony Huefner chimed in. I ignored
him, pretending not to hear, and walked over to the window
and a high counter where we kept our hill check paperwork.
"Hey, Dude! Talk to me," he chortled.

It didn't take long for others to join the chorus, initiating the typical good old boy razzing. "Tell us how it went," another one urged.

"Come on, we're family," Jeff urged, laughing. And in a real sense, we were. We'd spent so much time working, playing, skiing, hanging around at Bump, riding chair lifts, changing into uniforms and gear in the locker room, and eating meals together. After four seasons, we knew each other's quirks, strengths, and weaknesses, of which there were plenty.

"We better do our hill checks," I answered with a smirk.

Scott Hoffman, our skip patrol supervisor, cut me off with a grin, "I'll take care of that, Johnson. You can sit right down and tell us your love story." And turning to several other patrollers, he said, "Hey, rookies, suit up. Mike, you take Miracle Mile. Josh, you've got Summit Run. Chris, shut down Westridge from the top here, and then close off the road to six, seven, and nine." He turned back to me and smiled. His teeth showed through his big bushy red beard, and his eyes sparkling through his glasses. "All right, Johnson. We don't have all day."

I was eager to recap the events of last weekend *again*. The record kept playing over and over, so I might as well share it with someone. They each would interrupt at critical points. Knowing my faith and standards about sex before marriage, several made inappropriate remarks in foolish jesting. I kept talking, ignoring each of their trite remarks and answering only genuine, sincere questions.

I loved sharing all the details with them, and I could see many of them reflecting as I did. This wasn't the usual young-man-gets-some-time-with-the-girl-he-loves story, and story, and the way it played out was far different from what it would've been if any of them were the pursuer. I knew this, and they knew me. Respectfully, several expressed awe that it was even possible to find such a girl.

That evening, I called Jenise and summarized the events of the day. Her voice made me weak in the knees. Then, she shared her day. Our hearts were one. Three thousand miles changed nothing. My brief flash of concern before calling was for naught. This was for real. Speaking before we signed off for bed became our nightly routine. We talked about what we learned, did, and thought, along with our dreams, plans, ideas, and spiritual insights—we talked about everything!

At the end of that first week back, I found myself driving down the mountain to Fullerton on Saturday. *Knock, knock.* I waited. Were they home? How would they react to my being there? What was I going to tell them? Joy Johnson, Jenise's mother, opened the door, interrupting my thoughts.

"Hello, Mrs. Johnston!"

"Oh my!" she exclaimed, surprised. "Call me Joy," she instructed. She was as direct as Jenise.

"Well, come right in." She turned and called loudly to the back of the house, "Gene!" She wiped her hands on a small apron. "Come on in," she said briskly, her waving her hand at me. I almost felt like a little boy being reprimanded. She took a few steps back and waved me toward the front room. "I'll get Gene." She briskly walked through the dining room and down the hall calling his name, "Gene!"

"Yes, Joy," I heard him say quietly.

"Chad's here," she said crisply.

I heard Gene's inquiry, though muffled. "Chad who?" *Guess I didn't make much of an impression on him*, I thought to myself.

"Oh, come here, Gene," Joy said.

I heard them both coming back down the hall toward me. I remained standing and took a step forward when they entered. Gene Johnston looked like what he was—a very successful businessman and investor. He was wearing khaki pants and a white dress shirt. He had a full head of grey hair, a handsome square jaw, and grey-blue eyes set the right distance apart, which looked at me now with a calm, assured, but inquisitive manner.

"Hello, Mr. Johnston," I said, extending my hand.

"Gene," Joy corrected me again.

Gene said nothing but nodded as we shook hands before motioning to the chair behind me. Upon sitting, I turned to face Gene and saw both Gene and Joy sitting on the sofa across from me. I didn't wait but spoke right out. "I'm sorry to drop in on you. I tried to call, but nobody answered." They both said nothing but nodded, and I continued, "I was in Atlanta this weekend."

"We know," Joy interjected with a cheeky smirk. I was grateful Jenise had already informed them. I continued, "My whole point in going was to get to know your daughter better. When I called you back in August, Gene, you mentioned I could ask her out but that she lived in Atlanta."

Gene had virtually no expression on his face, at least none that I could read, but he nodded. Joy leaned forward from the couch seat-back and seemed to be immensely eager to have me continue.

"I flew to Atlanta a week ago, Thursday, and spent time with her Friday through Monday at various times. We went up to Gatlinburg for a big singles' retreat. She sang for the whole event. It was so much fun. I was also able to be there for her birthday on Monday."

Joy registered her surprise by raising her eyebrows and letting out a little gasp. "That's right! Her birthday was Monday. Oh, my," she said softly, while looking at Gene.

Gene didn't seem to notice and looked at me as if waiting for me to continue.

I went on. "You've raised an amazing daughter. I know you know that, but I wanted to let you know how grateful I am for what you've done. She's truly unlike any other young lady I've ever met. I'm very serious about getting to know her much better. I brought you a couple of pictures from our weekend. Would you like to see them?"

Before I'd finished asking, I could see Joy's smile brightening, eyebrows raising, and head nodding while she scooted forward on the couch. I got up and walked around the glass coffee table between us and sat down by Gene. "Here is when we were ice skating and one of her singing at a concert with Wayne Watson."

"Can you believe it, Gene? Wayne Watson!" Joy was clearly pleased as punch about it. Gene nodded, saying nothing.

"Here she is, the two of us, at her birthday dinner." I had made copies of the pictures, so I left them there on the coffee table and walked back to my chair.

"I know you're busy, Gene and Joy, so I don't want to take much of your time. My whole purpose in coming here is to let you know that I'm very interested in your daughter. I respect her so much. I respect both of you, the roles you've played in raising her, and the roles you continue to play now as her parents. It was important that you hear it from me—that I'd like to continue to get to know her. I want to honor her and both of you in everything I do." I stopped.

Every word of that was straight from my heart. I firmly believe you don't marry a woman—you marry a family. I'd never been more intentional about pursuing someone. Everything would be clear, honorable, and trust-building in the very best and purest sense. I had a particularly clear vision of marriage. My whole intention was not only to date but also to see where it went and to pursue Jenise with the explicit purpose of marrying her and building a wonderful life together. This life would, God willing, be filled with a multitude of precious little blessings.

Everything mattered—it would lay a foundation of respect, trust, and honor, or it would undermine the very future I aspired to create. I'd never had a conversation that was even close to this before, and if I had my way going forward, I never intended to have another one like it. I think my directness took them a bit off guard. After all, I'd barely spent any time with Jenise, and here I was in their living room, telling them my heart's desire and in a stunningly clear way, asking for their blessing to move forward.

Gene said a few words about how "fine a young lady" Jenise was, and that he appreciated me coming by. He didn't specifically say, "Sure, Chad, go ahead and pursue my daughter," but he also didn't say no. The implication was that he and Joy weren't opposed to me getting to know Jenise better. He stood up, and I followed him to the door. Joy, beaming, thanked me for the pictures. It seemed as if she were very approving of the whole thing.

As they walked me to the door and stopped, I turned and gave Gene a big hug. He stood still and seemed shocked by my embrace. It was like hugging a telephone pole. His arms stayed right by his side and didn't seem to even hint at returning the gesture. His response, or lack thereof, also jarred me a bit. I've always been a hugger. It's what I do. I hug—not in a weird way—but when I like people, I hug them. I'm used to them embracing me back, at least a little.

Thinking Joy would be much warmer, I turned and gave her a big hug too. Wrong! If Gene was uncomfortable and stiff, Joy was uncomfortable, stiff, and like a block of ice. Oh, my, I thought to myself. Hugging is not a very popular sport around here. That's going to need to change. Then, I said a final thank you and jogged down the concrete stairs to my waiting 4Runner.

It felt right that I'd visited them. I really did see Gene and Joy as my future father- and mother-in-law. I had no idea what they thought of me, but I guessed time would tell. Later that evening, I rehashed the whole scenario to Jenise. "That's so much like my mother," she said. "I can just see her." Jenise got the biggest kick when I told her I hugged both of them, and I was going to have to work on them so they could learn how to give and receive hugs.

"I believe in miracles, Chad, but I'd have to see that to believe it. If you ever get my mother to like giving and receiving hugs, you'll be a miracle worker, indeed." She giggled. It was easy to sense the love and respect she had for both of her parents, and I could tell it meant a lot that I visited them. "That's so sweet, Chad. Nobody has ever done anything like that. Why did you do it?" she asked.

"Dating is a huge deal to me, Jenise. I've never done any of the things I'm doing right now. But I want to honor and respect you and your parents so much in all of this. Who knows, they could be my father- and mother-in-law someday." I finished.

"Chad!" she exclaimed, laughing.

"You know I'm serious, Jenise," I said.

"I think I better change the subject," she replied. "Are you going to church with your parents tomorrow?"

"Yes," I responded. "Guess I better hit the sack. Goodnight, Jenise Cheri."

About a week later, during a nightly touch base, Jenise seemed a little quieter than usual. At one point, she paused, saying nothing.

"Are you okay?" I asked.

She was slow to reply. "Yes, but—"

"Jenise," I interrupted her. "What is going on?" I asked, with a bit of fear creeping into my voice.

"Well, I guess I need to see you, to be with you. This whole thing happened pretty fast, and I want to know it's real."

"Oh, believe me, it's real, Jenise. I've never known anything so real. But I'm all for getting us together. When can I fly you out?" And two weeks later, she ran down the hall at LAX and into my arms. "Is this real, sweet girl?" I asked her, holding her close.

"I know it seems silly," she responded. "But you really did come into town and sweep me off my feet. It all seemed like a dream. It was so fast! Doubts kept rising in my mind as if it were too good to be true."

"Fast for you, Jenise, but I've been thinking about you, trying to figure out how to make this happen from the first moment I met you. For me, this seems like it's taken a very long time! In only one month, we're coming right up on a year since we met! Crazy, huh?"

"I'm glad to be here," she said, snuggling into me and looking up with soft, warm eyes.

"Me too! Me too," I agreed, holding her firm.

The weekend flew by too fast—time with her at her home, time with several members of her family, time with my family at my parents' home, and way too soon, we were saying farewells through tears, not wanting to let go, and waving goodbye once more.

By then, we'd determined that we would go to the JH Ranch for the summer. We thought living closer to each other and working and serving together for the summer would be a good thing. Jenise's older brother Bruce was like a second father to her. I could tell he wanted me at the ranch, probably as a vetting process.

I also had quickly picked up that Bruce didn't like the thought of a JH Ranch summer without Jenise on his team. She was an MVP and had been a key part of making the whole thing work for quite some time. The thought of being in that environment with Jenise sounded like a complete and total blast! My ski season would wrap up on April 15, which would give me plenty of time to get ready for the camping season to start at JH in June.

* * *

CHAD'S REFLECTIONS

Going to see her parents was very important for me. I wanted to honor them so much! The Bible in Exodus 20:12 highlights the importance of honoring your father and mother, even naming it among the ten commandments, and it is reiterated throughout Scripture. There is a blessing of long life that goes with it.

Well, I figured if Jenise and I were to end up married someday—as I so strongly hoped and expected we would— then Gene and Joy were going to be my parents.

Earlier, I mentioned that you don't just marry an individual, you marry a family, a history, a legacy, a family tree. To me, the more support a relationship or marriage has, the better. My vision had always included close, loving relationships with parents-in-law and receiving their blessing (although I really messed this up later in the story).

In a way, my framework of dating included winning not only the heart of a woman but also the heart of her family. From her parents, siblings, and friends—if someone was important to her, they were important to me.

I think this is an integral mindset for young people to develop and one that has lost much ground in our current dating culture. The idea that you can show up and take the girl or guy and leave the rest of the family is just misguided. I know that, in a real sense, every family is dysfunctional, and parents of all stripes have their issues. It can become very easy to dismiss the need to win their hearts, to honor them, and to bless them with your love as a suitor of their child. My encouragement is that you give yourself the goal of winning not only the girl or the guy, but the parents, siblings, and friends of the one you love. It is a loving thing to do, and there is a huge blessing that goes with it.

A quick note on hugging. My goal of turning Joy into a hugger was for real. I think hugging is good for people. Some people don't grow up hugging, and it makes them feel uncomfortable, but I have found over and over again if I am patient, sensitive, and sincere, before very long, even non-huggers can become proficient and enthusiastic huggers. Joy did! Today, I get a warm hug from Mama Joy whenever I see her.

CHAPTER 27
THE RIDE OF A LIFETIME

On my list of "100 things to be, do, and have," was riding my bike across the USA. David and I discussed this during our night shifts on ski patrol. Oh, man, the challenge and thrill of accomplishing such a feat—what a rush. After sending Jenise off at LAX, I gave David a call.

"David, if we'll ever do this whole biking across the USA trip, we better go now. I'm madly in love with a beautiful blonde woman that you mistakenly counseled me to get over. I'm convinced now more than ever—she's the one and only woman for me. We said if we're going to do this, it must be before we get married, and marriage is big on my mind, brother. So what do you say?"

He was in! I think it had everything to do with the fact that he negotiated our route to include a stop in Boulder, Colorado, where Jodi Thompson, his girlfriend, attended the University of Colorado in exchange for swinging far south through Atlanta, Georgia, on our way to Savannah and the Atlantic Ocean. We set our epic adventure departure date for April 17, two days after Snow Summit's seasonal close. Between ski patrolling and daily conversation and letter writing with Jenise (and the thought of being with her for the entire summer), my days flew by in anticipation of our upcoming ride. Before I knew it, our journey was upon us.

Our youngest brother, Dwight (sixteen at the time), decided he wanted to go. Our parents said if we were up to it, he could go, which shocked David and me. We told Dwight that as long as we didn't have to wait for him, we'd be glad to have him along. One of the most determined young men we'd ever known, we knew if he wanted it badly enough, he'd make it happen. All three of us bought brand-new cross bikes (a cross between a road bike and mountain bike) from the same place our father used to purchase bicycles for us on our birthdays as children, Tony's Schwinn Bike Shop on Atlantic Boulevard in Commerce, California.

We stocked up on gear to trek safely across the country: REI for panniers, an ultra-light tent, sleeping bags, a small stove, and, of course, a journal, camera, and camcorder to ensure we'd never forget this trip. Fully loaded, my bike weighed in at over 110 pounds. A well-wisher advised a weapon for protection, so I also packed a .357 Magnum revolver. It was virtually a hand cannon and weighed a ton. Fortunately, we never needed it, not even for a rabid squirrel. However, I did feel safer having it along.

Gene, our grandpa, loaded us up in his camper and drove us north to Fort Bragg, north of San Francisco, where we stood with our bare feet ankle deep in the Pacific Ocean, snapped a photo, and headed east. The first day, an uphill battle and pouring rain kept us under thirty-five miles. Dwight lagged, and all our rear ends killed by the end of day one. We gave Dwight the big talk that night.

"Dwight, you fell behind. This is only day one." We pulled out the map and showed him how little we had progressed and how far we had to go. Dwight pleaded for one more day, and we agreed. In fact, he promised us that if we ever had to wait for him again, he would quit and go home. The next day would be the test. Could he keep up with a sore rear end and burning legs from our ride the day prior? Throughout the six-week journey, we never again waited for Dwight, not once.

This young man had a fire burning inside, and once locked on a goal, he made it happen. I was so proud.

The adventure took us on the highest of highs and lowest of lows, with lessons learned daily. Each night, I found a payphone to call my love—the highlight of my day. We spent a week in Boulder, Colorado—just long enough for Jodi to break up with David. Massively gifted in many areas but not famous for his positivity and joyful demeanor, David's heartbreak made him even more sure to reprimand Dwight and me for misbehaving and having too much fun.

Little moments turned into some of the best memories of our lifetime. As we crossed the desert in Utah just outside Salt Lake, we hit the flattest stretch of land I'd ever seen. It was endless. Alongside the elevated road was an embankment reinforced with boulders and stones ranging in size. I pulled aside and hiked down the boulder embankment to the flats below. "Come on down, boys," I yelled. Then, I began gathering rocks and spelling out a message on the blank canvas.

From top to bottom, each letter spanned about eight feet, requiring a ton of rocks. Catching on to my plan, Dwight scampered down to assist, whereas David wanted nothing to do with it. Instead, he provided motivational words of select intention. He peppered them about my head and shoulders, attempting to get me back to my bike and away from my energy-sucking rock engagement. The more the rock masterpiece took shape, there was no way on earth this hopeful romantic would leave the desert canvas unfinished.

Realizing his banter's futility, David grumbled his way down and helped Dwight and me finish our project. He helped me finish, but his perfectionistic eye took over, ensuring the highest standard of completion. Then, he followed it up by taking a photo of me and my rock message, "I [shape of a heart] JENISE." The message turned out to be grand, beautiful, and symmetrical too. Deep down, I think David really enjoyed it. I know Dwight and I did. Taking time to smell the roses, move the rocks, ride the cows, and jump in rivers is a critical key to life. It certainly makes a 3,000-mile bike ride a lot more enjoyable and memorable.

After clearing the Rockies, the Great Plains, and then Nashville, we headed south to Atlanta for a wonderful reunion. The Gables welcomed us with open arms and their familiar warm, Southern hospitality. The first evening we were in Atlanta, Jenise and I united once more. What a joy to see my girl! Absence truly can make the heart grow fonder. She liked everything about me except my five weeks of bearded manliness. Like her mother, she much prefers a clean-shaven man.

We parked our bikes in Atlanta and spent a week at the lake with Jenise and some of her dear friends. One in particular, Steve, owned an equipment rental company boasting of RVs, ski boats, and jet skis. He generously brought all his toys. It was a joy to be out in God's creation waterskiing, wakeboarding, jet skiing, and camping along the shores of a beautiful lake. Jenise and I walked hand in hand, visited around the campfire, and played in the sunshine and water.

One key element I looked for in a wife and lover was a playful companion who'd work and play alongside me. I desired someone who'd be willing to take on a grand adventure or go skinny dipping (after marriage, of course). Having fun is a vital part of life and love; many married couples forget how to play. We discussed the importance of how a lifetime of play keeps you young and close. We had no trouble feeling young and close at that point!

It happened that my twenty-second birthday, my golden birthday (I was born on May 22), landed that week, and what a celebration we had! Jenise planned such a fun evening with thoughtful gifts, a dessert of my choice, and the whole gang helped me bring in my twenty-third year. Jenise gave me a custom-made wire-frame bike about five inches long and three inches high on a trophy platform with a little placard that commemorated the ride: *Coast to Coast, 3,200 miles, May 1992*. What a treasure!

The following day, Jenise had to play the harp at an event in Atlanta. I stayed back because of the planned activities. My heart felt so full, so satisfied, and so completely at ease as we walked hand in hand to her car. We'd become friends, good friends. There was nobody I'd rather spend time with, nobody I'd rather talk to or get counsel from. She was such a solid and deep person who anchored me. When I was with her, I felt freer to be me and felt confident about the future.

I opened her door. Leaning in, I gazed into her warm, soft eyes. "I miss you already, Jenise. Please drive safely. No way I want to do life without you in it." My head bent down through the open window of her car, and her lips welcomed mine with a warmth and softness I'd never known . . . it was breathtaking, overwhelming, lovely, and beautiful all at the same time. Though we wanted it to last forever, we knew the wisdom of not tarrying long here, and she pulled back.

"Wow!" we both said at the same time and laughed.

"You're way too hot!" I exclaimed. "You better get out of here."

"Okay, but one more kiss." She leaned her head out of the window, looking at me with the most forlorn look on her face.

"Nope, no more kisses! Not one. Because I want a thousand more, Jenise," I said truthfully. The aching I believe we both felt was a lovesick pain—an ache to hold, to love, to never part, to become one, and to stay one. Before He formed the earth, God created this desire for a man to love a woman and all its wonder. It was that desire that was fueling my heart.

I interrupted our longing silence. "Our day is coming, Jenise Cheri. We have a future so bright; I need shades even thinking about it. Go, do your work, sweet girl. I'll be right here, missing you something fierce!" I smiled. She waved as she drove off, a piece of me going with her.

Leaving Atlanta, our journey to the Atlantic Ocean spanned a short 200 miles. Arriving on the shores of Savannah, Georgia, we took a picture with our feet in the water. Mission accomplished. What a rich experience it'd been.

My brothers and I packed up our bikes and gear and shipped them back to California. Then we helped Jenise and her younger sister Jilinda pack up their belongings. We all piled into the Wondersled and headed back to Southern California. After a couple of days in Los Angeles with our families, Jenise and I packed up the 4Runner and headed north on Interstate 5 past Sacramento, Redding, and Lake Shasta. We turned off in Yreka to head west to the small town of Etna, California. Just ten miles away was the JH Ranch.

As I pulled across the bridge and saw the old wagon and the stunning valleys and rolling landscape, it felt like a welcome home. It was a beautiful meadow of lush green grass with grazing horses surrounded by tall timbers poised like sentinels, on guard and watching.

Summer, here we come!

* * *

CHAD'S REFLECTIONS

Writing down goals is powerful! Taking the time to think through what you want to be, do, and have in your life is such a fun, creative, and worthwhile exercise to do.

Psalm 37:4 says: "Delight thyself also in the Lord, and he shall give thee the desires of thine heart."

Pray that the Lord will direct you and dream away. Hold your dreams loosely should He direct you in a new and different way.

Dream without limits. What would you do if you had all the time in the world? What would you do if money were no object? Who do you want to become? What do you want to learn? What skills do you want to develop? What group of people do you want to bring the most value to?

Where do you want to live? What mountains do you want to climb? What language do you want to learn? Where do you want to travel? What do you want to give?

Taking the time to write these things down is exciting and empowering. It helps you see what is possible. Yes, some of them will happen, and some may never happen. Some will change over time as you mature and grow in wisdom.

So many of those 100 things I wrote down so long ago came true:

- Marry the woman of my dreams
- Have ten children together (we have eleven)
- Teach them to love God and people
- Ski steep and big mountains
- Live in the country
- Travel to other countries
- Run a marathon
- Complete an Ironman
- Obtain my private pilot's license
- Bike across America
- Write our love story (here you have it!)

CHAPTER 28
"FALL IN LIKE" AT JH RANCH

I t was late in the day when Jenise and I arrived; we were both tired from the twelve-hour drive. Having the 4Runner's windows down invited in the sound of French Creek rushing over the rocks beneath the bridge. The sun cast its yellow glow across the horses grazing peacefully in the pasture before slipping behind Etna Summit. A lone sprinkler shooting its arching geyser some 150 feet over the meadow beat out a welcome rhythm. The scents of pine, grass, and pure spring mountain air tickled our senses.

"Honey, we're home," I called over to Jenise. "This place is amazing." I stopped alongside the big river rocks lining the gravel road. I helped Jenise out, and we both turned, stepped over the river rocks and onto the lush green grass, and walked to the fence between us and the great expanse of JH Ranch's main pasture and valley. Leaning up against the fence, I asked her, "Is it good to be back?"

She took a deep breath. "It never gets old," she whispered. "This place is so special, and I'm so glad you're here." Her eyes turned to mine. I bent down and kissed her lightly.

The sound of a motorcycle moving fast startled me. It was Bruce! "Hi, Chad and Jenise. When did you guys get here?" he asked, a big grin on his face.

I was a bit embarrassed. Bruce had previously mentioned that I was good to work at the ranch but that we'd have to keep our relationship low key and not let it interfere with our job, which was to serve others. Then, right off the bat, he caught us kissing. He said nothing then, but I knew Bruce, and he never missed a thing. I guessed we might talk later.

Instantaneously regaining my composure, I replied, "Just pulled in, Bruce."

"Great! Are you hungry? I know Jenise is. She's always hungry!" he teased. Bruce and Jenise laughed. "It's that Johnston metabolism," Bruce added. "Better get on up to the lodge to see what's left for dinner. We just finished up."

I came to understand the importance of getting to meals on time at JH Ranch. They took pride in feeding a staff of over 100 and all 350 campers within thirteen minutes. The process defined the old adage, you snooze, you lose! We needed the energy and calories to work as hard as we did, and you can be sure everyone, including me, figured this out quickly. The chef had some extra food, and I quickly realized my association with Jenise Johnston would have its perks. Something told me that, alone, I would've been praying and fasting, not by choice.

From dinner, we headed to our respective staff housing quarters. Some early birds had already grabbed the prime spots, if that's what you call old, metal bunk beds with metal bars for support under a two-inch thin, grey plastic-lined mattress. I threw my stuff onto a bed. A young man about my age with a big grin on his face stuck out his hand and said, "Hello there. My name is Brad," with the thickest Southern drawl I'd ever heard. It sounded as if he were trying to be funny. That was maybe the only time during the summer Brad did not try to be funny.

I shook his hand and replied, "My name's Chad Johnson."

Brad was attending Georgia Tech and had a college roomie along, Jeffrey Wallis. They asked me what school I attended.

"Getting all Cs at UHK," I answered. They looked perplexed. "That's the University of Hard Knocks," I said, laughing right along with them. "In all seriousness, I wanted to get out of high school early, but I couldn't spell GED, so I had to take the California High School Proficiency Examination to get out. I went to a local junior college to get my EMT so I could work ski patrol. That's what I'm up to now. Cool career, huh?" By now, they didn't know what to think of me and made up some excuse to go to the lodge to get something.

Throughout the evening, more guys poured into the cramped cabin from schools all over—Auburn, Alabama, Duke, Georgia, and Mississippi, to name a few. I was the least educated of the bunch; I felt I had left my country and visited another planet. Talk of fraternities, sorority girls, college sports, and other sophistications were all unknown to me. All the guys seemed friendly, like they loved the Lord, and accepting of the challenge to grow, learn, and lead for the summer at JH Ranch.

Erle, a veteran staff member and Bruce's right-hand man, played a key role in leading staff and making JH Ranch run. As the guys' staff ringleader, he helped me adjust and orient me as a team member. Having worked side by side over several summers, Jenise and Erle were great friends. The support the new guys and I had from Erle made all the difference. He was a guy we all respected, a man's man, and a truly humble leader; he was full of adventure, loved God, and loved people. Several times throughout the summer, I marveled at how Jenise somehow liked me and hadn't run off and married Erle. I measured him up as twice the man I was, though I never thought of bringing that to Jenise's attention—it wasn't my job to do that, now was it?

Winter and nature wreak havoc on a place left unattended. The first week entailed preparing the property for guests—cabins were painted, decks and bridges stained, pine needles cleared from pathways, Big Top raised, lawns mowed, weeds whacked, broken equipment and buildings repaired. I learned to dread patching the cracks in the "Wish of Death Flusher," a name I concocted. That concrete water slide felt like a cheese grater when you lost your mat and finished on your hips, elbows, or knees. Our days were long and filled to the brim. Jenise and I rarely saw each other except at mealtimes. Just knowing she was near, working diligently in her role, somehow made each moment more enjoyable.

The second week kicked off with a bang. The staff loaded the vans, bus, and trailer with rafts, life jackets, and paddles. From French Creek Road, twisting through Etna, turning at Fort Jones, and heading onto Scott River Road, by the time we hit the confluence of Scott River and the Klamath, every one of us wanted to pitch our breakfast. The roads twisted, turned, wound, and then wound some more.

Jenise and I were together. She held my hand and squeezed on every turn and corner. She wanted to go ten times slower, but Erle knew the road like the back of his hand and drove it like a race car. Jenise visibly relaxed when we turned to drive along the Klamath River, a straighter path. Our next stop was Happy Camp for a snack and a cold drink.

Like her health-conscious mother, Jenise didn't drink soda, alcohol, coffee, or tea. She was a water girl, through and through. In some of our serious talks, we discussed what we'd allow and abstain from; it surprised me that Jenise shared my standard of not drinking alcohol. This was rare. Our parents both steered clear of alcohol. I had several friends and acquaintances who suffered destruction of career or relationship, injury, even death, because of misuse. I knew my tendencies to go all in and thought it'd be wiser if I left it alone; so I'd never even tasted beer. I did have one sip of wine, just enough to know that I'd have to develop a taste for it and decided not to.

Jenise leaned toward healthy snacks like fresh carrots or a bell pepper. Yep, she eats bell peppers like apples. Joy was always taking whole food supplements, bee pollen, or other health products. She had the energy of a youngster. Impressive! On the other hand, I lived on a ski patrolman budget and was too busy to cook. So if Dixianne wasn't cooking or I wasn't visiting my parents, I was eating at Carl's Jr. or all-you-can-eat pizza night at Village Pizza. Jenise was already rubbing off on me.

A few miles down the road, we threw out our river mats and camped for the night. Seeing the bazillions of twinkling stars in the night sky made it so easy for me to worship God. I believe in a God who created the Heavens and the Earth, a God who created me and has great things in store for my life. Being in nature and surrounded by His handiwork, praise came quickly to my lips, and I felt my soul being enriched and my awe of God expanding. I was asleep before my head hit the pillow that first night on the river. Always moving, the Klamath River's sound created sweet, hypnotic music that calmed the soul.

Over the next several days, Erle and Bruce taught us all the art of being river guides. We learned how to spot the three dangers on the shore—snakes, slippery rocks, and poison oak—all of which we'd see or experience over the summer. We learned how to fill, deflate, maintain and bail out the boats. (This was before the amazing self-bailing Sotar rafts they have now.) Then the commands for movement and navigation: forward paddle, back paddle, right side back paddle, left side back paddle, stop paddle, rock side, and lean in. We learned to make the river an engaging experience with games, information on wildlife, humor, and stories. After a practice run, staff members loaded up the boats and used one another as guinea pigs. Jenise was in my boat, of course. I always had so much fun with her along.

Along the way, we stopped and jumped off rocks and bridges. I've always enjoyed jumping off high places. It's not that I was fearless; I enjoyed the adrenaline rush I felt when I thought about the leap. Whether snow skiing or jumping off bridges, the freedom of flying delighted me! Bruce led the way as we pulled our boats to the class four rapids (named Dragon's Tooth) that we'd take campers down. He climbed a steep section, pointing out the poison oak growing in the cracks and ledges. Then he performed his scary belly flop approach from the forty-foot ledge before jackknifing into the water.

Before heading back to the ranch to prepare for our 300-plus campers, we hiked a scenic trail that wandered inland from the Klamath River and alongside a snow-melting creek that rushed over rocks and fallen trees, finding its way back into the main river. Near the top, we swam a short forty-foot section in crazy cold, crystal clear water that literally took our breath away. Then we took our winding route back to JH Ranch to welcome the campers. They piled out of the buses, stretching their legs after a long drive from Sacramento.

When we took our campers to the river that week and every week after, I adopted a personal mission as a river guide—we'd have the best boat! We'd give it our all, yell the loudest when we hit the rapids, work as a team, engage in water fights with other boats, and we'd leave it all on the water. We built team spirit and camaraderie with our students, and, in the end, I'd send them back on a mission: find the prettiest blonde girl in the world and tell her you were in the best boat and your river guide has a huge crush on her.

It was so fun to send a bus full of young camper girls and guys back to the ranch with a message for Jenise. This was our form of cell phone and text messages. These fine young carrier pigeons spread messages of love and anticipation all week long.

As discreet as our relationship was coming in, Bruce gave me the talk right after our arrival. It was okay to "fall in like" at the ranch, but you had to wait for the end of summer to "fall in love"—there's so much wisdom in that. We had amazing guys and girls spending three months in the most romantic and beautiful environment; love was bound to take root!

Jenise and I kept the burner on low and let our relationship simmer, which, by the way, was and is boiling hot! Something about liking and not being able to express fully is crazy fun and electrifying. Anyone around us could sense sparks flying, but I believed we could keep the main thing as the main thing. Know what I mean?

The summer swept us into an adventuresome whirlwind with days of group action, enjoying rodeo, lake, river, ropes, and wilderness. We also had time for solo work, growing, leading, and learning. There was never a dull moment. Campers coming in from miles apart became fast friends.

It's almost impossible to wrap up this amazing experience into a book. We road-tripped to the river, explored other stretches of the river, found new rapids to challenge us, swam at a clear creek, jumped off Independence Bridge, floated rapids in our life jackets only, and visited around campfires. When it was just the guys, campfire topics included girls, life, *girls*, faith, *girls*, what we were learning, *girls*, what we struggled with, *girls*, our dreams of future careers, and school, and stuff like that . . . and *girls*.

We opened up and shared our strengths and weaknesses; many nights, we prayed for one another, lifting our burdens to the Lord. One particular evening, I shared my struggle with pornography and my desire to walk in purity. I was exposed to this life-sucking monster at age fifteen; it plagued me off and on until I met Jenise. Wanting to marry her motivated me to live life in purity and not fall prey to the sin that'd provoked me in the past. I found freedom in sharing as James 5:16 tells us: "Confess your sins, one to another, that you may be healed."

Back at the ranch, the guys woke early and took turns leading military-style workouts, taking on the steep mountainous trails aptly named Cardiac and Heart Attack, or hitting the weights in the gym in the barn. We followed our increased heart rates with quiet prayer time, reading the Bible, and praising and thanking God for His goodness. The ranch, a spiritual refreshment, was a place of purpose to know God better, hear His voice, and feel His presence. Although away from the distractions of city living hustle and bustle, ranch life gave way to its own fast pace yet offered a rhythm that brought me closer to the Lord and strengthened my faith. I wanted to bottle it up and take it with me at summer's end.

Amid serving, there were times of recreation—from square dances at the end of each week to sports nights to treasure hunts and scavenger hunts and even haunted houses we set up in an old barn to scare the girls. We made so many fun memories, and in the middle of it all, Jenise and I grew closer and closer.

* * *

CHAD'S REFLECTIONS

Anybody who has experienced a summer at JH Ranch or something similar can attest to the power of being out in nature, in an undistracted environment, and with people of like faith, all desiring to grow spiritually. It makes for a truly life-changing season, and this time at the ranch did just that.

Jenise and I grew closer and closer working together, serving together, and seeing each other in all kinds of different trying circumstances and situations. I realize that is a rare situation, but if you are ever offered the opportunity to work alongside the one you love in that type of setting, take it! It was a gift to both Jenise and me. It enabled me to understand her so much better, seeing her in the environment and forces that had shaped her.

Witnessing Jenise at the ranch gave me a greater sense of appreciation for who she was (and is)—capable, strong, dependable, responsible, and a woman of character. Situations like that reveal so much about person, and every bit I learned drew me deeper.

Putting yourself in situations where you can see the good, the bad, the ugly of how a person responds to difficulty, disappointment, and fatigue is invaluable. Sometimes when dating, you find yourselves only in places or events that bring out the best in you—all dressed up, on your best behavior, doing only things you enjoy, eating great food, and finding entertainment.

That is not the total picture of what marriage looks like. Yes, it is fun. Yes, it is full of adventure, romance, and fine dining moments, but it is also full of chores, bills, dirty diapers, and vomiting children at 2:00 a.m.

How does the person you are dating function in the day in, day out of life? It has been said you fall in love with personality but marry the character of the person. Character is revealed in hardship.

CHAPTER 29
DATE NIGHT

O n turnover day, in between rounds of campers, we readied the ranch and had the afternoon off for down-time. Bruce and Erle gave me permission to take Jenise on a date off the property. I had scouted and picked the perfect spot—a scenic overlook just up French Creek Road, up into the wilderness toward the trailheads that led to Payne's and Duck Lakes, two mountain lakes far above the ranch.

I found some props in the barn such as a four-by-four-foot card table, two chairs, a white tablecloth, a full set of nice dishes, candles, CD player (complete with batteries), a four-by-sixteen-foot swath of red carpet and a piece of eight-by-ten-foot brown carpet (don't know why they were rolled up in the barn but glad they were). The chef was even in on it to make the whole event special.

"Jenise," I called, as she was coming out of the lodge, "you've been working way too hard recently. Would you be willing to go out with me tonight?"

"Did you ask Bruce?" she responded quickly. I loved the way Jenise was so responsible! She honored her brother so much and took her job so seriously.

"Yes, I did, and he said no, but I'm doing it anyway!" I said jokingly. "In all seriousness, yes, I did, and he was all for it. Are you in?"

"Of course!" she said. "What should I wear?"

"That's the fun part. Nothing at all. Just kidding! Just kidding!" I said, but not before she whacked me solidly on the shoulder.

"Be good!" she demanded.

I advised her to be ready at 4:30 p.m. and to wear something nice.

The next two hours had me running full steam to ready the spot. I had my props, the meal, and Sterno cans to keep it warm. I took great care to set it up and then headed back to the ranch to get cleaned up. Hygiene is a big deal for me. Some guys don't seem to notice the way they look, smell, or come across. A good shower, shave, deodorant, and aftershave made me feel great! Once all shined up and in my nice duds, I was off to get Jenise.

I pulled up in front of the Convent (fondly named female staff housing) that was technically a broken-down trailer home that smelled of mildew. It was 4:30 p.m. I was on time and proud of it! Knocking on the door, I heard a chorus of giggling, laughing, and yelling. "He's here, Jenise!" All of them seemed to be very much in love with Jenise. Jenise won their hearts, and they rallied behind her.

As usual, she took my breath away. Would I ever get used to her beauty? Would it ever become commonplace? Would there be a day I'd see Jenise and not think, *Wowzah, hawt thang*? "I'm ready." Her voice interrupted my thoughts.

"Let's go!" I turned, grabbing her hand, and guiding her to the 4Runner. I opened her door as I always did, and told her I always would, and she got in. I leaned in for a quick peck, and an encore of girls' voices, clapping, cheering, and egging us on erupted from behind me. I turned and saw twelve or more heads peering out the window, gawking at us. I saw huge smiles on their faces, some giving me the thumbs up, and all lovingly gave me a hard time. I flashed a smile and thumbs-up, ran around the vehicle, loaded up, and backed out onto French Creek Road.

It was a quick ten-minute drive up the winding dirt road, surrounded by a pine forest on all sides with an occasional meadow along the way. I drove slowly so as not to make Jenise sick. We wound our way up the side of the mountain, switchback by switchback. I knew we were getting close, so I used a wide spot to turn the car around and backed the last couple hundred yards up the road to our destination.

"Close your eyes, Jenise; I want this to be a surprise." Backing the remaining 100 feet, I parked, got out, and opened Jenise's door. "Keep your eyes closed and wait right here for just a moment. No peeking!" I ran to the table and lit the candles sitting on the white cloth. I pushed play on the CD player and Ronnie Millsap's "Lost in the Fifties Tonight" started. I turned to Jenise, held her hand, and said, "Okay, Jenise Cheri. You can open your eyes now."

"Chadwick Buford! You're too much. This is amazing!" she exclaimed joyfully. "You're so dear!" She turned to look into my eyes. "You have got to stop this."

"Stop what?" I asked innocently, meeting her gaze.

"Being so nice to me," she said.

"I haven't even started, Jenise Cheri. I'm going to spoil you rotten the rest of your life! And there is nothing you can do to stop me!" I grinned back at her. Putting my arm out as an escort, I turned and said with my snootiest voice, "May I escort my lady to the ball?" She laughed, and we walked down the red carpet laid out like a royal welcome to the white-linen-covered table fully set with fine china and silver. I pulled her chair out for her to sit while the music played softly, and the candles flickered a warm ambiance.

A canopy of pines fell away beneath us, protecting a beautiful carpet of deep green. We could see the big meadow of the ranch far below and the white outline of the Big Top. Rolling far beyond, the mountain ranges surrounding Etna,

Fort Jones and Yreka, and to the south, the bright white snow tip of Mount Shasta, soared above the green. We sat across the table from each other, holding hands and soaking in the view. She whispered, "It's so beautiful."

"Yes, you are," I whispered back. Her coy glance me made me feel like a million bucks. We were in love, and everything seemed perfect.

"I know better than to ask, but are you hungry?"

"How did you know?" she laughed.

"Well, you came to the right place," I said, jumping to my feet. "My lady, could I interest you in a glass of sparkling apple cider?"

"Why, yes," she replied. From behind a bush, I grabbed from my stash of surprises and good eats.

We offered thanks to the Lord for His bountiful blessings and His goodness in both of our lives. We shared how we felt the favor of the Lord and couldn't believe how blessed we were with the parents and siblings we had and the health we enjoyed. The Lord gave us gifts and abilities and His grace beyond understanding. His salvation gives us hope and the opportunity to be at the ranch and enjoy His creation in such a powerful way. What a blessing to be a small part of the massive transformation in the lives of others. Amen!

I served my girl a feast prepared by the chef earlier in the day, and everything was spot on—hot, tasty, and in abundance. We started with a salad and some bread (Jenise loves bread), followed by the main course of chicken parmesan. For dessert, we enjoyed a chocolate brownie, and, yes, even ice cream. Amazing what a little dry ice can do. I knew this was one of her favorites, and the look on her face when I brought it out to her was so worth all the work in getting it there.

As was always the case, endless conversation blessed our time together. Catching up on ranch life, who liked whom, what we were learning, things the Lord was showing us, and challenges we were facing. As the sun set behind us, it made the most amazing glow in front of us. The view changed moment by moment as we witnessed God's evening painting of glory.

"Would you like to dance?" My voice broke the stillness.

"Here? Now?"

"Sure, why not?"

"Okay."

I reached behind me to the CD player nestled against a small shrub and popped in another CD. Then we danced. Wow! Talk about romance. Sweet music, the girl of my dreams in my arms, and a setting sun casting its warm blanket out across the valley, wrapping us with a balmy comfort while our hearts beat to the rhythm of the music. I wanted it to last forever. The temperature started to drop the second the sun had set, and we worked together to pack up our date-night equipment.

"This was so much fun! How did you find this place?" Jenise asked.

"Just did some scouting around," I replied. "I knew this was the place when I saw it."

"Where did you find all this stuff? In the barn?"

"Yep, that's right! That place has everything."

Our drive back seemed much longer in the dark. I dropped Jenise off back at the Convent. She thanked me profusely for the magical evening, gave me a sweet peck as she hopped out, and she was gone.

"Hey, you didn't let me get your door." I felt my voice riding on the wind, and it never seemed to reach her. I drove away, imagining the conversation she was having with all those curious girls of the Convent, and a huge smile swept over my face.

Lord, you sure did make a good one when you made her.

* * *

CHAD'S REFLECTIONS

Is chivalry dead? I know it is popular for women of this day and age to get their own door, pay their own way, and all of that. Personally, I don't buy it. Yes, I'm old school. I like it when men act like men, finding ways to protect, provide, and all that. I also like it when women are ladylike and feminine. Some think these things are out of date. But I have seen time and time again that when we fulfill the roles God laid out in Scripture, there is a beautiful synergy that makes one plus one more than two.

I believe a lady still appreciates being treated with respect. The simple act of getting a door for a lady tells me a lot about the man who says he loves her.

But let me go a little deeper here. I can show my love for her by getting her door but still be unkind with my sarcastic words. When it is all said and done, how does your woman or man feel loved and appreciated?

Find out, and then do that.

CHAPTER 30
FRIGID JENISE

Two weeks later, I learned that I had much to learn about women. Jenise and I had left on what I thought was the very best of terms after our date, which seemed a great success. Then our schedules got very busy in the next two weeks. When I returned from four days on the river, I was met with a somewhat frigid Jenise. Seeing her for the first time in a while, I ran up to her and hugged her. I didn't pay much attention initially, but she didn't give me a warm hug I was used to, more of a quick side hug, and not much in the way of response. I wrote it off to other staff being around.

"Hey, you." I poked her as I went through the chow line.

"Hi," she replied with a hint of ice. *Wow! What is going on?*

"Everything all right?" I asked.

"Sure, fine—" she cut me short and turned back into the kitchen area where the rest of the staff couldn't go. I took a couple of steps to follow her but sensed that it might not be the best thing to do. I ate dinner with the rest of the staff and didn't see Jenise until after the talk at the Big Top. She was visiting with some other female staff, and as I approached, she turned as if to walk away.

"Jenise?"

She turned. "Yes?"

"Can I speak with you?" The girls made a few comments under their breath that made them laugh, but I focused on Jenise and her response.

"I think we should talk," she said, her voice icy.

I walked up beside her, and we headed up the road that led to the lodge hill. "What's going on?" I asked.

"You tell me," she snapped.

"Whoa, Jenise, I have no idea what's going on. Are you mad at me?"

"Should I be?" she asked.

"No, I'm sure of that! You should never be mad at me. You should only love me, adore me, and want more of me!" I said, trying to be funny. It didn't work. She turned and stomped off, away from the direction we were going. "Jenise, wait! I was joking! I'm trying to be funny; you know, lighten things up a bit." I retreated with a nervous chuckle.

"I don't think it was funny, and I don't think things need to be lightened up!"

"Please forgive me for making light of it. I'm all ears. Talk to me. What's going on, Jenise?" I implored. This was much more serious than I thought. What she said next floored me. It came out of nowhere.

"I don't think we're right for each other." The words rolled right off her tongue like she meant it.

I couldn't believe my ears! "What? For real? Are you trying to be funny?" My response was explosive. Far more than I meant it to be. I went on. "What on earth makes you say that? Have I done something wrong? Have I offended you?" Fear was creeping up in me. Surely, she couldn't be serious.

The thought of us not being *us* was crazy to me. I never had even a whisper of a thought that we might not be right for each other. I knew beyond all shadow of a doubt that not only were we right for each other, but we were perfect for each other! How could this be happening?

My world was spinning as I realized she was serious. She really was questioning us. *Take a deep breath, Chad. Slow down, stay calm, and find out what's really on her mind, what the root of this is.* But my heart was beating out of my chest. Everything in me said speed up, talk more, fix this, make this go away. I knew I needed to understand a lot more than what met the eye in that moment.

"Jenise, I want to understand what you're saying. Could you explain? What makes you say that?" I asked, much more in control of my emotions.

"Well, you seem very capable of doing life without me—"

"What do you mean by that?" I interrupted.

"Can you let me fin—"

"Yes, but I need some kind of explanation or clarification," I interrupted again.

"If you'd stop interrupting, I'd tell you what I mean."

"Okay." I held my hands out, open palms upward, with my eyebrows raised in a questioning look.

She continued, "I know you're the cool river guide, and the high school girls can't stop talking about you. '*Chad* this, *Chad* that, our river guide *Chad* is amazing!' and on and on and on. And I know you and Alaina are coaching together, getting along great, taking long hikes into the wilderness together, winning all the events with your special team. Maybe you and Alaina should be a couple." Her voice was sharp and full of emotion.

"Jenise Cheri! Now, you must stop. You're being ridiculous! I'm doing my job and making sure all the little campers have a great time on the river. But come on; they're little girls! And Alaina? She's a champ! I agree with that, but she isn't for me, not for a second. We're doing what we're supposed to do, coaching our campers, and giving our best. But there's nothing between us. Nothing!"

I continued. "I could say the same thing about you and Erle, tramping all over Mount Shasta, special trips with the elite Track II Students, all of you in a league of your own.

Don't you think I hear the way the Track II guys speak of you? They all adore you. They probably all have a crush on you; only I know better. You're mine, Jenise Cheri Johnston—all mine! There's nobody on earth that comes even close to you, girl! Please know this! Not even close.

"You have all of my heart, Jenise, and always will. I can see that I've done a poor job of letting you know this. Yes, we have both been busy and going a million miles in opposite directions, but that has nothing to do with us. You've got to know this, honey. I adore you." I pulled her close and held her. She was crying softly. "Are you okay?" I whispered in her ear. She nodded, keeping her head on my chest.

"Jenise, how long have you been feeling this?" I asked her.

"Just the past couple days," she answered softly. She continued, "It's that time of the month too," looking up into my eyes sheepishly. I nodded and smiled warmly.

"Jenise, we're going to be okay, aren't we?" I asked.

She nodded again, and I felt her head move reassuringly against my chest.

I walked her down to her cabin and held her face in both hands. I told her, "Jenise, thank you for sharing with me. Please don't let anything get bottled up in you. Get with me. Share it with me. I want to know the good, the bad, and the ugly. All of it. I love you so much and don't want you to suffer alone."

"I'm so sorry for sounding crazy," she said.

"Not crazy, you just sound like a woman."

She slapped me good. "You turd!"

"I can't believe you use foul language, Jenise!" I teased. "Good night, Alaina, oops, I mean high school girl, oops, I mean Jenise Johnston."

"You're lucky you're too far away to slap; I'd knock you silly, boy. Good night, Chadwick Buford. *My* river guide."

"More like your life guide!" I laughed.

"Get out of here!" she laughed back.

* * *

CHAD'S REFLECTIONS

Communication is a big deal! Learning how to share and express your thoughts, hurts, ideas, visions, and dreams in a relationship is critical. Learning how to listen well and truly seek to understand the other is a skill worth having.

We grow up in different homes, with different parents, learning different approaches, ways to communicate—or not.

Some family dynamics blurt it all out. Some stay silent and stuff it all down.

All of this naturally comes to the surface as a relationship deepens.

I encourage every young person to set a goal of becoming a master communicator. Regardless of what you learned or did not learn growing up about healthy communication, it is a learned skill and will serve you greatly in all relationships.

CHAPTER 31
SUPERMAN RETURNS

A couple of weeks later, the summer was halfway through, and singles week was upon us. Jenise invited a bunch of her Atlanta friends (many who'd also become my friends) to join us at the ranch for the week. Will, Dayne, Anne, Jill, Steve, and Glenn, and several others drove up the lodge hill that evening.

The week kicked off with a rodeo and a day at the lake. These guys and gals were all very gung-ho and so much fun. Will was the guy Jenise dated for a short while when she first arrived in Atlanta, the guy I dubbed Superman due to his ability to hit high marks in every area I considered important for manhood.

Some of the ranch staff guys had heard our love story, and on those nights out by the river when they heard the name "Will" several came straight over to ask, "Chad, is this the guy who was dating Jenise in Atlanta?"

"Yep," I replied. "He's probably out for one last shot at her." I said it jokingly, but some part of me wondered.

At the lake that afternoon, a competition between Will and me may have ignited. He took a turn on the super swing and pulled a beautiful layout backflip. The crowd went wild. I climbed the ladder to the top and performed my best double backflip, going in clean. The folks on the beach started razzing

Will: "Can you do a double?" Being the great sport he was, he made his way back up the ladder to the top and sure enough, nailed a double backflip, clean as a whistle.

Now all the staff guys started getting into it. "Come on, Chad, bust a triple!" To be honest, I didn't know if I could pull a triple clean. I'd tried before and had come up a bit short. It was painful, and the thought of busting right then wasn't appealing. So I passed. Yes, the guys razzed me a bit, but soon enough, we were all on to other things.

The competition seemed to continue in every activity we did. While out on the river, it was skipping rocks. On our hike to the clear water pool called Little Hawaii, the cliffs almost begged us to jump from them. All the river guides and several of the guy campers climbed the cliff next to the waterfall, and two of them jumped from the top of the falls. Four of us remained and kept climbing to the highest point possible, well over fifty feet and over double the fall's height. One of the staff guys jumped feet first, and he landed cleanly in the foaming water of the falls. Another followed suit.

After standing there for a sufficient time to ensure everyone down below was watching, including Jenise, Will dove forward off the edge. To everyone's surprise, he landed a precise front flip into the water below. I knew Jenise was watching along with all the other campers. In moments like that, my adrenaline really gets pumping, my breathing slows, my mind focuses, and I lose all thought and vision of those around me. I carefully stepped to the furthermost edge of the rock. Wow, it was a long way down. I knew better than to think long while standing in such a place. It was easier just to go. So I jumped.

I threw my feet straight out in front of me and slightly up. I held my arms straight out from my sides and threw my head back. I fell backward toward the water below. Not a moment too soon, the water came into view, and I pulled my body back into alignment as I hit the water, pulling a gainer clean and true. What a rush! Amazing! I'll never get over that sensation. It made me feel truly alive! As I walked up from the foam of the waterfall spray, the group on shore was cheering. I really enjoyed entertaining people. As a kid, I put on a circus and involved all my siblings and cousins. I guess I have a bit of showman in me.

The following day back at the ranch, while on my early morning run, I came across Will returning from his run. "How far did you go this morning, Will?" I asked him.

"I only did thirteen miles this morning, not time enough to do a long run," he said nonchalantly.

What? Thirteen miles wasn't a long run? This guy was a beast! He was training for his next Ironman, and every part of him looked like it. My three-mile loops around the Wagon Wheel felt small and insignificant that morning. What was worse, it seemed every time I turned around, Jenise was there, talking to *Will*, laughing with *Will*, smiling, and having a great time with him. Now, it was my turn.

"Hey, Jenise, what's up with Will?" I asked her as we walked into the lodge one evening.

"What do you mean?" she asked.

"You tell me. It seems like you two are getting along just fine, always chatting it up, laughing, having fun."

"Chadwick Buford, are you jealous?" Jenise said jokingly.

"Should I be?" I quipped. "I don't think this is funny, by the way."

Her expression changed, and she drew me close. "Chad Johnson, I can't believe it. You're jealous."

"Hey," I defended myself. "I need to know that you and I are still okay. Are we okay?"

"Yes, you silly boy!" she laughed. "I'm so in love with you, I can't stand it! Will is a great guy, but not for me, no way. No way on earth! Chad Johnson is my man, right now, and forever!"

"That's all I needed to know. Guess it's just that time of the month for me . . ." I laughed.

We walked hand in hand into the staff dining area, letting go as we walked through the door as the rules required. But I knew we were holding hands in our hearts; the look she gave me confirmed that in a million ways. The rest of the week came to a climax on Friday when the lake opened one more time. By this time, the entire staff and all the campers knew that Will and I had a little running competition, or maybe more like a friendly feud.

It didn't matter what event, activity, or game we were playing; it was game on. The highlight of the week came that afternoon at the lake when Will took his acrobatics game to the super swing. Ready to witness the latest stunts, eager onlookers surrounded the whole lake. After warming up on a single laid-out backflip, Will raised the stakes once more with a clean double. People started talking about a triple backflip, and then the challenging and jesting of voices echoed around the lake.

Will took to the ladder and climbed to the top. His tan, strong, and lithe body, a masterpiece of manly function and fitness, was on display. The whole crowd silenced as he grabbed the rope handle and took a deep breath. As if in slow motion, he took the first step and activated the long arch down. You could see the g-forces acting on his shoulders and arms as he steered through the apex of the swing and headed up the other side of the sweeping arch. He let go of that handle, snapping his body forward feet first and transforming into a tight tuck. His first flip happened fast! Snapping into the second, then third, and he opened up, then worked to slow and stop rotation. Stopping rotation, he met the water with a horrific sound of flesh slapping its surface. The whole crowd roared their empathy and joy of the courage on display. He'd gone for it and gave his all, and that was heroic.

People think life is all about winning, victory, and success. It's not! Life is about doing, risking, trying, and going for it despite the chance of failure and defeat. It's being in the arena, not in the stands. It's about being a participator and not only an observer. Will was a true champ in my mind. He'd grown on me all week. I witnessed a man of character, strength, and true manhood. And since I was now secure in Jenise being mine, I could even like him. I thought this while standing right next to Jenise and several of our Atlanta friends, when I realized they were all looking at me and saying something to the effect of "your turn."

"My turn?" I joked. "You want me to go so you can hear my body splat all over that lake? One isn't enough for you sick people?" Erle and Stuart were walking my way, and I knew what was on their minds.

"All right, Chad, your turn! Dude, don't let us down. All the guys are betting on you. You've got this, brother! Triple it, dude! Think of the glory."

Will joined us on the shore, "Come on, Chad, you've got this. I just made it look hard." He laughed. He turned and showed me the cherry red skin covering his entire back. He looked like a lobster. "Really, it's not that bad. It only hurts for a day or so," he said, laughing again.

I had a choice. Isn't life like that, full of choices? Do I cave in to peer pressure and go sacrifice my body for their enjoyment, or do I stand on the shore with the onlookers and wait for someone else to take the risk? I didn't even have a choice to make. I decided long ago that I'd push my boundaries, take some hits, feel some pain, miss the mark, and fail trying. I'd been thinking all week about that triple flip. I knew the time was coming when I'd have to try it. I believed I could pull it off, and I enjoyed that kind of challenge.

If these guys were pressuring me to slam a drink or take drugs, something that breached my standards, then disappointment would've been theirs. I wouldn't have budged. But this was a no-brainer. I'd climb that ladder, jump, and give everything I had to make that triple flip. I'd be good with whatever the outcome was.

That all sounded great in my head on the beach. But as I climbed the ladder, I remembered the times I opened too soon or too late on this same super swing, which brought to mind the crazy pain that followed with deep bruising that had me hobbling around for more than a week after. Pushing past the fear, I climbed higher.

The handle felt solid in my hand, and the adrenaline was in full force. I inhaled deeply and stepped off the platform. The wind rushed through my hair. The g-forces tugged at my arms, pulling me toward the mirror of the lake. Flying upward, the point of release came fast. I whipped into a tuck and let go of the handle while throwing my chin up. Spinning tightly, I tried to keep up with the rotational count. One, two, I held my tuck and prayed for an upright landing. The blast of water hit me before I expected. I didn't make it all the way around, clean, but had entered while still in a ball, with my shins and toes hitting the water first. I didn't back flop or front flop, which was a cause of celebration and victory in my book! A triple flip with no pain. It'd score nothing at the Olympics, but then again I don't think the super swing is a sanctioned event . . . yet.

The crowd cheered as I surfaced from my deep submerge. They saw it as a victory! And glowing in the crowd, Jenise held two thumbs up and wore her wake-up-the-world smile. Will congratulated me first, "Man, you did it!" he said, slapping me on the back—a little too hard. He must have wanted matching lobster backs!

My river guide buddies surrounded me with high fives and under the breath comments. "Dude, you showed that guy! That was stinking awesome!" These guys were like brothers to me, and the way they had my back, man, I was glad to be one of them.

Watching the video under the Big Top that evening brought our epic week to a close. Saying goodbye to our Atlanta friends was full of mixed emotions for me. I'd grown closer to each of them and really loved and admired them. As for Will, I must admit I was glad to see him go. He was a lot like Superman, and I felt a bit insecure in his presence, like a little boy around a man. Little did I know that his experience at the JH Ranch would alter the course of his career and life's work. He returned to Atlanta and began building a very successful Christian camp. He used his talents and God-given gifts to bless many people and make an eternal difference in countless lives.

* * *

CHAD'S REFLECTIONS

Friends who have your back are a precious gift in life. Relationships are not built in a vacuum. As much as it may seem like it is just you and her or you and him, your relationship will be surrounded by others, impacted by others, encouraged by others, or challenged by others.

As I mentioned prior, winning the support of those closest to you and your date is a powerful strategy for laying a solid and sound foundation.

The peers Jenise and I worked alongside at the JH Ranch were a huge support and encouragement to us both.

I have witnessed relationships suffer because of the wrong kind of friends surrounding them. It has been said that you will become like the five individuals you spend the most time around. This makes a person look around and pay attention to who they are doing life with.

Good friends pressure you to do better. Bad friends pressure you to do things that tear you down.

Seek out and connect with others who will encourage you in your faith, your vision, and your life goals. Your relationship and your whole life will be impacted by your choices.

Our summer at the JH Ranch was loaded with great friend support. To this day, almost thirty years later, we are connected with many of those we volunteered alongside that summer of 1992. We still attend "River Guide Reunions" every five years back at the ranch. We jump on the phone and send email blasts several times throughout the year as well.

CHAPTER 32
THE ENGAGEMENT RING

With summer closing and each adventure in the books, Jenise and I grew closer and closer. I had the biggest, most serious, almost unbearable crush on that girl, and she seemed to feel the same about me. I was completely smitten.

All was going really, really well—and then, well, it happened like this . . .

I woke to another stunning day of God's magnificent glory with bright rays of sunlight piercing the high trees and reflecting the meadow's dew-covered deep green grass. It was Friday, another day of helping campers on the ropes courses and out at the lake. We'd just returned from four days on the river, and I was full of anticipation for the final night. It'd be full of celebration and fun activities such as the banquet night, awarding the best teams, the boys' tie, and girls' hairpiece contest, watching the highlights video, and the square dance.

The Lord spoke to me in such a powerful way during prayer time that morning, encouraging my heart through His Word. I knew the God who created me truly loved me and had great things in store for me. He put me on earth with unique gifts, abilities, and talents. The world was my oyster, and I had big dreams, including marrying the girl of my dreams.

I'd met her, knew her heart, and was more in love than I ever thought possible.

I dreamed of a big family—with at least ten little ones—filled with joy, life, and adventure. Jenise thought maybe five or six. Either way, I envisioned a close-knit bunch of rad little people to do life with and whom I could train up in the nurture and admonition of the Lord. My family would love to work hard together, love and serve others, rat pack big ski mountains with Jenise and me, jump off bridges into cold water, and stay up late around a campfire talking about dreams and what God has in store for them.

I knew I was cut from a different cloth, and a life of the masses had no appeal to me: go to school, get good grades, go to college, get a good job, make enough money, buy the right house and cars, have two babies (one boy, one girl). Yuck! Yuck! Yuck! To me, the average life represented a slow, boring death.

No, the Lord built me for something else. What exactly? I didn't know. I journaled about these things in my time alone that morning. All I knew was my destination was for success, and life would be a grand adventure. I was sure of that. All the details would work out in time. After all, they were only details. Magic saturated the air that day—the feeling that all is well in the world—and I'm sure love had something to do with it.

After my quiet time, I headed to a place we called Rusty Gains. It was a modest gym inside the barn that sported an old weight bench, barbells, and dumbbells. It had everything a growing young man eager to add some bulk needed. Moving through shoulder presses, a little plastic bubble thing behind the bench against the wall caught my eye.

When I popped open the shell, something fell to the floor. I picked up a petite diamond ring (fake). The band didn't connect to make it adjustable. I inspected it carefully; it was actually beautiful. A thought hit me. *I'll give it to Jenise. The thought evolved. I'll propose! How fun would that be? I could ask Jenise to marry me tonight! We'd be engaged!* I tend to have a lot of thoughts, and some are good, but this one really excited me. Being the spontaneous guy I am, I put the ring in my running shorts, cut my workout short, and dashed back to my bunk to stash the ring.

My heart sang the entire day. I pondered, *Should I do it? Is this crazy?* We both knew we wanted to marry. We'd spoken as much several times. There'd be so much meaning in getting engaged at the ranch, such a special place for her, and now a special place for me too. Her parents and some of her siblings were there. It felt right.

What about that ring? It was a piece of junk and not a real diamond. Would that matter to her? It'd be a placeholder until I could purchase a real one, an eyepopper. This could totally work for now. Focusing on my work was such a challenge. And on top of that, even though Jenise and I always had crazy-fun electric energy that sparked into flame when together, we burned even hotter that day. Our commitment and actions to keep ourselves sexually pure and wait until marriage was a huge part of that authentic joy and energy we had.

Almost before I knew it, we were cleaned up for the banquet dinner, the grand finale feast of the week. Putting that plastic bubble holding my "engagement ring" in my pocket shortened my breath. Without telling a soul, I walked to the lodge. During dinner, I could hardly contain myself. I wanted to pop, shout, tell everyone I was going to ask Jenise Cheri Johnston to marry me. My secret was killing me! "Sharing the joy doubles the joy," Bruce had said so often, and here I was suffering from solo, uncontainable joy.

Joyful campers raised the bar of gleeful energy throughout that final dinner. The exuberance of the audience made announcements barely audible. Jenise, so beautiful and animated, wore a one-piece spring-floral shorts and blouse. With her blonde hair pulled back, Jenise's bright eyes, high cheekbones, and radiant smile stunned! I stole countless glances at my breathtaking beauty, not wanting to give myself away but daydreaming how she would be *my wife*.

I must have zoned, or maybe I drooled, but I suddenly woke to Jenise looking straight at me. "Are you okay, Chad?" she asked, looking concerned while waving her hand slowly in front of my face.

"Uh, yeah. Just fine, really fine. In fact, maybe too fine!" I said, laughing.

"What were you thinking about?"

"Oh, let's see. I don't know what to think anymore," I joked. Ever since she'd said, "I don't know what to think anymore," after the concert on that rainy drive in California, we lovingly used that line to say we were thinking good thoughts about the other person but weren't ready to share out loud. I changed the subject, stood up, and held my hand to her in royal welcome to escort her away. "We'd better get going if I'm going to get you to the dance."

We walked down the trail toward the tennis courts, along with a rapid exodus of campers. I leaned over and whispered in her ear, "Tonight is going to be a good night," and winked.

"What are you up to, Chadwick Buford?"

"All good things, Jenise Cheri. Ready to dance, girl? Cuz I'm ready to take you for a whirl."

"Let's go then!" She grabbed my hand and pulled as she ran the rest of the way.

We danced several square dances before resting. We took to a corner with the music still playing and couldn't help but dance the swing dance moves we stole the show with while in Gatlinburg. It seemed like a million years ago, like we'd known each other forever, but it'd only been six months! In such a short time, how could this woman win my heart, soul, and mind (and yes, the body was eager to be won when the time was right)! It hurt to be apart. Together, we were natural, right, and meant to be.

We were well on our way to becoming one. Without hesitation, I had her heart, and she had mine. I took her hand. "Come with me, Jenise. I want to show you something." We left the bright lights of the tennis courts and headed into the darkness, across the torn-up pasture, and toward large tractors sitting dormant, waiting to turn it into a sports field. I led Jenise to a large tractor on the edge of the pasture. My anticipation expanded with each step.

"Where are you taking me?" Jenise asked sweetly.

"Not far, Jenise, just a little further. See that tractor? We're going there."

I climbed onto the tractor, gently pulled Jenise up with me, and held the cab door open. "You can sit right there in the tractor seat," I told her. Reaching into my pocket, I wasted no time. I pulled out the little plastic bubble and opened it up. Getting down on my knee, I looked up into my beloved Jenise's eyes, which were opening wide with wonder.

"Chad, what—"

I held up my hand. "Jenise Cheri Johnston, will you marry me?" The words came out just like I'd thought them in my mind so many times. The look on Jenise's face as her hand came up to her mouth, eyes widened with shock, with joy, with wonder . . .

* * *

CHAD'S REFLECTIONS

It was August 14, 1992, when I asked Jenise to marry me. We had met almost sixteen months earlier on April 13, 1991.

From the moment I met Jenise, I found myself unable to be even slightly interested in any other woman. It felt as though I were taken from that day forward, even when I wasn't sure she really knew I existed.

Late December of 1991 was when I had dropped her off at the airport to fly back to Atlanta after spending time with her and her family in Fullerton. That was the first time I felt confident that we were absolutely going to be married.

That was confirmed to me on our drive from Gatlinburg to Atlanta after Valentine's Day in 1992.

I never mentioned that the Lord had shown me this. I just treasured it in my heart and prayed that I was hearing Him correctly and waited to see what came to pass.

Again, if you feel like the Lord has shown you that someone is right for you, it might be wise to keep this to yourself. I have seen both young men and young women share this information, causing undue pressure on the person they are dating. Let the Lord show them in His timing. When you both know, then you can share in that.

There was never a moment since then that I did not have every confidence that Jenise Cheri Johnston was the only girl for me. Not once.

Every story is different. Some struggle with doubt, unknowing, fear of proceeding, indecision.

May I encourage each of you reading this to pray that the Lord would give you wisdom, clarity, confidence, and speak to your heart regarding the one you are dating? He has promised to give wisdom to those who ask.

CHAPTER 33
THE BIG MISTAKE

"Yes! Oh, yes! Chad, yes, I will marry you!" Tears streamed down her cheeks, her smile true and glorious.

The joy of that moment remains forever in my heart. I took her left hand, held up the bubble gum diamond ring, gazed into her eyes, said, "This is just a placeholder. I found it this morning and didn't want to wait until we were back in LA to ask you. You're worthy of the rarest, largest, most precious diamond that ever existed, but for now, this is the best I can do." She smiled and nodded as I slid the ring on her beautiful, slender finger, claiming her as my own. I stood, and leaning over the edge of the tractor seat, gave her an awkward embrace.

She laughed, saying, "Let's get out of this tractor so that we can hug right." I helped her down, and then once on solid ground, we embraced, and her sweet lips met mine.

I'd never been so at peace. *Thank you, Lord.* I prayed as we held each other. *She is a precious gift from you. Help me to treasure her always, as I do right now, and even more.*

As we came up for air, Jenise exclaimed excitedly, "I can't wait to tell everyone! Let's go back to the dance!" I grabbed her hand, and we took off running through the plowed field.

We'd taken only a few steps when Jenise slowed and asked me, "What did my father say when you asked him?"

"I haven't asked him yet," I replied.

Her face showed shock and then concern. "You didn't?" she said slowly.

Realizing I'd made a massive mistake, I told her, "Jenise, I'm a total knucklehead. I thought I should ask you and make sure you were up for it before I asked him. I don't even know where I came up with that; it sounds crazy! It is crazy! He was so hands-off when I asked to date you and later when I told him we were dating. I wanted to honor him and your mama. They seemed so indifferent, cool, and distant, and they've remained that way the whole time we've been together. Oh, Jenise, I'm so sorry."

It was so obvious how badly I'd blown it. What was I thinking? Clearly, I wasn't. Surely, he'd say yes. "Jenise, you know how much I love and respect your parents. You know I want to honor both your father and mother very much. Please forgive me for this. I'll find him right now and ask him if I can marry you. I'll ask for his blessing. I think both of your parents know that we're right for each other. You do think he'll say yes, don't you?"

She nodded. I saw joy returning to her face. "Okay, let's go find him," she said.

When we walked back onto the tennis courts, Jilinda and several of the female staff ran over to Jenise, who was beaming from ear to ear. I couldn't believe my ears when she squealed in delight, "We're engaged!" She held out her hand, showing the ring that graced her finger.

The girls erupted! "Oh my gosh!" they shrieked. They jumped up and down. Their jubilation drew a crowd. People slapped me on the back, asked to see the ring, which Jenise showed as proudly as if it were the finest piece of jewelry known to man.

My river guide buddies jostled for position to give me high fives and fist pumps. "Congrats, man!" they said.

"Jenise," I said, catching her eye. "We need to get out of here." I nodded my head toward the gate on the far side of the tennis courts. Taking her hand, I said loudly to everyone gathered around us, "Sorry, guys, we've got to run!" We zigzagged toward the gate with the crowd thinning behind us and took off running on the trail.

"Jenise, I need to speak to your father. This is totally out of hand, and the whole world knows, except your parents. I've made a terrible mess of this!" I said, my breath coming in short blasts. We ran down the dirt road through the pasture to where the main entrance road passed the old wagon. Then we ran back up the road, heading to the good old Green Bean, which was part girls' housing and part Gene and Joy Johnston's place. We slowed to a walk to catch our breath before knocking on the door.

The foolishness of what I'd done was hitting me full force when I walked through the door of that home. How would I feel if someone approached my daughter, my little girl, and asked her to marry him, before asking me and before getting my blessing? I know I wouldn't feel respected; I wouldn't feel honored. When we entered the living room, Gene was sitting in the corner in his big chair, and Joy was sitting on the couch close by. I immediately regretted not communicating with Jenise before entering. It seems like I was doing a good job of not communicating well.

She ran toward them, held out her hand, and blurted out joyfully, "We are engaged!"

Gene, who I'd never seen upset, yell, or ever seem ruffled at all, didn't appear phased. In his very calm and steady way, he said, "Well, you can just get unengaged."

"But Daddy—" Jenise started to say.

"Jenise, we're officially unengaged," I interjected.

"Chad, are you serious?" she looked so unbelievably hurt, and I was so sad I put her in this awful predicament.

"Yes, Jenise. It's the right thing to do." Turning to Gene, I asked, "Can I speak with you and Joy?"

Gene nodded. Jenise and I sat down on the couch across from Gene and Joy, and I began.

"Before I start, will you please forgive me, Gene and Joy, for not honoring you and showing you the respect you're due in asking Jenise to marry me before I asked you?" They both looked on with questioning looks on their faces. I continued, "From the beginning of our relationship, I wanted only to honor you and respect you, and here I've done the very opposite of that. Please forgive me."

Gene and Joy both nodded. "We do," Joy said, speaking for both of them.

I took a moment to explain my faulty and poor logic to them of why I did what I did, and even in the explaining, I marveled at my cluelessness and impulsiveness. I wanted so badly to convey that I truly did love, respect, and honor them, and in no way was I trying to circumvent them or be dishonorable by what I'd done. Sheepishly, I ended by telling them I loved their daughter so much; I think love had gone to my head.

Gene began to speak, and I shut up and listened. "Chad, Joy and I can see that you and Jenise seem to really be taken with each other. From our perspective, you've been good for Jenise, and we aren't opposed to you dating each other. That said, I don't believe you're ready for marriage." I swallowed hard and continued listening. "You're twenty-two years old; you haven't graduated from college. You ski for a living, and I don't believe that provides a wage that will provide for a wife or family. How do you expect to provide for a wife and children someday?" he asked.

"Oh, I have no doubt I'll be financially successful, Gene. I'm a student of life, and while I haven't graduated or earned a degree, I'm a hard worker, a voracious reader, and love learning. I'm confident I can do whatever I set my heart and mind to. I've always been a dreamer and will do whatever it takes to be successful. I'm considering starting a business of my own. In fact, I already have a network marketing business called Melaleuca. While it isn't making me any money yet, it has a lot of potential." I paused, realizing how lame that must have sounded.

He didn't seem impressed. "Chad, let's give you some time to find your way. By not being engaged, you won't have a timeline or pressure that may cause unneeded stress." He seemed finished.

"Gene, I hear what you're saying and will do as you direct. As you mentioned earlier, Jenise and I are officially unengaged. Please understand how serious I am about your daughter. I adore Jenise. It's my utmost conviction that she's the perfect spouse for me and me for her. Not another soul comes close. I won't bring up marriage again—I want your blessing and full agreement. I want to marry your daughter right now and will only want to marry her more every moment forward until you say I'm ready. When that time comes, will you please let me know?"

I didn't pause for response and continued, "Until then, I'll put my head and heart into becoming a worthy provider. Gene, I mean this—I'll wait as long as you make me wait. If it's seven years like Laban in the Bible, I'll wait seven years." Jenise lightly elbowed me. The perplexed look in her eyes let me know I had some clarifying to do. Returning focus to Gene and Joy, I continued, "I love you guys and am sorry for the way I handled this. Thank you for your forgiveness and patience with me. Someday, I hope to make you proud."

We all stood, and I approached Gene and hugged him, getting a warmer response than in the past, but definitely not a hug. Same with Joy, although she did give me a pat on the back. "All right, you better get back up to all the action. Tonight is a big night, and everyone will wonder where you two are," she said in a way only Mama Joy can.

Leaving the house, Jenise turned to me, "Seven years? You'd wait for me for seven years?" Tears were in her eyes. She fell into my arms, and I held her close. "That is the sweetest, most romantic thing ever."

Pressing my cheek against the top of her blonde head, I assured her, "I'll wait for you seventy-seven years, Jenise Cheri. There's no other woman for me. I'd rather die lonely and single than not be with you. I'll do whatever it takes to prove to your father that I'm right for you."

"You're so amazing." Turning her face upward, she whispered, "I'm still engaged in my heart."

"You little rebel," I whispered back. "Me too."

* * *

CHAD'S REFLECTIONS

So there you have it! I made a colossal mistake. How could I have skipped such an important step in the process? I felt terrible for putting Jenise in such an awkward position and not honoring her parents the way I wanted to.

What was I thinking?

It has been thirty years, and I can't help but wonder those same things as I look back.

An Epictetus quote often spoken at the ranch is, "Circumstances don't make or break you; they just reveal you."

Losing doesn't make you a loser. Failing doesn't make you a failure. What happens after you make the mistake makes all the difference in the world.

I made an honest mistake and got ahead of myself. My desire to honor Gene and Joy in this whole process somehow got overlooked in my zeal for the moment. It is so embarrassing and humbling to look back on.

What I learned from this is the quickest way back to strength, healing, and forward progress is to humble yourself and acknowledge your error. Own it 100 percent! Don't blame, complain, or explain. (I did try to explain to Jenise at first.)

If you can, undo it. If you lost something, find it. If you took something, give it back. If you lied, confess and tell the truth.

Apologize. Say you are sorry.

Ask for forgiveness.

Then, ask what it will take to make it right. Gene said, "Get unengaged." So we got "unengaged."

We had to go back up to all our excited and celebratory friends and tell them that we were not engaged but were going to wait for Gene and Joy's blessing before getting engaged.

My love for Jenise was unfazed by this mistake, and, by God's grace, her love for me was unchanged too. I knew we were right for each other, and I had a long-term mindset. I was not worried about six months, a year, or even seven years. I knew I wanted Jenise for a lifetime, and any steps needed to prove that were okay by me.

CHAPTER 34
A GROWN-UP CHALLENGE

The marvelous summer of '92 ended as we loaded our belongings and a treasure chest of memories. We left behind new friends and the beauty of the JH Ranch and Scott Valley and headed south to the hustle of Los Angeles.

Jenise moved back into the Fullerton House with her parents and enrolled at Cal State Fullerton to finish her BA in early childhood development. She wanted to be a teacher. She'd make a perfect homeschool teacher to our many children yet to come, I thought—perhaps out loud.

I went to work at Ceramic Decorating Company, Inc., a screen-printing business in glass packaging that my grandfather, Wilbur Johnson, had started with his brother, Lyman, in 1934, during the Great Depression. My father, Burnell Johnson, his brother Allan, and their cousin Ralph Johnson purchased the business from their fathers.

Growing up, I worked for them on and off during my summers, in between construction jobs, and at the close of the ski season. This time was different—I knew it, my father and uncle knew it, and the team at Ceramic knew it. Chad was here to get serious, to grow up. They decided it'd be best for me to learn the business, department by department.

The business printed labels onto glass bottles for customers like Grey Poupon mustard, Bob's Big Boy salad dressing,

Beringer Estates winery, Fabergé, and Revlon cosmetics. I began in the art department, learning how to create artwork for labels and develop the film used in our screen making.

After two months of the basics, they moved me to screen making. I found it fascinating the first week. Then, after getting the gist of it, I was ready for a new challenge, but my father and uncle insisted I stay longer to ensure my competence. Next, I moved out to the shop floor for color mixing, where I learned the science and art of ceramic colors. Then came small order production and hand machines, followed by large order production and automatic machines.

It didn't take long to realize I loved the people part of the business: communication, teamwork, problem-solving, and conflict management. The mechanical part of the whole process was an exercise in futility and frustration. I didn't impress my father and uncle with my ability to set up a machine, produce high-quality prints, or grind a squeegee with any precision. Whenever I had the chance, speaking with customers really lit me up. Hearing problems, finding solutions, calming anger or frustration, and making a customer's day—I loved connecting!

I did great with all the steady forty- and fifty-hour work-weeks during September, October, and even November. But when December rolled around, the weather turned cold, snow started falling, and the mountains called my name. It hurt even to think about missing a winter season of skiing in the mountains: the nature, the adventure, the camaraderie, and the joy of doing work I love. Yet my love for Jenise compelled me. There was no contest. She won my heart completely, and any sacrifice seemed insignificant in the face of that love.

I told Terry McDonald, the ski patrol director, no when he called me for the third time. "Are you sure, Chad?" he asked. "You'd be 507." He tempted me. Patrol staff members were numbered, starting at 501, which was his number; 502 and 503 were assistant patrol directors; 504–506 were supervisors; and 507–509 were shift leads, which meant you got your pick of the good shifts, made a higher wage, and had more seniority and perks.

"Terry, I've got to win my girl," I told him. "You met her. Jenise. Her father needs to see me step up as a provider, and ski patrolling is not his idea of my bigger future. I want to show him I can stick with something that I'm not passionate about."

"The door is always open, Chad," Terry replied.

Jenise and I spent every evening possible on the phone and at each other's homes. To save money, I moved back into my room above the garage at my parents' home. Our love and physical desire grew each moment we were together. Even though I took full responsibility for the purity of our relationship, we thought it wise to add this accountability of proximity by being so close to our loved ones, where in community, iron would sharpen iron.

It was so fun to plan creative dates, take her out to dinner, and spoil her rotten (as she liked to say). We spent fun evenings with my family, played games, visited in the front room, sang with the family, all of which gave my family a better view of who this amazing woman I loved was. My parents and siblings immediately liked Jenise the moment they first met, and that only continued to grow. Likewise, the Johnstons welcomed me with open arms from the beginning.

I noticed my admiration for her brothers growing, especially as I paid more and more attention to business. They seemed so fearless in the marketplace. They were doers, risk-takers, and entrepreneurs. They made good money and had freedom to involve themselves in other pursuits, be it ministry or other adventures. Being quite a bit younger, I wanted to be like them and learn from them. Gene, too. What a wise, humble, and confident man. Kind, gentle, and quiet. When he spoke, he was always worth listening to, such a great example for me.

I filled my days pouring my heart and energy into eight-, ten-, twelve-hour days of running production at Ceramic

Decorating Company, Inc. in between the daily grind of battling traffic from Hacienda Heights to Commerce in Los Angeles. Jenise was dutifully completing her courses at Cal State Fullerton, and she was only a few credits shy of graduating. I often joked with her about what I wanted her to do with that education.

The days passed quickly with us spending time with her parents, my parents, family time, friend time, but the common denominator was we were together. Our hearts knitted together as one; we were a perfect fit. There was no doubt in our minds. It was a season of normalcy in most ways, yet it was lit by the glow of two hearts aflame. Every task seemed easy, doable, and routine if accompanied by the one who made the world go around, my Jenise. Days became weeks, and weeks became months, and nothing more was mentioned by anyone about the engagement of Chad and Jenise.

I was confident that both Gene and Joy would see in time that I wasn't going anywhere, and my heart was set, my mind fixed, and my goal was clear. Jenise Cheri Johnston would someday become Jenise Cheri Johnson, and the simple thought of it made my heart soar. Jenise and I were growing ever closer. We shared everything but our bodies and living spaces. We were becoming one.

December turned to January, January to February, and just before March, I received an unexpected call.

* * *

CHAD'S REFLECTIONS

Do Hard Things is the title of a book and could make for a good life slogan. Saying no to the "good life" of mountain living, ski patrol, and fun-loving ways of my youth was hard for me.

I didn't like Los Angeles traffic. I didn't like working in a factory. I didn't like being away from the mountains. But I did like the idea of getting married to Jenise. I did like the thought of having a family. I did want to see some of the dreams I had written down come true.

Today, many young people I meet want to live the dream, now! Right now! No delay. No months or years of hard work, just sweet and easy now. Every person I know who has accomplished much, gone far, or seen unusual success in any endeavor, has intentionally gone through seasons of hard.

Hard is hard, but hard is good.

CHAPTER 35
THE CALL

Jenise called the house, and my mother answered the phone. "Chad, it's for you. Guess who?" she asked cheerfully.

"Huh, I have no idea. Let me see," I joked. "Hello, lover girl," I said into the phone.

"Chad, can you come over to the house?" Jenise was always direct and to the point.

"When?"

"Right now."

"Sure. You realize it's almost 9:00 p.m.? It'll be half an hour before I get there. Is everything okay?" Concern began to knot in my stomach.

"Yes, I know. Just come on. Everything is fine."

"I'll be there as quickly as I can. See you soon. Mwah," I said, finishing with a kissing sound. I wondered what was up as I jumped into my 4Runner and pulled away. At the Johnston house, Jenise answered and pulled me inside, giving me a quick peck and a hug. I looked over her shoulder and saw both Gene and Joy sitting on their sofa, looking directly back at me.

"Hello, Gene and Joy." Jenise and I parted. I took a few steps into the living room, but Joy waved me to sit across from them before I could get to them.

"Hello. Have a seat," she said. Jenise and I sat in the two chairs facing them, and Joy, looking as happy as a clam, looked over to Gene and paused. Nobody said anything.

"Well, go ahead, Gene," Joy urged him.

"Chad, Joy and I wanted to have you over . . ." He paused. "We think it's time that you and Jenise get married."

The shock had to have filled my face. *What? Really?* My mind raced. *Amazing! Already?* I had put the whole engagement thing out of my mind and prepared myself for at least a year before I'd hear anything like this from Gene and Joy. To say they'd surprised me was a massive understatement. Only six months had passed. This news was thrilling!

Jenise turned to me excitedly. "Chad, let's get married at the ranch!" She was beaming.

"On the tractor?" I questioned wryly.

"Very funny, Chad." She punched me in the arm.

Joy broke in. "If you want to marry at the ranch, you better get with Bruce right away. The whole summer is booked solid, and I don't know if he'll be able to fit you in."

"Hey, now, everybody needs to slow down just a bit." I laughed. "I haven't even asked Jenise, and you all have the wedding all planned."

"Well, we're waiting," Joy chuckled. "No need to waste time now," Joy spoke directly in her quick quipping way.

I turned to Jenise. "Jenise, can you please leave me alone with your parents for a moment?" I asked.

She nodded. Smiling and standing up, she let go of my hand and left the room.

I turned my attention back to her father. "Gene, I really messed this up the first time, and I want to make sure I do it right this time," I said. "Your daughter is the most amazing woman I've ever met. I love her with all my heart and am confident I always will. I adore her and promise to do my very best to nourish and cherish her all the days of my life."

Looking at him directly in the eye, I continued asking him what I'd failed to ask in proper order six months prior.

"May I marry your daughter, Jenise Cheri, Gene? May I have your blessing to ask for her hand in marriage?"

"Chad, I want you to know that Jenise isn't your average woman. She has a good business head on her; she's so incredibly capable. She could be the president of the United States, run her own company, be a famous singer—she's that kind of woman." I knew the love and pride Gene had for his daughter. He continued, "She could be anything she wants to be, but I do believe she wants to be your wife."

He paused.

I waited.

"Yes, Chad, you may marry Jenise. Joy and I give you our blessing. We do think you're right for each other." And that was it. He said no more.

I stood and approached them both, and, as they stood, I shook Gene's hand and hugged him. Maybe it was only my imagination and optimism, but I felt like he was a little less stiff than the last time I hugged him. Joy too. That was a good feeling. After all, we were going to be family.

Jenise was waiting down the hall where she'd been listening to the whole thing transpire in the living room. She ran to meet me; we were both off the charts giddy. We ran out the front door of the Fullerton house and down the steps to the jacaranda-lined street below where the antique streetlights cast their warm glow on a still and silent neighborhood—silent except for the couple bursting with love.

Holding both of Jenise's hands in mine, I faced her.

"Jenise Cheri, can you believe what just happened, sweet girl? I have permission to ask you to marry me!" I proclaimed.

"Well?" she said with her head tilting sideways, eyebrows slightly raised.

"Oh, no, you don't, Jenise! Don't look at me like that! I'll be asking you in my own sweet time," I said in mock sternness.

"But, Chad, if we're going to—" I put my finger to her lips.

"Shhh . . . I know, if we're reserving the ranch, I need to ask you this very moment, right?" She nodded, all sweet and doe-eyed.

"Well, that's something we'll have to risk because I'm not asking you until I have a ring. I'm doing this thing right. It's important. That said, what are you doing this Friday night? Will you go out with me?" I asked innocently. "Expect nothing, nothing at all, okay?" I laughed again.

"I'd love to go out with you, Chadwick Buford."

I pulled her close, and she rested her head on my chest. I felt her hair on my neck and chin, her smell, and the firmness, yet softness, of her body so close. Oh, how I loved this woman. Though her father just said she could be mine, I felt like she'd been mine for a long time. Honoring her parents by waiting would lay a foundation for a lifetime of love, romance, and adventures in marriage. I'd never been so happy, so content. This was the way life was meant to be—full hearts, a grand future, love overflowing, and divine blessing.

"Someday, Jenise, I won't have to say goodbye," I whispered. "Someday you and I will fall asleep in each other's arms, naked," I said it quietly, but Jenise gasped and shoved me back.

"Go home, young man!" she ordered, jokingly.

"It's true, Jenise Cheri. Just saying, and I'm living for that day. Good night, sweet girl of mine." I pecked her on the lips, then pulled her closer, kissing her warm lips, soft and full. "Yep, I better make like a tree and leave. See you Friday." The words flew over my shoulder as I stepped hastily into my 4Runner and waved to her while welcoming the kisses she blew my way.

As an eternally hopeful romantic, a marriage proposal is a big deal. Planning romantic, creative, fun, and unique dates brings me pure joy. We've experienced so many beautiful meals in creative places with treasure hunts and surprises. I wanted so badly to pull off something wonderful for Jenise. She was worth the sun, moon, and stars! What could I do to bless her, to let her know how much she meant to me?

As I drove home, my thoughts kept me company. Boy, I didn't expect this tonight! "Thank you, Lord," I prayed out loud. "You've blessed my life. You've shown me the woman I get to spend the rest of my life with. She's perfectly perfect for me and everything I've ever wanted in a lover, wife, companion, and friend. She is amazing! Thank you, Lord."

* * *

CHAD'S REFLECTIONS

Patience is a fruit of the spirit. We live in a day of immediate gratification. We want it now—all of it. Things that are worth having taken time. A good relationship is no different.

"How long would you wait?" is a good question to ask yourself.

How long would you wait:

- to meet the right one?

- to have sex if it meant a richer lifetime of sexual intimacy and romance?

- to really get to know your future partner?

- to prove your love and commitment?

- to receive their parents' blessing?

It has been said that true love waits. Actually, it does.

I am completely confident that the awesome sex life Jenise and I have experienced for twenty-seven years has only been enriched and more fully blessed because we waited until after marriage to express ourselves that way.

I am sure that the blessing we received from Jenise's parents by waiting until they thought we were ready for marriage has contributed greatly to the well-being of our marriage and the massive family support we have enjoyed.

CHAPTER 36
THE GREATEST SHOW

The next few days flew by as ideas for our engagement popped in and out of my mind. No, that won't work. Maybe this one? No. A personal flight to Catalina Island fell through. Chartering a boat in Newport Harbor was a no; the weather was too bad. Time was running out, and work was brutal that week.

After work on Wednesday, I went to the jewelry district in downtown LA where there were several blocks of buildings selling jewelry of every kind. Jenise and I had perused jewelry stores on our dates, and I knew what I wanted. Our tastes, like our souls, matched. I navigated my way unsuccessfully through the crowds inside this shopping circus. As I was about to leave one building for the next, a man waved me down.

"Here, look at this one, sir!" He held up a ring, and curiosity drew me in.

The one he presented was nothing like what I wanted but looking down in the display case full of wedding rings, there it was—the exact ring I wanted that I knew Jenise would love! I tried to play it cool. Had I given myself away? Did he know how badly I wanted it? He wanted $12,500. My jaw hit the floor.

"What? $12,000?" I asked.

"No, $12,500," he answered.

"I'll give you $3,000," I said flatly.

The number $12,500 bounced around my head. That's like six months of take-home pay as a ski patroller. It's not that Jenise wasn't worth it, but I wanted to have a little in-pocket to invest in a memorable honeymoon. I knew Jenise was okay with us starting small and growing financially; otherwise, she would have latched onto one of the many rich dudes that came her way. That wasn't her priority. She wanted to begin the journey from scratch with me. It sounded romantic, but I had no idea how difficult it would be.

The man behind the counter jarred me back to reality with his response. "You're crazy, man, no way. I'll give you a special price, best price, how about $9,500?" We bantered back and forth, getting down to $6,800. It was still not low enough, so I walked. "This ring worth $25,000. I already gave you best deal. Don't go!"

As I left the building, he called after me like a drowning man wanting a rope. I pretended not to care, even though that was the ring I wanted. I went down the street and got a Philly cheesesteak sandwich. I decided to go back one last time and offer $5k. I wanted to spend no more than $5,500. I knew I was close.

He lit up like a Christmas tree when I walked back into the building. I pretended not to notice him, walking right by his booth toward the other end of the building like I was on a mission. He almost leaped over the counter to stop me. I kept on going, his voice calling after me. "Sir, I can do better, just a little. I can do better," he said, his voice trailing off.

I looked back over my shoulder and nodded at him, possibly rolling my eyes just a little, registering that I heard, but left the other side of the building and waited outside for almost ten minutes. Finally, I entered the door and walked briskly toward him.

"So you want to do better? How much?" I asked.

"$6,000 is my very best deal! Such good deal." He had the ring out and was presenting it to me.

I didn't take it from him but answered, "$5,000," for what seemed like the twentieth time.

"No." His hand went to his forehead as he rocked back on his heels, grimacing as if in pain. "No, no, no! I can't do that." He moaned.

"Okay, you wasted my time," I said and turned to go.

"$5,500."

I turned. "You have a deal." I was running out of time, and he hit my number.

His hand felt cool and clammy as we shook hands. He told me he'd mount the diamond I'd selected earlier. He picked up the diamond, which I confirmed to be the correct one by looking through the scope and identifying the single minor flaw. He began to turn toward the back where a door was ajar leading to the back room.

I interrupted him. "Please mount the diamond here, at this table," I told him. "I'd like to watch. I've never seen how it is done."

He paused, then continued walking to the back of the booth space. "My tools are here," he replied as he sat down at a small workstation located well out of my line of sight. His head and shoulders were visible, but his body and the upright wooden part of the workstation concealed his hands and motions. I wondered what was going on. My gut didn't trust this guy. Everything seemed slimy. After a minute or two, he stood and walked to a buffing wheel and shined the ring until polished. He took a small black velvet box and prepared to place the ring into it.

"May I see the ring, please?" I asked.

"Uh, oh sure, beautiful ring, she'll love it," he assured me as he held out the ring. I held it up close to my eyes. I immediately noticed the center diamond, the big one, appeared yellowish and not nearly as clear, white, and bright as the one

I selected. I mentioned this to the man, who was eyeing me carefully. "Oh, yes, that's very normal," he explained. "The gold color from the ring reflects in the diamond. What a beautiful ring! She'll love this!" He raised the volume of voice as if to be convincing to himself as well as me.

"May I please see the scope?" I asked, looking him in the eye.

"Oh sure," he answered, turning to the counter in front of me, where the scope had been. It was gone! He looked all over the counter, and then down on the floor, appearing to be searching earnestly. "I'm so sorry, but it's gone." He shrugged his shoulders as if to say, *What's a man to do?*

I was starting to get upset. This whole dog and pony show was beginning to feel like a house of scams. "No problem," I said, turning to the booth to the right. I asked the woman behind the counter if I could borrow her scope. She nodded, said nothing, and handed me the small silver object with a magnifying glass. I held it up close to the light and peered through the scope.

"You have got to be kidding me!" my words exploded out unchecked. "You're a total scam artist!" My head came up, and my gaze fixed on Mr. Jewelry Scam Man. "You switched my diamond. This thing is a piece of junk! Yellow, four major flaws. So glad I paid you nothing! Where is my diamond?" My voice had risen above the usual noise level of the space, and I realized that all eyes in the room fixated on Mr. Scam Man and me.

He realized this too and began to apologize profusely. "So sorry. I must have accidentally picked up the wrong one. Let me see." He took the ring from me and stepped behind his work counter. His scope suddenly appeared in his hand, and he looked through the lens intensely at the ring. "Oh, my," he exclaimed. "I made a mistake. This isn't the right diamond."

"No, duh!" I shot back at him. "Remove that piece of junk diamond and show me the diamond I picked out. Once

I confirm it's the correct stone, you'll mount it right here in front of me." My intensity surprised me. I'm not usually a bossy dude, but I was irate. What a snake!

He rummaged around his workstation, and after several moments of moving things around, he looked up, "I don't know where the other diamond went."

"Most likely it got lost like the scope did when we needed it," I said sharply. "Find it, or I march to the nearest payphone to dial the police!" I was sick of his shenanigans but wasn't about to start over. I realized he had intended to scam me the entire time. The reason he went so low on price was he never planned on letting me go with the good diamond. "I'll help you look," I offered and threw my leg up on top of the counter. By now, I was causing quite a scene, and he seemed very uncomfortable with all the attention attracted by my antics.

He stepped around his workstation and almost ran toward me with both hands out in front of him. "No, no, you stay there. I'll find it. It must be here somewhere," he said, his voice weakening. Sure enough, moments later, he held up a diamond and brought it to me. "Is this the one?" he asked.

"You tell me, you're the expert," I retorted. I held it up to the light once more. It was the right diamond. "Yes. Now, I'll hold it while you get your tools and bring them to me. We can mount it right here, right now." He nodded, went to the bench, and came back quickly. After confirming once more, prior to mounting, and again after mounting, I counted out the fifty-five one-hundred-dollar bills. I left feeling like I was carrying all I owned in the world in a little two-inch felt box.

Driving home, I felt drained. I'd never had the purchase of something be so taxing. The thought of Jenise and how delighted she'd be, how beautiful this ring would look on her graceful hand, and its significance made me smile. It was worth it all for Jenise, so worth it. Next, the proposal.

I booked the finest table in the house at The Candlelight Pavilion Dinner Theater, which I'd been to once before when I was young. At that time, *Oklahoma!* was showing, and my father took our entire family. Now, *The Sound of Music* was in lights. Jenise looked stunning, dressed in her favorite classic cut dress and sparkling diamond earrings with her hair pulled up, which allowed her face to radiate her beauty. During intermission, I asked her to walk outside with me. I felt so proud to have her on my arm as we passed by tables to the exit.

White twinkling lights lined the path leading to an arched bridge overlooking a charming pond. The lights reflected and played on the water. As we reached the bridge's crest, I got to one knee, pulled the ring out of my pocket, and said the words I'd been longing to say for so many months. "Jenise, my love, will you marry me?"

"Yes!" she cried, bending her face down to mine, kissing me sweetly. "Yes! Yes! Yes!" she exclaimed, holding my face with both hands.

I slipped the ring on her finger. "By the way, Jenise, I did ask your father this time." We both laughed. "I told you I'm a learner and a grower." Our warm embrace became a dance as we moved with the music playing softly through the speakers somewhere nearby.

I'd found her. Proverbs 18:22 says: "Whoso findeth a wife findeth a good thing, and obtaineth the favour of the Lord." Boy, did I feel favored. My heart was full. It was so right. Everything about this woman was right for me.

Once we were inside, people cheered and clapped. Someone had seen me on my knee outside and spread the news. Our waiter brought us a special dessert drizzled in chocolate that spelled "Congratulations!" Snuggled in our booth, we enjoyed the rest of the show, but most of all, I enjoyed seeing Jenise's eyes constantly returning to her left hand and the sparkling reminder that we'd soon be together, forever.

* * *

CHAD'S REFLECTIONS

After my first failed attempt at a proposal on the tractor at the ranch, I really wanted to dream up and execute a proposal to beat all proposals.

In my mind leading up to our engagement, I had envisioned picking her up at a local park in a helicopter, flying to the roof of a fine dining place in downtown Los Angeles, all the while a special love song I had written just for her was being sung by the live band while we ate in candlelight bliss. A Porsche 911 would be waiting at the curb when we were done. You'd find us driving down the PCH with the top down, enjoying the balmy air. Jenise would see the billboard towering overhead that read: "I can't get you out of my mind, Jenise. Love, Chad."

We'd pull into a scenic overlook around Pacific Palisades and stand on a rocky bluff looking out over the ocean, holding each other close. I would walk her a little farther down the path. She would cry out again, pointing to the rocks so neatly laid out, spelling the words: "Will you marry me, Jenise?"

She would then turn, and I would be on my knee with my hand holding out the ring, asking her the words again.

The sun would be setting behind us as we basked in the glow of our glorious future together.

It is good to have dreams. Ideals. Many of them will even come true.

What about the ones that don't?

When it came time for me to ask Jenise, I was tired from working long hours and felt pressure to ask right away so we could lock in the date at the ranch. So my vision of some incredibly crafted, unique, and highly orchestrated proposal did not happen. Guess what? That isn't what marriage is all about. We got engaged. She said yes. It was sweet and meaningful. Sometimes, letting go of perfection allows you to proceed.

CHAPTER 37
WE NEED TO STOP

Couples spend gazillions of dollars as they plan ceremonies, celebrations, and parties to mark the glorious milestone in their lives. According to Scripture, this grand event is the making of a covenant, which is more than a contract—it's a lifelong commitment to love, cherish, nourish, and respect each other. Couples submit to each other and the Lord, modeling Christ's love for the church. It's powerful.

Jenise and Jilinda led the way. I answered questions: How many groomsmen, bridesmaids, candles? No candles? Outside? Under the Big Top? Bruce gave us the okay for the ranch wedding. The date was set—August 15, 1993. Friends and family could come early to enjoy the fun activities at JH Ranch. Destination weddings weren't yet a thing. We were both raised and lived near LA, where most of our friends and family lived.

Many thought we were crazy for trying to pull off this twelve-hour drive north of LA. We weren't sure how many would make the trip. We selected twelve groomsmen and twelve bridesmaids to ensure at least a modest crowd, thinking that with our large families and the JH Ranch staff, we'd for certain not be standing alone in the woods getting married. Okay, that's a slight exaggeration, but we were a bit concerned.

The weeks and months between our engagement on March 12 and our wedding day on August 15 crawled by slowly. Prior to receiving the go-ahead from Gene and Joy, I seemed able to endure our nightly goodbyes. Though difficult, they were bearable. Once we had the green light, that changed, and I was ready to get married now—right now!

"Jenise, let's elope," I begged one evening. "Let's get married now! Four and a half months is forever!" Never for a moment did I mean it. I had waited almost twenty-three years at that point in my life and laying a foundation for a great married life was a consistent theme and dream. There were a few things, if any, I wanted more. I knew this time of planning, waiting, and preparing was important, but don't get me wrong—I'm a huge fan of short engagements.

My parents' teaching bears repeating. Date for as long as you need to confirm he or she is the right one, and only date if you believe this person is a potential spouse and at a point that he or she is ready for marriage. As soon as you realize they aren't, call it off—no matter how much you like, respect, or think it'd be fun to date him or her.

Our romance continued filling the air throughout the summer. Wedding talk was all the talk: plans, ideas, buying, showers, excitement, and joy. Jenise continued her schooling while my work at Ceramic was going well. The love and passion we shared grew while our boundaries on physical affection became more challenging to maintain. I'd never received instruction on the power of a kiss, but, boy, its powers had me! Jenise and I vowed to each other that we'd remain pure and virgins until our wedding day. This included no inappropriate touching, petting, or anything we'd regret. It was extremely difficult.

After a day of wedding errands and dinner one evening, Jenise and I pulled up in front of my parents' home. I parked the 4Runner near the curb and turned toward Jenise. She was sitting there just being her, and I was just being me, smitten.

"You're so amazing, Jenise," I whispered.

"Really," she said coyly, her eyes teasing.

"Come here," I said, leaning toward her. Our lips met, and nothing further needed to be said. Every part of me electrified, and all energy ignited where our lips touched—passion surging, rushing, and roaring. I felt a hunger for this love of mine that knew no bounds and laughed at containment. She drew me in with a hunger all her own, making my entire world spin. I felt myself losing control. I wanted her, all of her, now, not later, not on our honeymoon, but something held me in check.

I wanted something more—her respect and her trust. I wanted to walk down the aisle to a waiting virgin. I wanted a foundation that would make forever better and stronger. I wanted to share our story with our children and not have to skip parts or pretend parts didn't happen. I wanted to encourage my sons one day that it was possible to see God's strength and receive it. I wanted to tell my daughters about their mother and how she kept herself in honor, in purity. Pushing myself away, Jenise looked into my eyes, and she knew.

"We need to stop, huh?" she whispered.

"Yes, we do," I whispered back, breathless. Whew! Exhaling deeply, I leaned back into the driver's seat, threw my head back, and looked at the ceiling of the 4Runner. "Yes, we do, Jenise Cheri. You're way too much. Someday soon, I'm getting you, all of you, and there'll be no stopping me, my lady," I said with a laugh. "But right now, I must remove myself from this car and put myself to bed before—" My words fell off. I opened the car door and stepped out, closing it after me. Coming around to her door as I always did, I opened it for her.

"Before what?" Jenise said coyly.

"Before, well, uh, I . . . before we fall far short of what we aspire to be. We have way too much to look forward to. I've waited far too long to take a shortcut. I want so much for our marriage, Jenise. So much! I want it to be beautiful, long-lasting, rich, real, romantic, and built on God's richest blessings.

I wrapped my arms around her, and with her nose touching my nose, we stood on the curb with her back against the vehicle. I kissed her again and instantly tore myself away. "I can't kiss you, my love. I just can't! It's overwhelming! I need to take a break completely! You slay me, girl," I groaned.

"But, Chad, we can kiss a little here and there. We can handle it. I know we can," Jenise countered.

"You may be able to, Jenise, but I can't. So, for my sake, we need to stop. Maybe just for a while, but we still have two months until we marry. Two months! That's forever. Let's not kiss for the next four weeks. Then, we can see what we think is best at that time," I suggested. "Want to kiss on it?" I teased. My smile widened. "Just kidding!"

She reached out her hand and shook mine. "Deal," she said thoughtfully. We turned and walked up the steps and across the pathway that led across the lawn to the front door of my parents' house. Jenise turned and stopped me. "Chad," she said, looking straight into my eyes, "Thank you."

"For what?"

"For wanting what's best for us, for loving me enough to wait for me. For leading our relationship in a way that honors the Lord. That means so much to me."

I pulled her close, hugging her with her head resting on my shoulder. Her hair felt so soft and feminine near my face. "I love you so much, Jenise. Nothing but the best for us. I truly want the best."

A couple of days later, while in LA to pick out flower arrangements, we took time for lunch at a street café. Jenise reviewed fun details she'd been putting together for the big day. She pulled out several sheets of paper. "What's this?" I asked.

"A love song written by Rick. He wants us to sing it to each other at our wedding." Yikes! Jenise is a singer. Me? Well, I like to say I have a beautiful voice. I tear it up, getting it out. Rick is a true composer, and he'd written this love song just for us and our day.

"Jenise, I don't want to ruin his song, or the wedding, or our lives, or . . ."

She laughed. "It'll be sweet," she said.

"Or sour," I muttered dryly.

Changing the subject, she asked, "Did you know I have fifty white doves that'll be released during the ceremony and a horse-drawn carriage to take us away? Your cousin, Lynette, has agreed to sing "Can I Have This Dance?" and Dick Johnson will play the guitar and harmonize with her."

"Maybe Dick and Lynette would want to sing Rick's song," I suggested. "That'd be sweet." I raised my eyebrows.

"You really don't want to sing, Chad?" She looked dispirited.

"I just don't want to mess it up, Jenise. You have such a beautiful voice, and I want everything to be perfect. My voice is a singing-in-the-shower kind of voice, but if you want me to, I'll do it."

"Let's do it!" Jenise stated firmly. "It'll be great as long as it's from the heart."

"If it were from the heart, I'd be great!" I laughed. "Unfortunately, it needs to come through my mouth."

"Stop it! You don't sound that bad!" she consoled. Then I knew just how bad it sounded, for she could have said, "You sound great, or good," or something like that, but she didn't. Oh, dear.

Changing the topic in my mind, I thought about how August at JH Ranch was spectacular, making it a perfect time and place for an outdoor wedding. Hot days and warm balmy evenings, cooling off nicely into the night. It was such a beautiful time and place. Details, one by one, fell into place.

Jenise broke the silence by saying, "You realize we only have two-and-a-half weeks to go?"

Wow! The time had truly flown by. The past several weeks, I'd been doing a cleansing fast for my health, as I'd been struggling with my energy levels. My all-you-can-eat 100 percent vegetable diet helped me lose over fifteen pounds and a couple of inches around my waist. "I need to fatten you up before the wedding," Jenise joked. "Here, eat the rest of my salad." She pushed two small pieces of lettuce on her empty plate toward me.

"Why, thank you, I shall try to get it all down. Are you saying you don't like me skinny?" I inquired.

"I like you any way you are, Chadwick Buford. Can you believe I'll be your wife? That sounds so amazing! Chad's wife. I will be Chad Allan Johnson's wife! Can you believe this? We're really getting married. This is it! How crazy is that? Married. Like husband and wife—"

"Like sex," I said, grinning, interrupting her.

"Stop that, bad boy." She slapped my hand that was resting on the table. "But you're right, that too. Are you ready for all this?"

"You kidding me? I've been waiting my entire life to find you, convince, coerce, and beg you, and finally get you to marry me. Yes, I'm ready for all of this! I'm past ready for all this. Now, I think the question is, are *you* ready for all this?" I laughed. I opened my arms wide and pointed my fingers back toward my chest.

"You don't have any reservations, concerns, or fears about getting married?" she asked seriously. She wanted to see my conviction, and it was easy to share.

"Jenise, I'm 100 percent convinced that you're the only one in the world for me, that God, in His perfect way and time, has destined us to be together, forever. He made you for me, and He made me for you. There's zero doubt in my mind. I've not had one moment of hesitation, fear, worry, or concern since the moment God showed me at the John Wayne Airport that you were indeed the one. You remember, the time—"

She interrupted, "Yes, I do. When you were seeing me off and started crying because God showed you I was the one."

I looked into her hazel eyes. "What about you, Jenise Cheri? Are you sure? Do you have any doubts or fears?"

She looked down.

"What is it? Talk to me, Jenise. You can't honestly have doubts about whether we're to be together. Can you?" My voice revealed my concern.

"I know we're meant to be together," she whispered, then paused.

"Yes?" I urged her on.

"I hope you never grow tired of me." A tear spilled down her cheek.

"Come here, my love." I took her face in my hands and held her close. "Whatever do you mean by that?" I asked, looking deeply into her eyes.

"Oh, I don't know," she searched for the right words, with a sniffle. "I don't want you to get bored or tired of me . . ." she said as her voice trailed off.

"Jenise, I don't know where that comes from, but I can assure you this. I will never, ever, get tired of you. You're going to take a lifetime to know, figure out, discover, unwrap, experience, love, cherish, nourish, and when I get done with that, it'll be about time to start over again. You have nothing to fear, my bride. Forever won't be long enough to get my fill of you."

Sweet, lazy tears rolled down her cheeks, and I kissed them one by one as they spilled. Moments like this could only be more precious if they lasted so much longer than they do. Jenise always seems so tender, lovely, precious, and dear when she's crying. Her tears seemed tears of gratitude and joy, not pain or sorrow.

My lips met hers, and her eyes opened wide. She pulled back with a gasp. "I thought you said we shouldn't kiss!" she exclaimed.

"I did, and that was almost six weeks ago. If we'll be married in two weeks, and we will be, I believe a little kissing might be in order because kissing seems a little tame compared to—"

"Chadwick Buford, you can stop right there!" She gave me the cutest little tough girl stare that melted into a warm and generous smile. Her eyes lit up the whole area where we sat.

"Let's be wise and careful, but a peck or two over the next two weeks is something I believe we both can handle. God has us," I assured her.

We left twelve dollars to cover the salads and tip. Holding hands, we made our way to the car. The drive home found me looking over at Jenise, thinking of the joy of being with her. What a wonderful day this had been, doing errands, visiting, talking of the future—nothing big, fancy, or dramatic, but doing life together. I couldn't wait to get used to this.

As I dropped her off at her parents' home on Brookdale Place that evening, we talked quietly about how we'd only have a few more nights, and we'd never have to say goodnight and part ways again. Our wedding day was fast approaching, a day that'd change all other days. It'd be a day that would unite us in holy matrimony, a covenant before God and other witnesses, a new way of life, of two becoming one. We'd become a family, the beginning of a new generation of witnesses to God's glory. Yes, our wedding day was fast approaching.

* * *

CHAD'S REFLECTIONS

This chapter is loaded with things I would love to talk to every single young man and every single young lady about. Sex before marriage doesn't make for a great marriage.

Dating just to date and have fun doesn't make for a great marriage. I often ask couples who have been dating for several years if he or she is the one. They surprise me by saying they don't know. It should not take years to figure out if someone is right for you to marry.

I advise the following: Date only people you believe have strong marriage potential. Date intentionally. Ask the hard questions earlier in the relationship. Have a list of make-or-breaks or non-negotiables. Date as long as it takes to determine whether they are the right one for you (or not).

Treat each other as if you are someone else's spouse. Treat each other in such a way that you have no regrets and in such a way that you will feel free to share your full story with your children someday.

Keep the Lord first in your personal lives, and let Him draw you together in wisdom.

Guys, you are 100 percent responsible for the purity of your relationship.

Ladies, so are you. Give yourself the blessing of a foundation of purity and respect.

If you have fallen short of what God's standard is in this area, God has total and complete forgiveness and restoration if true repentance is yours.

All marriages are made up of imperfect people. We all need grace and forgiveness.

There is no promise of not getting hurt in dating. It is the risk we take in loving another.

My heart's desire is to see more and more young couples start their marriage in the beauty of purity with passion. The blessing of the Lord is awesome!

CHAPTER 38
OUR BIG DAY

The rain beating on the roof of my small cabin woke me with a start. No! Rain? Today of all days? Surely not. It's summer in California, and it doesn't rain in August! The sound of steady falling rain pulled me up and to the window of The Oaks cabin, which sat so grandly by the edge of French Creek on the JH Ranch. I had my own cabin the night before our wedding, and looking out the window, I found gray, dull, and rainy weather staring right back at me.

The phone rang. It was Jenise. "Chad," her voice sounded stressed and slightly panicked. "What are we going to do? It's raining!"

"I know it is, and I know what we're going to do," I said confidently. "We're going to get married! Today is the day, Jenise Cheri! We're waterproof, and no matter what, by the end of today, you and I are going to be husband and wife!"

"But it's supposed to be outside . . ." Worry plagued her voice.

"Jenise, please be at complete rest. Have a fantastic morning with your bridesmaids and leave the details to me. I'll make sure everything is alright. We may need to improvise and have it under the canopy tent area where we eat instead of out on the grassy knoll. I'll head up there right now and get with Bruce, but please don't think another thing about it. It'll be a beautiful wedding. The rain will only make this day more memorable, okay, Honey? Will you let me take care of it?" I asked.

"I love you, Chad." The fear in her voice retreated. She sounded soft and warm, so much calmer.

"Jenise, today will be everything we imagined—our big day. I can't wait to be yours. Enjoy your day, sweet girl, and miss me. Next time I see you, you'll be in white, walking down the aisle to me. Speaking of, I better get going!"

"Hugs and kisses, Chadwick Buford. *Mwah, mwah!*" She kissed me through the phone.

"And a whole lot more tonight, Jenise." I laughed. "Bye!"

A brief meeting with Bruce and we had all the solutions we needed. "Let's get staff and groomsmen to move all the chairs and arbor under the canopy. We'll have the wedding ceremony under there," he pointed out. The rain showed no signs of stopping, and the forecast called for rain through the night and into Sunday.

Many hands made light work, and in no time the transition was complete. As young men do, we all engaged in a show of strength with how many chairs we could carry. The banter and jokes created a jovial and light mood.

Towels suddenly appeared, drying the 250 chairs, while a crew squeegeed the cement area under the canopy. The rain had flooded the space, including what would be my bride's walkway. Someone suggested we place some folding tables down with legs unfolded, which would create a three-inch-high raised platform from the lodge to where the ceremony was taking place. We covered the tables with white cloth, illuminating the path my bride and her procession would walk down.

The crew strung beautiful large ferns from the canopy along the edges at twelve-foot intervals. We transported the arched trellis to the backdrop for our ceremony on the grassy knoll to the canopy. Before I knew it, David, my brother and best man, tapped me on the shoulder. "Hey, dude, you better get going. We have pictures in less than forty-five minutes."

"How long do you think it takes me to get ready?" I gave him a sly grin.

"I don't know," he responded. "I never saw you get ready for a wedding before. Can you believe this, Chad? You're getting married! This is crazy! You sure you're ready for this?"

"You kidding me?" I shot back. "I've been ready for this since I was twelve years old! It just took me this long to find Jenise and convince her father to let me marry her."

David and I had shared a room our entire life, even after moving out on our own and often working for the same employers. I loved our relationship and knew life would be different going forward—we were tied at the hip. I figured it must be harder for him since I was the one leaving, getting married, and moving on with a new best friend. He and Jodi were dating again. It was only a matter of time before they, too, walked down the aisle.

The canopy guys got dressed in a flash and went to meet our photographer. Allan, the JH Ranch videographer and photographer and a professional wedding photographer away from the ranch, was ready to work his magic. "I just finished getting Jenise and all the ladies' photos done," he said as I approached him. "Jenise looks amazing! But you already knew that." He chuckled. Allan was a true romantic and had taken many pictures of Jenise and me during our summer at the ranch. He was such fun; it was a no-brainer to have him take our wedding photos.

We selected a longtime friend of the Johnstons, a pastor named Bill Birch from Scott Valley, to perform our ceremony. He was also Jenise's tennis coach while growing up. He reminded me a lot of a mentor of mine, Dwight Thompson, in his manly, athletic build, his zest for life, and his love for the Lord and people. We met several times before the wedding day to prepare, learn, and share our desires for our wedding. Today, he and I met briefly before the ceremony.

"You excited, Chad?" he asked, a grin spreading across his face. He shook my hand, then placed his arm around my shoulders. "You sure have done well," he went on. "I can think of no finer woman than the one you're marrying today. She's one of a kind, a truly godly young lady."

"I know. It's still kind of surreal. I've adored her since the moment I met her. To think she'll become my wife today . . ." I felt my eyes filling, and a tear spilled down my cheek. I brushed it away with my hand. "I pray that the Lord will make me a worthy husband for her. I want to bless her and enjoy a marriage full of blessed richness, real relationship, passionate intimacy, authentic friendship, and pure joy. I want a joyful marriage we both can delight in, one that brings glory to God and blesses others. I want our marriage to encourage and inspire others in marriage." My voice trailed off as my emotions welled my eyes even more.

"Let's pray, Chad." With his arm still around my shoulders, Bill began to pray. When he finished, I prayed too.

"Lord, wow! Today is the day! I thought this day would never come, but here it is. Lord, thank you for putting all of this together, for bringing Jenise into my life, for allowing her to see past so many of my shortcomings and find the good. Thank you for drawing our hearts together in such a powerful and sweet way. Pour out your blessing, Lord. Give me the wisdom to be the husband you've called me to be, to lead in love, and to nourish and cherish Jenise. Lord, today, may you be glorified and honored in this wonderful celebration. In Jesus' name, Amen."

Bill gave me a strong hug. "Take a deep breath, Chad, and enjoy your day." He smiled and patted me on the back as we parted.

Walking back up toward the lodge as the time was getting close, I met my father and mother. Both hugged me tight.

What a precious gift—the unconditional love of parents, the parents who raised me, poured their love into me, and modeled for me what marriage was meant to be. I was the most blessed man on earth. Nobody, it seemed to me, had parents as amazing as mine. Maybe everybody feels this way. All I know is my heart overflowed with gratitude as we shared that moment. *Lord, let me have a marriage like Daddy and Mama's, and let me love my children the way my parents have loved me.* I knew of no higher standard or better way.

The excitement and energy were palpable as friends and family piled into the ranch and up to the lodge area. Many had stayed in cabins and enjoyed the fun activities of the ranch the day before. All dressed in their finest, they signed the guest book and were ushered to their seats under the green-and-white-striped canopy.

The audience, now seated, watched as music lured the bridesmaids down the aisle. The rain slowed, and our witnesses smiled in awe as Jenise came through the door of the lodge and stood there with her father. As the wedding march signaled Jenise to begin her procession, the rain stopped, to all of our surprises, and the sun burst through the sky in radiant glory! It was as if God Almighty were smiling brightly at this very moment and joyfully celebrating with us.

My heart was bursting in the glory of my love for Jenise, bursting with joy, with gratitude, and with every good thing a heart can burst from! I couldn't contain it all, and tears flowed freely down my cheeks as my eyes tried to take in all the wonder of the woman who, adorned in white, was gracefully gliding down the aisle toward me.

Surely music was playing, and surely people were present, but the entire world slowed to a blissful, dreamlike pace. The radiant Jenise Cheri Johnston, with her long, slender arm draped through her father's arm, gracefully walked down the long, white tapestry. That smile began mesmerizing me on April 13, 1991, twenty-six months earlier at another wedding, where it all began. The realization of all that God orchestrated in answering my prayers for a woman who seemed far too good to be true or real—and yet was in living color, right here, right now—was warming me with the light of her lovely countenance and ever closer proximity.

"Who gives this woman to be married to this man?" Those words jolted me out of my grinning trance.

"Her mother and I do," Gene said, as he shook my hand and placed Jenise's hand in mine.

I don't know why I was crying, but I was. My heart almost hurt with happiness, I was so full of joy and so overwhelmed. Pastor Bill immediately put the crowd at ease with his warm humor and a sincere zeal for marriage that came through as he spoke. He told us to turn and face the audience to see the loved ones, family, and friends who'd come so far to witness our vows and celebrate what the Lord had done in bringing us together. It was a delight to scan the crowd seated under that green-and-white-striped canopy.

The sun rays warmed the area, and the smiles and eager expressions of the faces of so many family members and friends created pure joy. The energy of the moment was palpable. It was energy you could sense or feel, almost as if people were buzzing. Bill commented, and everyone laughed out loud as if they needed to release their bursting happiness too. I looked over at Jenise, and she was beaming. My radiant, glorious bride was pure, lovely, graceful—all I imagined her to be on this day.

We heard God's Word, and the foundations of marriage were made clear by God's beautiful plan laid out for us so long ago—the simplicity of His design and His purpose in making two one—His desire for fruitfulness and blessing, the differing roles of a husband and wife, the synergy obtained by one plus one becoming much more than two, the mystery of Christ and His bride, and the role marriage plays in proclaiming the wonder and glory of the Gospel.

Jenise and I stood in rapt attention, although we knew these things and had seen the blessing of these truths born out in our parents' lives. I'd witnessed the testimony through five generations of my parents and grandparents walking these things out in powerful life-giving ways. I saw first-generation believers grasp these truths and had observed the marriage and family transformation that comes from the Holy Spirit of the living God working in and through a marriage surrendered to Him.

Bill spoke of the marriage covenant made before God and how it differed from a contract or government document. All these truths meant even more to us as the bride and groom, rather than as witnesses to matrimony, as they were spoken profoundly and directly to us.

We shared our wedding vows, which we'd written beforehand, in solemn awareness of the significance of what we were committing to. Yet we were full of joy with the realization of the lifelong relationship and the blessings our vows would bring.

Grasping her hand, I slid her ring gently into place on her slender finger at the direction of Bill. She returned the giving, doing the same with my ring.

We turned and lit the unity candle—the symbolism simple, yet powerful, in two becoming one.

I turned and found David handing me a microphone. "Good luck, George Strait," he whispered, smiling.

Our special song, "All I Need Is Your Love," written and composed by Jenise's brother, Rick, with full background music began to play:

Was it the sparkle in her eyes, or the sunshine of her smile,
that brought a love I never knew, attracting me to you,

We'll join in marriage,

Spellbound attraction, I can't believe my dreams came true.

With God above, we'll make our house a home,

Visions of spending my life with you, are just about to pass and come true.

Yes, come true.

Chorus: All I need is your love, your lasting love. Your love, your lasting love.

Jenise asked me to sing, and boy, did I sing—straight from the heart, and I meant every word. My eyes locked on hers, and Jenise, with her lovely rich voice, carried me. Our harmonies rang true, and my solo part left everyone eager for Jenise's voice to return. The rich emotion of the moment seemed to elicit the audience's forgiveness, for which I was grateful.

Pastor Bill, smiling ear to ear, proclaimed, "I now pronounce you husband and wife. Chad, you may kiss your bride!"

The sounds of those simple words washed over me. Husband and wife! We were married! And kiss, we did!

With matching smiles, matching hearts, and matching souls, already one, we turned, hand in hand, and marched triumphantly into our glorious future, together at last.

* * *

CHAD'S REFLECTIONS

Weddings today are a big deal. I get it. Love, romance, ceremony, and celebration all make for a fantastic party, and rightly so.

We spend small fortunes on pulling these events off, and months and years planning.

A book title that I love, *After Every Wedding Comes a Marriage*, speaks to the fact that great weddings are not the goal. Great marriages are.

Sadly, over 50 percent of marriages end up in divorce. Of the 50 percent that stay together, I think it would be shocking if we knew how few are actually great. Marriages that are rich in love, really united in oneness, romantic fun, and life giving, are a true blessing.

Houses fall down if they don't have a good foundation. Marriages too.

I would love to see Christian couples spend far more attention on dating well, laying a strong foundation for the married years to come.

Oh, that every young couple would desire such an awesome marriage that they would be willing to delay gratification, invest the time and energy needed, date with clarity and intentionality, seek godly wisdom and counsel, and realize their vision.

SIMPLE GUIDELINES FOR
INTENTIONAL DATING

This **BONUS** ebook will equip you to navigate your adventurous journey of finding and building a love that glorifies God and delights you for a lifetime.

Free at
HowToWinAHeart.com/Bonus

The
Newlywed
Workshop

**The perfect wedding doesn't guarantee
an awesome marriage.**

The ceremony is over and you want to build a healthy,
long-lasting marriage. What's your first step?

Join us at our next Newlywed Workshop!

Chad and Jenise share how to prepare for the inevitable
challenges coming your way. You will leave equipped to ...

- ♥ Use a biblical blueprint for marriage.
- ♥ Navigate your new roles.
- ♥ Work through communication issues.
- ♥ Manage marital finances.
- ♥ Stay on the same page of intimacy.
- ♥ Implement a lifetime commitment.
- ♥ Build a strong foundation for your marriage.
- ♥ Tap into precious opportunities to grow deeper together.

Give as the Ultimate Gift for a Newlywed Couple you love.

For more information, visit
NewlywedCoaching.com

Are you the man you really want to be?

Young men ages 15–25 face many challenges today, including apathy, addiction, ease and comfort, lack of vision and ambition, and a devastating lack of purpose and meaning.

Achademy Boot Camp is an adventure-based, content-driven, life-transforming weekend event designed to help young men . . .

- » Break free from addiction.
- » Learn to lead others by learning to lead themselves first.
- » Begin the process of discovering their God-given talents and unique abilities that will enable them to create great value for others.
- » Learn and use tools, concepts, mindsets, and new language to aid them on their journey to live inspired and passionate lives.

Created and led by successful men, Achademy Boot Camp will equip you to be the man you want to become.

For more information, visit
TheAchademy.com

Create a plan that makes your good marriage *great*!

Marriage
MAXIMIZER

Designed for dynamic entrepreneurs, executives, and leaders, this two-day strategic getaway is a unique opportunity that allows you and your spouse to invest in your marriage and family.

As a successful couple, you need time to refocus and align your priorities of marriage and family so your business success does not crowd out your dreams for a future you will both love.

Your coaches Chad and Jenise Johnson will guide you and other like-minded couples to:

» Determine your Giant 5 Priorities-to ensure great teamwork and unity.
» Create, clarify, and commit to your next year's vision as a couple and as a family.
» Plan quality time as a couple in advance and stick to it!
» Take your communication and teamwork to the next level.
» Learn fun and creative ways to keep the spark alive in your marriage.

For more information, visit
MarriageMaximizer.com

Lightning Source UK Ltd.
Milton Keynes UK
UKHW041333130123
415275UK00025B/111/J